SAM KAPLAN

CHALLENGING
CHINA

SMART STRATEGIES FOR
DEALING WITH CHINA
IN THE XI JINPING ERA

TUTTLE Publishing

Tokyo | Rutland, Vermont | Singapore

Published by Tuttle Publishing, an imprint of Periplus Editions (HK) Ltd.

www.tuttlepublishing.com

Copyright © 2021 by Sam Kaplan

Library of Congress Control Number: 2020951447

ISBN 978-0-8048-5432-0

27 26 25 24 23 22 21
10 9 8 7 6 5 4 3 2 1   2102VP

Printed in Malaysia

Distributed by:

North America, Latin America & Europe
Tuttle Publishing
364 Innovation Drive
North Clarendon
VT 05759 9436, USA
Tel: 1(802) 773 8930
Fax: 1(802) 773 6993
info@tuttlepublishing.com
www.tuttlepublishing.com

Asia Pacific
Berkeley Books Pte Ltd
3 Kallang Sector #04-01
Singapore 349278
Tel: (65) 6741-2178
Fax: (65) 6741-2179
inquiries@periplus.com.sg
www.tuttlepublishing.com

Japan
Tuttle Publishing
Yaekari Building, 3rd Floor
5-4-12 Osaki Shinagawa-ku
Tokyo 141 0032 Japan
Tel: 81 (3) 5437 0171
Fax: 81 (3) 5437 0755
sales@tuttle.co.jp
www.tuttle.co.jp

Contents

Preface

One day, I sat sipping tea in a coffee shop while taking advantage of the opportunity to learn from the businessperson sitting across from me. She had recently moved back to Seattle after working and living in China for more than two decades. As she talked of her experiences, describing what she did in China and generally regaling me with tales of an expat in a foreign land, I asked her, "So what was the number one thing you learned about China, having lived and worked there so long?"

Surprisingly she didn't lean back, gaze into her coffee or up to the ceiling, or out the window into the busy Seattle street, pondering the question and how best to answer. She immediately said, "What I learned about China is…I will never understand China."

The long-time businesswoman did not mean that China is some strange, foreign land, an unknowable orient. No, she meant that China is too large, too complex, too fast changing to know entirely. Understanding China today, is not knowing China tomorrow. China under President Xi is a very different place than under President Hu. Understanding and spending time in Shenzhen does not mean one understands Tianchang. I know I certainly don't. China is like any large entity: there are many disparate parts adding up to an ultimately unknowable whole.

The United States is like that too. The Chinese tourists who travel to New York and Las Vegas have not seen America. Yazoo City, Mississippi, with its extreme poverty, is America, but so too is Medina, Washington, where Bill Gates and Jeff Bezos live (I imagine their butlers walking next door to borrow really expensive, fancy sugar from each other). India is similarly unknowable and complicated. In fact, any large country, any large entity, is ultimately beyond complete understanding.

So people, including "China experts," maybe especially China experts, who tell you they know China are not telling the whole truth. I won't claim to tell you the whole truth either in this book, but I will tell you what I do know and have learned. Just not necessarily as a China expert.

I don't speak Mandarin and cannot write simplified Chinese characters (or traditional, for that matter). But I have worked in international trade and international policy in one way or another for my whole career. I have been fortunate enough to have worked with China and on China issues over the last thirty years and have done so in policy positions, international trade and business forums, and education.

And what I have seen, learned, and experienced through the years, especially over the last seven, has compelled me to write this book. I watched China become an economic success story, achieving successes at a scale and rate not seen in history. But as China has grown economically, it has regressed politically. That would be worrisome but perhaps not a reason for this non-China expert to write this book. The challenge is that as it grew economically and regressed politically, China became expansionistic for the first time — not necessarily geographically, although occasionally in that way too, but certainly in working to export its system abroad and help tear down what until recently was a flawed and evolving liberalized world order. Worse yet, China has been aided and abetted by other countries in tearing down this order, countries including liberalized democracies, most especially the one of which I am a citizen.

Perhaps even that would not have spurred me to write this book, but even as all this happened, I read about, listened to, and watched the implementation of policies that I worry will either be ineffective, counterproductive or both in dealing with the new challenging China. So I decided to explain why a new strategy is needed for China, explain its economy in that regard, and tackle what the United

States should do, in concert with other countries, to deal with this new, challenging China.

When I write "China" in regard to its troubling actions and efforts, I am not referring to the 1.3 billion Chinese living there. I am referring to the party/state that runs modern-day China. This book and author are not against China, an amazing place, full of people who are good, bad, and indifferent just like any other country. They have achieved many great things and are as susceptible to the bad and corrupt as much as the rest of us. I may not be a China expert, but I have learned that much, at least.

And I have learned from and continue to read numerous Chinese experts whom I encourage you to read too (see the selected bibliography at the end of this book). These are some very smart people with vast experience in China who have keen insights. A few I have had the privilege of knowing personally, and who have been generous with their wisdom and ideas.

The best of them understand that China is not entirely understandable. They are not afraid to speak or write the three most underused words in the English language: "I don't know." I will use those three words more than once in this book.

So while I, too, will never understand China, I will never give up trying. And I hope this book will help all of us start the conversation of how best we engage with and confront China to create a more prosperous, peaceful world.

CHAPTER 1

Regression and Expansion: Why a New Strategy for China

China under Xi has Changed

In September, 2015, I was in the Westin Hotel in downtown Seattle helping to manage the Gala Dinner for the visit of President Xi Jinping of China. On my way to the hotel's grand ballroom where the dinner would take place, I walked by the escalators, which were supposed to be operational. They were not. President Xi's security team had shut them down even though they knew this broke the fire code. They had been told not to do this. More than ample security measures were in place to protect President Xi and all the other dignitaries in the hotel that day (There were lots of corporate executives from all over the country gathering around the President of China like teenage girls at the Beatles' Ed Sullivan Show in the early 1960s or, perhaps more relevant today, at a BTS K-pop concert.).

But none of this mattered to President Xi's security personnel, who did what they wanted when they wanted, even though they were not in their own country. U.S. laws were of no matter to them. This, of course, is a good metaphor for China's new assertiveness in the world in the Xi era.

The visit of President Xi to Seattle was far different from when President Hu Jintao came to Seattle nine years earlier, a visit I also worked on. During President Hu's visit, we worked with his advance team many months ahead of the visit. President Hu's team asked for suggestions on both the content and the logistics of the visit and in many cases accepted our suggestions. For example, our local host committee suggested they should not drive to a certain location during rush hour since it would disrupt traffic so badly that the story would end up being about angry motorists rather than the messages President Hu hoped to convey during his visit. Never, ever anger a commuter is always good PR advice in our experience. President Hu's team accepted this advice and adjusted the schedule accordingly.

In addition, we suggested that when President Hu visited Microsoft, he meet with kids using Microsoft software to learn Mandarin. The Chinese advance team loved the idea, and Bill Gates and President Hu together watched the young children speak Mandarin and write simplified Chinese characters using Microsoft software. I even got to pretend to be President Hu during a practice run-through with the children while a friend and Microsoft worker subbed as Bill Gates. This will presumably be the only time in my life I will have filled in as Chinese president, much to the relief, I'm sure, of 1.3 billion Chinese. The event and the whole visit went well from a Seattle perspective and from a China point of view.

The advance teams of President Hu were empowered to make decisions well ahead of his visit, and this included lower-level personnel from China who did the initial work of preparing for the President's visit to Seattle. Of course, as the time of the visit approached, higher-level officials came to Seattle and, for the most part, bought into the decisions already made. The visit was a partnership of local Seattle expertise, the Chinese Consulate in San Francisco, Ministry of Foreign Affairs officials, and President Hu's team.

But China in 2015 was a very different country than China in 2006. The year before, the Boao Forum, a sort of China Davos-type gathering held annually in Hainan Province, chose Seattle for one of its periodic satellite Boao-lite gatherings. I worked on that one, too. Midway through the organization of the conference, as Xi took over the reins of power in China, he instituted his corruption crackdown (much more on that shortly). Suddenly it became far more difficult for high-level Chinese officials to attend the conference as the new government instituted limits on how many days government officials could travel outside the country. The corruption crackdown impacted the conference in other ways as well. It was apparent, even then, that China was changing significantly.

By the time of President Xi's visit, I remarked to a couple of China experts I knew that it seemed as though Xi was the most impactful Chinese leader since Deng Xiaoping. They agreed with my assessment and deepened my understanding of what was happening in China with their words and counsel.

As with President Hu's visit, lower-level advance teams came to Seattle to prepare for Xi's trip. However, unlike in 2006, these teams weren't looking for advice on what President Xi should do during his stop in Seattle or how he should do it. They were telling us what he would do. And traffic? Who cares about your commuter? Not President Xi's team.[1] We're doing this China's way or the highway…a soon-to-be-very-jammed-with-angry-commuters highway.

We also found that these lower level teams were not empowered to make decisions. Of any kind. Large or small. Important or insignificant. No decisions were made until President Xi's small inner circle came to Seattle shortly before the visit of Xi himself. This, of course, made organizing for the visit more difficult. But it also revealed how China was now being run. Whereas in the past, power was more distributed, now decisions of all kinds were made by a small group of people close to the leader.

And, China was now much more aggressive and assertive. When President Hu came to Seattle, members of Falun Gong—a Buddhist sect—and other protestors gathered outside his hotel and shouted and banged drums in protest. President Xi's team did not want their president seeing or hearing these or any other protestors. Usually, when a head of state stays at a hotel, there is a one-block security perimeter around the hotel. President Xi's team insisted this needed to be three blocks. They told the U.S. Secret Service, who are responsible for such decisions, that this had to happen. The Secret Service consulted with the local host committee that had been assembled to organize the visit as to whether or not they should accede to China's demands. The host committee, which, full disclosure, I was on, said yes, extend the security perimeter. We made this decision even though we knew this would establish a precedent for a new perimeter for all heads of state, and not just China's but even our own. This would make all such future visits even more of an inconvenience for Seattleites. Though, of course, Trump was not likely to visit Seattle anytime soon.

China's security forces took additional extreme measures and asserted themselves in the name of security for dubious reasons. For weeks, Chinese security complained about the noise in the presidential suite of the Westin Hotel where Xi was to stay. Finally, Ambassador Gary Locke (former U.S. Ambassador to China, former U.S. Secretary of Commerce, former Governor of Washington, among a host of other accomplishments) and former Washington State Governor Christine Gregoire—the two co-chairs of the local host committee—asked me to accompany them to a meeting with Chinese officials and hotel staff in the presidential suite so we could hear the noise they were complaining about. When we got to the suite, some construction workers were building a wall in front of one set of windows. Not a temporary wall one might move in front of a window. No, they were drywalling, building an actual permanent wall in front of the windows as if one were remodeling one's house. Of course, because nothing in this world is permanent—not U.S. hegemony, nor China hegemony should they ever achieve it—after the visit of President Xi was over, the hotel tore down the wall so future visitors could enjoy the stunning views of the city and Elliott Bay.

While the construction workers took a break, we all sat there silently in the hotel suite…listening. And listening some more. For maybe five minutes we sat there quietly. I could not hear what the Chinese were complaining about, which was not a function of the many rock, rap, and jazz concerts I've seen in my life (though they certainly didn't help). There was nothing to hear. Of course, as I sat there quietly, sometimes with my eyes closed, sometimes gazing around the room, I wondered at how my life had led me to sitting in silence in a room with two high-powered officials like Governor Gregoire and Ambassador Locke, with a group of China's security and diplomatic officials and a few hotel staff in the presidential suite of a high-rise, four-star hotel. No one would have written a prediction of such a scenario in my high school yearbook.

Eventually the Chinese asked us about the noise they were complaining about. It turned out it was the slight hum of the fans of the adjacent office building. This building's roof, lower than the Westin Hotel, is stacked with high-powered fans because the servers for much of the West Coast Internet are below ground in that building. The Chinese officials told us we needed to turn off those fans during President Xi's visit. The Secret Service had already told them no. Ambassador Locke and Governor Gregoire did too. I'm sure the Chinese officials knew why those fans were there. Surely they knew it was not possible to turn off the fans. But in this visit, Chinese officials were far more assertive than during President Hu's visit, and if it had been possible for a Chinese security staff member to scale the adjacent building and turn off the fans Bruce Willis style in *Die Hard*, just as they presumptuously turned off the escalators despite all decorum, laws, and safety considerations, I'm sure they would have.

President Xi traveled to Tacoma (about 30 miles south of Seattle) right during rush hour, causing massive traffic jams and leading commuters to curse the day President Xi chose the Seattle area for his visit. They drove at that time despite locals cautioning them about the traffic disruption and resultant PR headache it would cause, just as we had advised President Hu's team. Hu's team listened. Xi's team did not care at all.

This is all to say that the visit of President Xi was an eye-opener regarding how China was changing under his leadership; at least certainly for me it was. It was one thing to read about President Xi's policies, such as increased censorship, corruption crackdowns, grabbing all the levers of power himself, and more aggressive economic nationalism. To see the differences in attitudes, policies and tactics up close underscored what one was reading.

And if you were paying close attention to China, much of the evidence was already there. When President Xi took office, he instituted a corruption crackdown. In December 2012, a month after Xi ascended to leadership, he issued the "Eight-Point Regulation of the Center," a set of rules aimed to curb the excesses of public officials—local, regional, and national. The eight rules—not seven, six or eleven—but eight rules passed from on high, range from leaders keeping in contact with the people to eliminating the elaborate ribbon-cutting and other ceremonial rites that Chinese leaders of all ages and stripes were prone to. Anyone who worked with and traveled to China pre-2012 has surely participated in an elaborate ceremony with tonnage of flowers decorating the stage, music playing, and a thousand speeches, followed by a bountiful number of toasts and drinks. Our liver can testify to such events it has participated in.

So, in many ways, Xi's anti-corruption measures made sense and were welcomed in some quarters. There was a tremendous amount of corruption in China, a kind of crony capitalism seeping into the earlier market reforms. Communist Party officials were getting rich from their positions of power and connections. A campaign against corruption was definitely needed (though recent research shows certain types of corruption are more damaging than others. See chapter 2 for more on this.).

But even from the beginning, it was clear the anti-corruption measures were also about asserting control more centrally, that is to say, giving Xi a tighter grip on power. The business nonprofit I worked for at the time was helping organize a trip for the mayor of Seattle to Chongqing, Seattle's sister city, around the time of the onset of the corruption crackdown. Chongqing is a megacity of 30 plus million people. Shortly before the trip, it was announced that Wang Lijun, the police chief of Chongqing, was being demoted. This, you may think, should not be a big deal for the Seattle mayor's trip to

Chongqing. But, Wang had been a top aide to Bo Xilai, the soon to be erstwhile Communist Party Secretary of Chongqing.

Bo Xilai was a charismatic leader—former mayor of Dalian, governor of Liaoning, Minister of Commerce, and overall ambitious guy, son of a prominent Communist leader—who was publicly clamoring to be a part of China's inner leadership circle. In Chongqing, he carried on a public campaign against organized crime, ruled at a time of double-digit GDP growth (and like all political leaders everywhere in good economic times, took credit for it, though it is true through massive state investment Chongqing grew faster during his reign than before or after), and yearned to bring back aspects of the Cultural Revolution. He could be and was seen as a rival for power in China.

So it was important news when Wang Lijun was demoted. It was bigger news still when one day he showed up at the U.S. Consulate in nearby Chengdu having asked for a meeting with the Commercial Service officer there, ostensibly to talk about economic development matters. I know and worked a bit with that Commercial Service officer, who tells the story that he sat down with Wang in a meeting room, expecting to talk about economic issues, when Wang looked at him from across the table and said he wanted to defect. The Commercial Service officer told me he stood up, left the room, and retrieved the proper personnel to deal with such a matter while he called Ambassador Gary Locke in Beijing to inform him of the development. Ambassador Locke has told the story of what he said when he received the call, which was the initial proper reaction, and I'm certain exactly what any of us would have said in such a situation: "Oh s***."

After the initial shock of the situation, consulate staff eventually persuaded Wang to leave the consulate, which, by that time, was surrounded by Chinese police. The Chongqing government announced Wang was receiving "holiday-style medical treatment,"[2] which, in China, is like saying Uyghurs are being re-educated. Wang was placed in jail and eventually sentenced to 15 years, a much shorter sentence than one would expect but given to him due to his cooperating in the investigation of his former boss, Bo Xilai.

By this time, Bo Xilai was in a whole heap of trouble of his own for alleged corruption and his family's alleged involvement in a mysterious murder case. Bo Xilai's wife, Gu Kailai, was implicated in the murder of British businessman Neil Heywood, a story too convoluted and tangential to go into here (but do look it up for all the strange and tawdry details), and she was eventually given a suspended death sentence. Bo Xilai himself was sacked as party boss of Chongqing, expelled from the Communist Party and Parliament, charged with corruption, bribery and abuse of power, and eventually found guilty of all charges.

The Bo Xilai saga began just before Xi took power, and he was found guilty as Xi announced and instituted his corruption crackdown. Bo Xilai, whatever his sins and crimes, (and being a high-level China Communist Party Leader, we are sure he has some), was a harbinger of what was to come.

And what was to come was "sweeping up some 2 million officials of both high rank and low.[3]" Begun shortly after he took office, President Xi's anti-corruption campaign has been expansive and is still ongoing. In 2013, there were 172,000 investigations, 330,000 in 2015, and 527,000 in 2017. Among the high brought low are seven people at the Politburo and Cabinet level. But the campaign has swept up a broad swathe of national, provincial, and local leaders throughout China. Richard McGregor calls it a "generational clean-out."[4] While there was plenty of corruption to clean out, the campaign also served the second purpose of solidifying Xi's grip on power. Political scientist Yuen Yuen Ang took the time to calculate the economic effectiveness of local leaders and whether that had any correlation with their being sacked. Her conclusion based on the data was that the performance of local leaders was not correlated with whether they were investigated. Being an effective local leader economically had no impact one way or another on the odds of being swept up in the corruption campaign. There was, however, a correlation to patronage. If a local leader's patron went down, there was a good chance they would too. Some of the corruption campaign is about actual corruption, some of it is about Xi extending his power. China was quickly becoming a very different place under Xi.[5]

I witnessed this firsthand. As Wang was trying to defect, with some colleagues I continued to organize our mayor and his delegation's humble trip to Chongqing. Our mayor was supposed to meet with the Chongqing mayor, whose police chief had just been arrested. So, we naturally wondered, given all that was happening, whether we should still go.

We talked with the Commercial Service officer who had met with Wang, and his advice was to talk with our main contact in the Chongqing mayor's office. Events were very fluid on the ground and perhaps this staff member could give us guidance, or, given the understandable reticence of Chinese officials to talk frankly in such situations, we could at least obtain some between-the-lines cues from him.

A few of us arranged a call with the staff person. We placed him on speaker phone and gingerly inquired whether everything would still work out for the planned agenda. I remember putting the phone on mute occasionally and asking a colleague who spoke Mandarin and was far more steeped in Chinese culture, politics and history than me, what he thought the mayor's staffer was trying to say. Nobody was certain, but by the end of the call we felt sufficiently reassured to send the mayor and delegation to Chongqing. And Chongqing's mayor did indeed meet with the Seattle mayor. I was not there, my travels taking me to another part of the world at the time, but my colleagues told me it was a long and strange meeting. At one point, the Chongqing mayor told a long parable about Jesus Christ. What he meant by it, no one was fully sure. Which I suppose is the point of parables.

The ongoing anti-corruption campaign is becoming encoded in China's government. In 2018, Xi's government created the National Supervisory Commission. This new organization "ranks alongside the central government and above the judiciary."[6] And tellingly, it does not just monitor and investigate the country's 90 million Communist Party members, but also "managers of state-owned enterprises, hospitals, educational and cultural institutions, sports organizations and even village governments and research institutes."[7] Further, as Yuen Yuen Ang notes, "…the central disciplinary authorities have expanded the scope of the campaign from policing corruption to monitoring policy implementation and ensuring correct political thinking."[8] Of course, state media has been ardent in discussing the importance of Xi's anti-corruption campaign. Indeed, in 2017, Liu Shiyu, chairman of the China Securities Regulatory Commission during that year's party national congress, praised Xi for "saving the Communist Party"[9] by taking down Bo Xilai and others in the anti-corruption campaign.

In Xi's Own Words

The anti-corruption campaign showed us, through Xi's actions, that China was changing. His words were just as indicative. When Xi become General Secretary of the Communist Party of China in late 2012, his first trip outside Beijing was to Guangdong Province, located in the south. China's media paralleled it to Deng Xiaoping's famous southern trip in 1992, which reiterated China's commitment to economic reform after the Tiananmen Square crackdown. Deng's speech was not covered by the Chinese media (although it was in Hong Kong) until several months later, perhaps because of some power struggles with Jiang Zemin, the General Secretary since 1989. As an aside, it is challenging to analyze and understand a country where the paramount leader gives a prominent speech on an important topic but it is kept secret for many months. The same was true with regard to Xi, as you will see in a moment.

In Xi's speech, he echoed the importance of China's continuing to progress. He pointedly noted how important the Chinese Communist Party had been to China's economic success: "Since its founding, the Communist Party of China has made great sacrifices and forged ahead against all odds. It has rallied and led the Chinese people in transforming the poor and backward old China into an increasingly prosperous and powerful new China, thus opening a completely new horizon for the great renewal of the Chinese nation."[10] He also both referenced China's corruption problems and foreshadowed the corruption crackdown: "… there are also many pressing problems within the Party that need to be resolved, particularly corruption, being divorced from the people, going through formalities and bureaucratism caused by some Party officials."

All in all, Xi's speech was perceived favorably by the world, with many holding out hopes that Xi would institute additional economic reforms and perhaps even political reforms. The BBC, for example, opined that mirroring Deng's southern trip, "Xi Jinping was sending out a message that he too intends to strive for economic reform."[11]

But it turns out that Xi gave another, secret speech to party members during that trip. It was leaked and reported on by Gao Yu, a Chinese investigative journalist in late January, 2013, more than a month after Xi's trip.[12] Just the fact that the leader of the country made a major speech that was kept secret from the people reminds one of the pitfalls of authoritarian governments and the advantages of democracy (more on that in chapter 4). But the speech made clear what we now know: there would be no forthcoming political reform. Indeed, the paramount leader's paramount concern was preserving the power and hold of the Communist Party of China. Xi's major point in the speech, reported Gao, was that the China Communist Party needed to learn the lessons from the fall of the Communist Party in the Soviet Union.

"Why did the Soviet Union disintegrate? Why did the Soviet Communist Party collapse?" Gao reported Xi asking in the speech. "An important reason was that their ideals and beliefs had been shaken. In the end, 'the ruler's flag over the city tower' changed overnight. It's a profound lesson for us!" Xi went on, finishing with a flourish, "To dismiss the history of the Soviet Union and the Soviet Communist Party, to dismiss Lenin and Stalin, and to dismiss everything else is to engage in historic nihilism, and it confuses our thoughts and undermines the Party's organization on all levels."

Xi and his colleagues in China were learning from what happened in the Soviet Union to ensure that it didn't happen there:

> *Why must we stand firm on the Party's leadership over the military? Because that's the lesson from the collapse of the Soviet Union. In the Soviet Union where the military was depoliticized, separated from the Party and nationalized, the party was disarmed. A few people tried to save the Soviet Union; they seized Gorbachev, but within days it was turned around again, because they didn't have the instruments to exert power. Yeltsin gave a speech standing on a tank, but the military made no response, keeping so-called 'neutrality.' Finally, Gorbachev announced the disbandment of the Soviet Communist Party in a blithe statement. A big Party was gone just like that. Proportionally, the Soviet Communist Party had more members than we do, but nobody was man enough to stand up and resist.*

Putting aside what our feminist friends would call Xi's patriarchal use of the term "man enough,"[13] it is important to note while the West was learning lessons from the fall of the Soviet Union, so too were China's leaders. Different lessons for different goals, of course. Rather than the hope that many of us had that China would evolve like Taiwan, South Korea and other countries—become more politically liberal as its economy developed—China was taking action to ensure it did the exact opposite: grow economically but remain authoritarian.

Just as significant was China's plan to take a more active role outside its borders, as Xi himself would outline in future speeches. I, like many others, figured China was relatively benign since they didn't have expansionist tendencies. But this has not turned out to be true, and by expansionistic we mean more than their regional goals in the South and East China Seas. China increasingly aims to transform the post-World War II, post-Cold War liberal economic order into one more friendly towards authoritarianism. An early indication of this was China's creating the Asian Infrastructure Investment Bank (AIIB). At the announcement of the creation of this rival to the Asian Development Bank and other multilateral lending institutions established after World War II, Xi said, "It will enable China to undertake more international obligations, promote improvement of the current international economic system and provide more international public goods."[14] This is all well and good and in many ways should be welcomed given that it could expand lending capabilities into the developing world. But as it turns out, China's ambitions are larger than helping developing countries succeed like China has succeeded economically.

Even as they created the AIIB, China launched its Belt and Road Initiative, the stated aim of which is to deepen trade and economic integration across Asia, Europe, and Africa. This also could be welcomed in many ways as China cooperated on additional infrastructure projects in countries along a new "Silk Road." Put aside that at least part of the real aim of the Belt and Road is likely to deal with excess capacity issues in China and that these projects too often hamstrung the recipient countries with burdensome loans they could not pay back, thus allowing China to appropriate their property, there is a deeper concern about China's efforts outside its borders. The challenge is that China is intent on changing a rules-based world economic order into one based on China's values, methods, and interests (see chapter 6 for much more on this).

China's stepping onto the world stage could and should be welcomed if it were another actor speaking helpful lines and acting constructively in a play about economic development and liberalization. But, instead, China is intent on tearing down the stage and erecting its own, on which a very different play with a very different plot will be presented. In 2017, at the 19th National Congress of the Communist Party of China, Xi gave a three-and-a-half-hour speech. Ignoring for the moment that only Bruce Springsteen should be allowed to perform for that long, Xi made clear that China planned to play a much greater role in the world. One must wade through 68 (!) pages of transcribed oratory, past riveting sections on "Seeing Socialist Literature and Art Thrive," "Giving play to the important role of socialist consultative democracy," and, of course, "Consolidating and developing the patriotic united front," (Xi was playing all the greatest hits and obscure B-sides of the CCP), to see the new world order Xi envisions.

In the foreign policy part of the speech, Xi talked about the world working together to tackle challenges, and he explicitly stated, "China will never pursue development at the expense of others' interests," but in the next clause he also states, "but nor will China ever give up its legitimate rights and interests. No one should expect us to swallow anything that undermines our interests." The problem is China's interests are the CCP's perpetual rule, which means the subjection of other views, alternatives and values—inevitably leading to abuses such as we have seen perpetrated on the Uyghurs in Xinjiang. But Xi also clearly stated, "No matter what stage of development it reaches, China will never seek hegemony or engage in expansion."

Xi's words were cloaked in cooperation but the challenge, as Bill Clinton said about the word "is," is Xi and China's definition of "hegemony" and "expansion." Vietnam and other countries would say the nine-dash line[15] is expansion, for example. The NBA and others would say China practices practical hegemony—to do business in China one must adapt to its values and assertions on human rights, even when not in China. China wants the world to adhere to its interests, to adopt its business practices. This is problematic to say the least, at least if one properly understands China's interest.

Elsewhere in the speech, Xi noted, "we have seen a further rise in China's international influence, ability to inspire, and power to shape." Indeed, through its size and economic growth, China does have greater influence and a larger ability to shape the world. It wants to use that influence and power to shape a world that has Chinese characteristics. Because China is so large, its economy so tied globally, and its large markets such a lure for companies all over the world, China can influence how the world acts. The U.S. has done this for decades, of course, and imperfectly so. But the U.S., with its allies, evolved the world towards a rules-based order. To do business with and in the United States meant to adapt to a civil society based on the rule of law. To do business with and in China is to adapt to the whims and wishes of the Chinese Communist Party, with far too little recourse to law. China's remarkable rise means, as Xi put it in the speech, that:

> *scientific socialism is full of vitality in 21st century China, and that the banner of socialism with Chinese character-istics is now flying high and proud for all to see. It means that the path, the theory, the system, and the culture of so-cialism with Chinese characteristics have kept developing, blazing a new trail for other developing countries to achieve modernization. It offers a new option for other countries and nations who want to speed up their development while preserving their independence; and it offers Chinese wis-dom and a Chinese approach to solving the problems fac-ing mankind.*

China's economic success is indeed worth studying, although how much of it was due to socialism and how much to market re-forms is debatable, and we'll look at this question in the next chapter. But it is clear Xi is ready to export the China system. He goes on to say in the speech that we are in a new era and it will be one of "building on past successes to further advance our cause, and of continuing in a new historical context to strive for the success of socialism with Chi-nese characteristics." After describing all the ways China will perfect itself, Xi closes this section of the speech saying, "It will be an era that sees China moving closer to center stage and making greater contri-butions to mankind." Again, that makes sense given China's larger economy and prominence. It is natural that such a country play a more central role in world affairs. Inevitably this will be the case. But it would be far better if China's contributions, as it takes center stage, were not authoritarian and lacking in the rule of law.

If China were a larger France or India or Brazil, its emergence on the world stage, although undoubtedly still unsettling for some, need not be worrisome or a reason to develop a strategy to mitigate its new-found prominence. But through its actions and words, China has made clear that there will be a new battle of ideas and systems.

This is not to say that there has been a vast and long-running conspiracy by China to take over the world, as some policy experts such as Michael Pillsbury argue. Pillsbury, in his book *The 100 Year Marathon*, implies that from the beginning, China has been biding its time, advancing its economy, and, when the time is right, will start to take over the world. This is not what we are arguing. And even Pillsbury, in his often contradictory book, doesn't really argue that. Rather, most of his arguments are about "hawks" in China who want to be more assertive in the world. And that most certainly is true.

But we argue something a bit more nuanced than even that. China is more powerful economically than it was thirty years ago, and it is the natural order of the world for the more prominent economic actors to have more influence. So China is naturally beginning to extend its influence around the world. Where before, China was mostly focused internally, today it is actively trying to mold the world to its liking. This is abetted by the United States abandoning world leadership and a policy that favors the rule of law. This is a problem because China continues to be an authoritarian state and its attempts to remold the world order will inevitably be authoritarian in nature. The Chinese academic Xu Zhangrun articulated it well in a critique of China's government he bravely published in February 2020 at the beginning of the corona virus crisis. The Tsinghua University professor wrote in a long essay, "No matter how complex, nuanced and sophisticated one's analysis, the reality is stark. A polity that is blatantly incapable of treating its own people properly can hardly be expected to treat the rest of the world well."[16]

Xi and China are working to change the world order, and they recognize there will be pushback on this. In the fall of 2019, China state media re-released an old speech by Xi from just after he rose to General Secretary on January 5, 2013.[17] In this speech, Xi talks about the cooperation and conflict China faces with what he calls capitalism (it's really far more than that—it's the liberalized, democratized world order). Xi notes the advantages, in the mid-term, of the West and the long conflict to come:

> ...*we must have a deep appreciation for capitalism's ability to self-correct, and a full, objective assessment of the real long-term advantages that the developed Western nations have in the economic, technological, and military spheres. Then we must diligently prepare for a long period of cooperation and of conflict between these two social systems in each of these domains.*

Xi then talks about continuing to improve socialism and having "strategic determination." Ultimately, he says, however, that China must lay "the foundation for a future where we will win the initiative and have the dominant position."

This was a new paragraph that was added in the republication of the old speech. But, in many ways, it parallels Xi's original secret speech that Gao reported on in early 2013. Oh, and what became of Gao in the system Xi aspires to grow into the dominant position in the world? She is in jail, along with many others, for exercising free speech.

Human Rights Are Deteriorating

China's ongoing and deepening abuse of the basic human rights of its people is too often ignored by policymakers in the U.S., Europe, and elsewhere. Instead, they concentrate on trade, national security and other issues. But as Xu Zhangrun wrote, how a country treats its people is a good indication of how it will treat other countries. As China has grown more powerful, and as the United States retreats from world leadership, China increasingly will be able to transform global institutions. Again, the worsening human rights situation in China is reason to be alarmed at the ways China will change the world order, whether economic, security or other institutions. So it's important to examine China's worrisome human rights record, which we do here, though, of course, not exhaustively. One could write an entire book about China's troublesome human rights record. We will focus on how human rights abuses have worsened in the Xi regime and what that means for the world. Later, in chapter 4, we examine why we should confront China on its human rights abuses and how to do so.

For now, a quick survey of those abuses, how they've worsened and how this affects the world. What we find is that from the beginning, President Xi gave a good sense of what was to come. President Xi began his regime by immediately arresting human rights activists. As Richard McGregor notes in his book *Xi Jinping: The Backlash*, more than 200 lawyers in China involved in human rights issues were questioned and detained after Xi became president.

China under Xi has not been shy about silencing human rights activists and jailing people of all types. As Human Rights Watch writes, "Human rights defenders continue to endure arbitrary detention, imprisonment, and enforced disappearance."[18]

In 2015, China initiated what became known as the "709 Crackdown" named for the date it started (July 9), with a crackdown on human rights lawyers and human rights activists around the country. More than 250 such people were arrested, with many still in jail and detained. One prominent example is Wang Quanzhang, who was originally arrested in 2015. Four years later, in 2019, he was found "guilty" of "subverting state power" and sentenced to four-and-a-half years in jail. From 2015 to his sentencing, he was held incommunicado, and, as Amnesty International noted, his family did not even know whether he was alive. Wang's crime was that he defended "religious freedom and represented members of the New Citizens' Movement, a network of grassroots activists who promote government transparency and expose corruption."[19]

There is, unfortunately, no dearth of such cases we could describe here, but suffice it to say that China brooks no opposition in regard to human rights, both in China and outside as well, where it has also occasionally disappeared people. For example, Human Rights Watch reports, "In January 2018, Guangzhou authorities forcibly disappeared Li Huaiping, wife of Chen Xiaoping, a US-based journalist for the Chinese-language Mirror Media Group. The disappearance came shortly after Chen interviewed Guo Wengui, a Chinese billionaire fugitive who exposed corruption among China's ruling elite." China's measures against human rights activities abroad are further evidence that China now has an expansionist policy.

The campaign against human rights activists continues with a group of five human rights lawyers and activists arrested in the last week of 2019. Why were they arrested? They met secretly in Xiamen in southeast China in early December, 2019. Freedom of assembly, freedom of thought are not allowed. One of those arrested was Ding Jiaxi, who has been active in pro-democracy, pro-human rights efforts and was jailed earlier, in 2014, for three-and-a-half years.

The sad fact of the matter is human rights abuses have grown worse in China under Xi Jinping. As Human Rights Watch put it in their 2018 report, "The broad and sustained offensive on human rights that started after President Xi Jinping took power five years ago showed no sign of abating in 2017." Spoiler alert: it hasn't abated since then either. Let's examine various facets of how China suppresses human rights.

Censorship

I am not a skilled photographer but managed to take a good pic on one of my trips to China and decided to post it on Facebook—except, of course, I couldn't, since Facebook is not accessible in China. This, I suppose, kept me in the moment as anti-social media folks like to say, so maybe China's government was doing me a favor. Or, maybe they are scared of their own people having the power to express their thoughts freely and access information from around the world. When traveling to China, foreigners must deal with the Great Firewall, the blocking of content on the Internet that China's government deems unsuitable. And increasingly that is becoming more and more content, more and more websites and digital platforms. We foreigners return home to a free Internet. Chinese grapple with a closed web every day of their lives. At the beginning of the coronavirus crisis, China's obsession with censorship cost many lives (more on that in Chapter 7).

Officially known as the Golden Shield Project, China employs more than 2 million people to make sure its citizens don't see any unsanctioned cat videos, or learn about Tibet, Hong Kong, Uyghurs, and other sensitive issues other than from the official organs of the CCP. Under Xi Jinping, China has become even more vigilant over the Internet. The Guardian notes, "…the government has invested in technological upgrades to monitor and censor content. It has passed new laws on acceptable content and aggressively punished those who defy the new restrictions. Under Xi, foreign content providers have found their access to China shrinking. They are being pushed out by both Xi's ideological war and his desire that Chinese companies dominate the country's rapidly growing online economy."[20]

In fact, at a speech on December 15, 2015, during the second World Internet Conference, Xi said, "Cyberspace is not a place beyond the rule of law…Everyone should abide by the law, with the rights and obligations of parties concerned clearly defined."[21] The law is the last refuge of despots. China's law of the Internet is one of an increasingly repressive nature, where a citizen cannot discuss protests in Hong Kong, the torture of Uyghurs, religious issues or a multitude of other concerns sensitive to the Chinese government. They're a sensitive, fragile lot, Xi Jinping and his team. Authoritarian rulers are always, and at all times, the real snowflakes.

The fear of free information has led to foreign news sources being even more heavily restricted in China. The Foreign Correspondents Club of China did an analysis that shows "…the Great Firewall bars Internet users in China from viewing the publicly-available websites of 23 percent of 215 international news organizations with journalists based in China."[22] Among those blocked in China are the *New York Times*, the *Times of India*, the *Wall Street Journal*, and *The Economist*. We expect the website for this book to be blocked too.

Censorship in China continues to be even more strict. In December 2019, China announced new censorship rules that took effect on March 1, 2020. The new law prohibits, among many other things, the following: "Content undermining the nation's policy on religions, promoting cults and superstitions; dissemination of rumors, disrupting economic or social order," as well as anything that "harms the nation's honor and interests." These are illegal to do online. It also has a list of content that is "discouraged," which includes "sensationalized headlines, improper comments on tragedies…bad habits or dangerous activities that might be imitated by minors."[23] Apparently, the latter does not include the bad habit of telling people what to think and do. As the United States debates whether to ban TikTok or WeChat (we weigh in on that later), it's important to remember that China years ago banned their foreign equivalents in their own country.

China is adept at keeping the outside world from having influence on China, as well as keeping its own people from influencing each other. In addition, China increasingly seeks to influence its own people, their belief systems, and their behavior.

China Social Credit System

It has become almost a cliché that China is becoming a *Black Mirror* episode come to life with its social credit system. Who isn't scared, worried, in awe of and confused—sometimes all at once—by this system to rate Chinese people's actions and thoughts, judge them with a resulting score, and mete out consequences as the result of the system's calculations.

China's social credit system started in 2014, and befitting its Orwellian aims, it is coordinated by the charmingly named "Central Comprehensively Deepening Reforms Commission," which was previously called the nearly identical "Central Leading Group for Comprehensively Deepening Reforms." Naming rights were surely determined by some committee of bureaucrats with, I'm sure, an equally astounding title. I might be willing to throw all my ideals away if I could get a mega contract from China to rename all its commissions, committees and organizations. The fact that the social credit system is under the supervision of such a supremely bureaucratically named commission, the words reordered from its former similar name, perhaps gives us the most hope that the whole thing won't work.

And it's fair to point out that as *Wired* magazine reports, "As yet, there's no one social credit system. Instead, local governments have their own social record systems that work differently, while unofficial private versions are operated at companies such as Ant Financial's Zhima Credit, better known as Sesame Credit...."[24] Of course, what is private is also public in China. Any data and judgements of individuals hoovered up by a private company can be and are gathered up by China's government.

China has stated it eventually hopes to have a unified system in which, as *Wired* reports, businesses will be given a "unified social credit code and citizens an identity number, all linked to permanent record." And there will be consequences for a low score. Indeed, even in today's decentralized system, Chinese have been denied the ability to fly or take trains based on their social credit score.

This is all part of a larger surveillance state China is building using new technologies, from face recognition to gait recognition technology. Yes, China is monitoring the way you walk to be able to identify you and "prevent crime." The biometric identification technology is used without people knowing it or giving permission. As you walk, stroll, drunkenly stumble down a Shanghai street past a surveillance camera, the gait recognition technology can identify you and alert the proper, or improper, authorities.

Again, that the most populous, second-largest economy in the world is using such technology on its own citizens with no checks or balances is concerning. But unlike what we thought a few years ago, China is expansionistic. They are exporting and helping other authoritarian regimes to use technology to keep their own bitter, iron grip on their own peoples. CNBC reports that "Chinese tech companies—particularly Huawei, Hikvision, Dahua and ZTE—supply artificial intelligence surveillance technology in 63 countries." Tyranny loves company. Of course, China has more than enough tyranny to spread throughout its own country, including and especially on the Uyghurs.

The Catastrophe of Xinjiang

As has been reported somewhat widely, China has engaged in the systematic repression of the Uyghur minority in Xinjiang Province in northwestern China. In the fall of 2019, the International Consortium of Investigative Journalists published a series of articles based on leaked classified Chinese documents that showed in detail "China's extrajudicial internment and compulsory indoctrination of Muslims as part of a sweeping program of mass surveillance and population control."[25] The documents show the oppression was planned in detail and comes from the very top level of China's government.

I won't belabor the human rights abuses here (although the world should do so continuously until China stops these abuses, as we'll advocate in chapter 4) but note that Human Rights Watch states in their 2018 China Human Rights report:

> *The Chinese government began waging a "Strike Hard Campaign against Violent Extremism" in Xinjiang in 2014…Since then, authorities have stepped up mass arbitrary detention, including in pretrial detention centers and prisons, both of which are formal facilities, and in "political education" camps, which have no basis under Chinese law. Credible estimates indicate that 1 million people are being indefinitely held in the camps, where Turkic Muslims are being forced to learn Mandarin Chinese, praise the government and party, and abandon many aspects of their distinct*

identity. Those who resist or are deemed to have failed to "learn" are punished.

In June 2020, The Associated Press (AP) reported on an extensive investigation they conducted on China's attempt to commit demographic genocide against Uyghurs. Through interviews and examining official data and state documents, the news service concluded:

> *The state regularly subjects minority women to pregnancy checks, and forces intrauterine devices, sterilization and even abortion on hundreds of thousands, the interviews and data show...The population control measures are backed by mass detention both as a threat and as a punishment for failure to comply. Having too many children is a major reason people are sent to detention camps, the AP found, with the parents of three or more ripped away from their families unless they can pay huge fines. Police raid homes, terrifying parents as they search for hidden children.*[26]

The AP puts a human face to this attempt to diminish the Uyghur population: "Another former detainee, Tursunay Ziyawudun, said she was injected until she stopped having her period, and kicked repeatedly in the lower stomach during interrogations. She now can't have children and often doubles over in pain, bleeding from her womb, she said."

The high-tech surveillance technology and techniques we described in the section above are all utilized against Uyghurs. But China also uses old-fashioned methods in Xinjiang: "...they have mobilized over a million officials to monitor people, including through intrusive programs in which officials regularly stay in people's homes." This includes sleeping in the beds with wives whose husbands are imprisoned in the detention centers. Talk about your unwanted houseguests. Imagine that instead of your in-laws during Thanksgiving, some dour-faced bureaucrat took over your easy chair, watched your TV, and ate all your leftover pie, and if you did anything about it, you would face prison, torture or worse.

Repression against Muslims in China is not new, but it has expanded and become systemized under the Xi regime. It is one of the more concerning and striking examples of China's increased authoritarianism of recent years. Not only has China not continued to reform, as many of us hoped it would as its economy continued to develop, it has regressed.

Let's not leave the persecution of Uyghurs (and other religious minorities) as a mere list of numbers and tactics. Let's allow the Israeli newspaper, *Haaretz*, to put a face to this widespread, systematic abuse, through interviews with Sayragul Sauythbay, who escaped from China and received asylum in Sweden (We urge you to read the entire article.[27])

> *Twenty prisoners live in one small room. They are hand-cuffed, their heads shaved, every move is monitored by ceiling cameras. A bucket in the corner of the room is their toilet. The daily routine begins at 6 A.M. They are learning Chinese, memorizing propaganda songs and confessing to invented sins. They range in age from teenagers to elderly. Their meals are meager: cloudy soup and a slice of bread.*
>
> *Torture – metal nails, fingernails pulled out, electric shocks – takes place in the "black room." Punishment is a constant. The prisoners are forced to take pills and get injections. It's for disease prevention, the staff tell them, but in reality they are the human subjects of medical experiments. Many of the inmates suffer from cognitive decline. Some of the men become sterile. Women are routinely raped.*

Is China Still Engaged in Forced Organ Harvesting?

Generally, we like our fiction grounded in reality and become annoyed when a TV show or movie makes it difficult to suspend disbelief. We're like that with the real world, too, which is why we've always been dubious about the allegations that China is harvesting organs from political prisoners—it seemed too crazy to believe. But a study analyzing the data of China's organ transplants gives us pause. By way of background, after international complaints that China was using prisoners to harvest organs for transplant surgery, China claimed to be using a new system in 2010 to prevent such abuse. (it always denied killing prisoners, political or not, just to take their organs, though there have been accusations of that as well.) Official Chinese statistics claim "volunteer deceased donors went from 34 to 6,316 annually," apparently proving that China was no longer using prisoners' organs. However, three authors, including Matthew Robertson, published a paper in the BMC Medical Ethics journal that claims this "data is manipulated, and done in the crudest of ways: …it appears that all of this data was manufactured using the mathematics one learns in high school: a quadratic equation."[28] Yes, they used math we learned in 8th grade to gin up data, making it look as though they were no longer harvesting organs from prisoners. Matthew Robertson concludes, "The goal of these elaborate efforts appears to have been to create a misleading impression to the international transplantation community about the successes of China's voluntary organ donation reform and to neutralize the criticism of activists who allege that crimes against humanity have been committed in the acquisition of organs for transplant."

An International Tribunal assembled by the International Coalition to End Transplant Abuse in China (ETAC) has also gathered evidence and listened to the accounts of witnesses (all of which are available on a website to allow others to make their own analysis). The tribunal's conclusion? "On the basis of all direct and indirect evidence, the Tribunal concludes with certainty that forced organ harvesting has happened in multiple places in the PRC and on multiple occasions for a period of at least twenty years and continues to this day."[29] Rarely have we seen a more chilling and damning conclusion of a country's current day practices. The principal group targeted so far for forced organ harvesting is the religious group Falun Gong, which is deemed to be a cult by China's government. The Falun Gong is not a group I would join, but there are many religious groups not to my taste, none of whom should be oppressed and deprived of the right to freely practice their beliefs. Certainly they should not be targeted for forced organ harvesting, as is currently alleged.

One of the many pieces of evidence presented at the tribunal was the fact that imprisoned Falun Gong have their blood tested and organs examined and other prisoners do not. Blood testing is needed so that donors and recipients can be matched. Falun Gong has been targeted, but it appears Uyghurs are being prepped: "Ethan Gutman gave evidence to the Tribunal in December 2018 stating that 'over the last 18 months, literally every Uyghur man, woman, and child – about 15 million people – have been blood and DNA tested, and that blood testing is compatible with tissue matching.'" The world faces important choices on how best to confront this conclusion. The worst option is to ignore it.

Hong Kong

In the fall of 2014, on the way back from Xiamen, I overnighted in Hong Kong. The Umbrella Revolution was fully opened, with young protesters camping out on the streets of the city. After dinner, I traveled down to where the protesters were congregated and watched with awe as thousands of young Hong Kongers assembled peacefully, holding signs and talking with people walking through the crowd, explaining their reasons for protesting, their calls for freedom. I talked with some of the protesters and asked one young woman, "Are you worried, scared to be doing this?" She assured me she wasn't. She was confident in the cause of universal suffrage, of democracy, of freedom.

Eventually, those 2014 protests ended, but new protests in Hong Kong erupted in 2019 and 2020. So is China's increasingly shortsighted reaction to them. But first, let's remind ourselves what the vast majority of Hong Kong protestors are asking for, just in case LeBron James, Steve Kerr or Steph Curry happen to pick up this book while LeBron takes a break from re-educating Daryl Morey (see chapter 7 for more on the NBA). We want to make sure we're all well-educated on the issue.

In 1997, Britain returned Hong Kong to China. During its long rule of Hong Kong since 1842, Britain never democratized it. Hong Kong was not politically free but it was economically, and it became one of the Asian Tigers in the 1970s. As part of the handover in 1997, Britain and China signed the Basic Law stipulating the terms, which created the "one country, two systems" principle. Hong Kongers were to have responsibility for running their internal affairs for the next 50 years until 2047.

As China became increasingly aggressive in recent years, Hong Kongers worried their freedoms were being taken away. The 2019 protests were tripped off when Carrie Lam, Hong Kong's Chief Executive, worked to get an extradition bill passed. This bill would allow the Hong Kong government to extradite, on a case-by-case basis, individuals deemed fugitives and criminals, including to the mainland. Hong Kongers worried that the Hong Kong government, increasingly controlled by Beijing, would send activists, protesters, business people, and others to China at whatever whim of the Beijing government, whose whims are driven by the need to control the aspirations for freedom of Hong Kong, no matter the one country two systems principle. There are, of course, reasons why people in Hong Kong were fearful of a law that would allow extradition to China, including a number of Hong Kong booksellers who mysteriously disappeared, only to turn up in jail in China.[30] In March 2020, one of those booksellers, Gui Minhai (a Swedish citizen!) was sentenced to 10 years in jail for "providing intelligence" to people overseas. So yeah, the people of Hong Kong had good reason to be worried.

Protesters in Hong Kong succeeded in thwarting the passage of the extradition bill. As the protests grew and authorities cracked down on the protesters, sometimes violently, a series of five demands emerged from the protesters. They were 1) full withdrawal of the extradition bill; 2) the formation of an independent commission to investigate police behavior; 3) the retraction of the term "rioters" for protestors—conviction for rioting carries a 10-year prison sentence; 4) amnesty for arrested protesters; and 5) the full election of Hong Kong's legislative council and chief executive.

China painted the protesters demands as an attempt to gain independence from China. None of these five demands do that and fall very much in line with the 1997 handover agreement. As with any movement that includes more than a million people, there are bad apples and extremists among the protesters. But the leaders and masses were remarkably restrained and consistent in their modest demands, all of which fall within the framework of the Basic Law.

Britain, as was typical of its colonization around the world, was criminally negligent in not introducing democracy to Hong Kong. That Hong Kongers, under the 1997 agreement, want to elect their own leaders, investigate police abuses, freely assemble, and shut down an extradition bill that would put human rights advocates in jeopardy should be a no-brainer. That we have to consider them brave for doing so reveals much about China's government and the risks of turning the post-World War II, post-Cold War world order over to such a regime. The Hong Kong protests did not occur in a vacuum. They are a reaction to China's increasingly heavy hand under Xi's rule.

The heavy hand fell like a ton of shackles in June 2020 when China announced and shortly thereafter instituted a national security law designed to criminalize "secession, subversion, terrorism and collusion with foreign forces." It allowed Beijing to set up its own security forces within Hong Kong. It has led to the arrests of human rights activists, raids on independent media, including the arrest of Jimmy Lai, the prominent entrepreneur, publisher of the newspaper *Apple Daily* and outspoken promoter of democracy.

The protesters in Hong Kong were right to be worried about encroachments from China on the Basic Law and on their freedoms. The Xi regime again showed its increasing aggressiveness and authoritarianism.

Taiwan

Many years ago, I worked for U.S. Representative John Miller in his Washington, D.C. office, handling foreign affairs, among other issues. I was young, like a Hong Kong umbrella protester. On a regular basis, I would hear from Shiru, whose last name I don't remember, but she was essentially a one-named star like Madonna, Cher, Beyonce or Rihanna. She worked for Taiwan's office in D.C. Back then, if I said the name Shiru, every foreign affairs staffer on Capitol Hill knew who I was referring to. On occasion, Shiru would take me to lunch at a fancy restaurant. She always chose a table in a discreet part of the establishment where we could talk quietly. Our discussions were far-ranging, and there was never anything untoward about it. She took all the young male staffers to lunch like this—we congressional aides often joked about it. Shiru and Taiwan wanted to develop a personal relationship with congressional staff, to establish a rapport.

Many, many years later, at a small dinner in Seattle for a visiting business delegation from Taiwan, I told the accompanying Taiwan government official based in D.C. that I once knew a woman named Shiru who had worked in his office and wondered whether he knew her. I assumed this many years later he would not, that surely she had been replaced or was doing something different. But the Taiwanese official smiled, even laughed knowingly, and said, yes, he knew Shiru. We talked a bit about her and I was glad to know Shiru's fame and work live on these many years later.

Taiwan has to work harder at diplomacy than other countries because of the position it finds itself in. Taiwan is very active in D.C. and in other cities in which it has offices (including in Seattle). These offices, of course, are not embassies and consulates because from the time China and the U.S. reestablished relations in 1979 until the Trump administration, U.S.–Taiwan relations were informal, and the U.S. recognizes a "One China" policy. Instead of an embassy, Taiwan has an Economic and Cultural Representative Office.

China, of course, does not recognize Taiwan as an independent entity and considers it a part of China. The world more or less accepts that. It's easy to forget that the world is accepting an illusion. After Chiang Kai-shek and his nationalist party were defeated militarily by Mao and his communists, Chiang fled to Taiwan (famously choosing to bring priceless works of art rather than another 20,000 people on the boats; this led to the founding of the remarkable National Palace Museum in Taipei, but presumably was not appreciated by those left behind).

Taiwan was ruled under the dictatorship of Chiang Kai-Shek for decades. But slowly, as it liberalized economically, it democratized until today it is a fully functioning democracy. Taiwan was one of the original Asian Tigers, growing at high rates in the 1960s and 70s until it became a fully developed country. It was an example of the model of many years of rapid economic growth, followed by democratic reforms, and eventually full democratization, that many countries adopted and that many of us hoped and assumed (wrongly) that China would follow.

At any rate, today Taiwan has a GDP per capita comparable to Sweden's and is an important economy of the world (as well as having played a role in mainland China's economic development). If an alien landed on earth and examined the world, they would assume Taiwan was a successful, independent country with its own duly elected government and a relatively successful economy.

But, of course, in the formulations of China, adhered to by the rest of the world, that is not how Taiwan is viewed or treated politically. There are sound geopolitical reasons for why the U.S. and other countries adopted the One China policy, and we need to think strategically if we were to abandon it. But the treatment of Taiwan is emblematic of the challenge of China. The world may very well sacrifice the rights of 22 million people living under a long-established democracy on the rock of China's new-found power and aggressiveness.

President Xi has been much more forthright in declaring a need to unify Taiwan with the People's Republic of China. "We will not tolerate anyone, using any means, at any time to separate one inch of land from China," he said. "Blood is thicker than water," Xi said at the 19th Party Congress, bringing identity politics to a new high (or rather, low). And Xi seems to be growing more impatient, saying the Taiwan issue "should not be passed down generation after generation."

Will China take the risk of invading Taiwan in the coming years? I don't know (2—Yep, we're keeping count). It certainly has tried to invade Taiwan politically and technologically. China has been conducting misinformation campaigns on social media in Taiwan.[31] And it has interfered in Taiwan elections.[32] It failed, however, in swinging the election to its preferred candidate in the most recent presidential election, a lesson from which we will apply in chapters 7 and 8. China has always regarded Taiwan as its own but in recent years has become more aggressive in its efforts to snatch Taiwanese from freedom and place them under the mainland's authoritarianism.

Tibet

Tibet is the original Xinjiang. That is to say, China for decades has worked to eradicate the Tibetan culture. China encouraged and facilitated the migration of hundreds of thousands of Han Chinese into Tibet, as it has now also done in Xinjiang. China has also made economic development in Tibet a priority, which generally is a good thing, but in this case, the Tibetan government in exile claims it is being done to marginalize Tibetan culture.

Of course, that exiled government is led by the Dalai Lama, and China now says it will determine who the new Dalai Lama will be once the current one, in his mid-80s, passes away.

Human Rights Watch reports that "Authorities in Tibetan areas continue to severely restrict religious freedom, speech, movement, and assembly…" They note that, as in Xinjiang, China is stressing political education in Tibet's monasteries and schools. What China has done and is doing in Tibet, they are also doing in Xinjiang, only perhaps amplified and with new technologies and techniques. Their hoped-for result is the same: cultural cleansing. Again, over the last ten years, China has been even more aggressive in its efforts in Tibet.

It can do this because it's more powerful economically, with greater sway in the world.

China is powerful, assertive, and a challenge

China has changed. It is more repressive, more ambitious on the world stage, and wants to export its values and system onto the world order. Xi amplified China's existing authoritarian tendencies while becoming more ambitious in projecting China's power and system onto the world. China is able to do this because of its remarkable economic growth and progress, a story worth celebrating even if it enables the great challenge China now presents to the world.

CHAPTER 2

The Economy is a Bakery, Not a Pie

We love pie. It's perhaps our favorite dessert. We make semi-regular trips to the best pie place in Seattle, A la Mode. The original one on Phinney Ridge, not the Johnny Come Lately in West Seattle. Along with stuffing, it's our favorite part of Thanksgiving. Agent Cooper's love of cherry pie was our favorite quirk of the TV show, *Twin Peaks*. Pie is good, it is important and we defend it against all dessert assailants.

But pie is the worst economic metaphor imaginable. People continually refer to pies in describing the world economy—as China's economy grew, there was less for the rest of us, they claim. But China's economic ascent does not mean there are fewer pieces for the rest of us. Just as the economic development of Japan, Singapore, Hong Kong, Taiwan, South Korea, and other markets did not harm the world or standards of living around the world, they enhanced it, China's economic rise also benefits the world.

The economy is a bakery, not a pie. The more goods and services China produces, the more entrepreneurs created, scientists trained, and artists mused, the more treats for the whole world. China's economic success is the greatest poverty alleviator the world has ever seen. Hundreds of millions of people are no longer in daily misery, no longer dying, no longer stuck in short, brutish lives, thanks to the economic reforms China implemented in the 1980s and the subsequent vast increase in GDP it created, leading to a higher standard of living.

The corollary of this fact, this truth, is that the U.S. and its allies should not seek to retard China's economy. America should develop a strategy to encourage China to liberalize. It should not have a strategy based on the notion that America should always, at all times, be larger economically than China. China's economic development is beneficial to Chinese, Japanese, Germans, Ghanaians, Americans, and the whole world, just as economic development everywhere is a positive. However, that we celebrate China's economic development does not mean we should not work to open up China's economy. We should point out and confront China's closed markets, its stealing of intellectual property, and other counterproductive economic policies. Dealing with China is not an economic competition. We want China to change for the better—for its own and the world's benefit—not to bury it.

Let's unpack all this some more.

China's Amazing Economic Success

In early October 2019, China celebrated the 70th anniversary of the founding of the People's Republic of China. And while we wouldn't have celebrated by featuring a parade of nuclear-capable missiles, soldiers marching in lockstep, and interminably long speeches (we would have hired a band or DJ and mixed some cocktails), it is true China had much to celebrate. For forty years, China has been an economic marvel, achieving high levels of economic growth and not coincidentally pulling hundreds of millions of men, women, and children out of abject poverty.

From the founding of the PRC in 1949 until late 1978, when communism was taken seriously by its leaders and Mao ran amok, annual GDP growth rates averaged less than 3 percent. From 1979 until 2019, after Deng Xiaoping launched economic reforms by de-collectivizing agriculture, allowing people to start businesses, and permitting foreign investment into the country, annual GDP growth rates averaged 8.2 percent.[1] (Don't worry we'll discuss China's unreliable data later.)

GDP per capita doubled from 1960 ($89.5) to 1979 ($184) but since then has gone up by a factor of 50, so that now per capita GDP in China is over $10,000. Today, China is the second-largest economy in the world as measured by overall GDP. It is a remarkable achievement. Over recent years, China has probably been the most important driver of global economic growth.

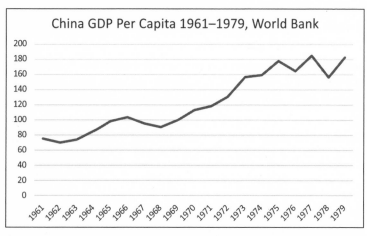

China GDP Per Capita 1961–1979, World Bank

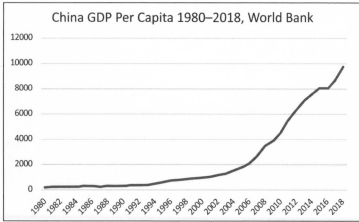

China GDP Per Capita 1980–2018, World Bank

Much of this economic success was built on international trade. In 1979, international trade accounted for about one percent of China's GDP. At its height in 2007, international trade was 64 percent of China's GDP but has since fallen to under 40 percent.[2]

China's economic success was the greatest poverty alleviation program in human history. The World Bank estimates that since 1979, 850 million people in China have been lifted out of extreme poverty (people living on $1.90 or less per day). That means the absolute poverty rate fell from 88 percent to less than 1 percent. Again, an amazing achievement, and for all of the world's many legitimate concerns about China, an achievement that should be applauded.

Andrew Batson, the research director for Gavekal Dragonomics, wrote an interesting blog post after three economists won the 2019 Nobel Prize for Economics for their work on alleviating global poverty. Batson noted that no one has won the Nobel Prize for China's poverty alleviation, even though those reforms led to more poverty alleviation than any other.[3] Unlike the three Nobel winners, China actually, well, reduced poverty for hundreds of millions of people. Batson quotes Harvard professor Dani Rodrik's tweet: "Remarkable how little today's development economics has to say about the most impressive poverty reduction in history ever." Batson chooses Xue Muqiao as the most likely candidate for China's economic and thus poverty reduction success. Xue advised Deng Xiaoping on economic reform, including de-collectivizing agriculture.

Certainly China's remarkable economic success is based on leveraging the market. Arthur Kroeber also of the economics research firm, Gavekal, wrote in his book about China's economy that "Between 1978 and 1990, the share of consumer goods whose prices were set by the market went from zero to 70 percent...by the end of the 1990s, 95 percent of consumer goods, and 90 percent of agricultural commodities and producer goods were purely market-priced."[4] State-owned enterprises still play an outsized role in China's economy but only account for 35 percent of China's GDP with private firms accounting for 65 percent. It is the market that drove China's remarkable economic success and in turn the astonishing lowering of poverty and other social goods achieved.

Of course, this all occurred within a self-proclaimed communist government. It also was accompanied with the usual developing country corruption. Some experts on China, and non-experts like myself, are often confused by how China managed to be so successful economically while having large amounts of corruption and outsized state involvement. In other developing countries, such high levels of corruption have retarded their economic growth. A recent book by Yuen Yuen Ang, a political science professor at the University of Michigan, sheds some much needed light on this dark matter subject.[5] She breaks corruption into four categories: *petty theft*, the kind where police and small-time bureaucrats shake you down for small bribes; *grand theft*, which is when a political leader absconds with millions of dollars; *speed money* where you grease a bureaucrat's palm to get a permit; and *access money* where businesses pay, often large sums, to higher level officials to construct projects or obtain near monopolies for a series of projects. Ang argues that while all four types of corruption are harmful to an economy, the fourth one, access money, can often encourage economic growth in the short-run. She also argues that while early on in the post-1979 reform era that China had all four of these types of corruption in abundance, in the last few decades access money corruption has been the predominant mode of corruption. It essentially functioned as a successful profit-sharing tool for government officials, and provided incentives for them to implement policies and projects that encouraged economic growth. Of course, this type of corruption distorts the economy and as China enters a new stage of economic development, could be even more problematic going forward.

There are undoubtedly many fathers and mothers of China's economic success, and the world should applaud them and continue to conduct research to understand how this success came about. Maybe the Nobel Committee will finally even bestow one of its awards on someone who helped make them happen. China has not just alleviated poverty but has also become a powerful driver of innovation.

I'm always amazed at how many people believe China is still a copycat economy—stealing intellectual property and creating nothing new of its own. While it is true that China still steals intellectual property, there is also plenty of innovation taking place. Both things can be true at the same time. Anyone who has traveled to China knows they are far ahead of the United States in mobile payment systems, for example. In 2016, according to a Brookings Institution Report, Chinese consumers spent $22 trillion on mobile payment systems. The United States? Only $112 billion.[6] One of the reasons for China's innovation in this technology is scale. China has as many 4G phone users as the entire U.S. population (with 5G controversially coming along with Huawei). China now has more than 800 million mobile Internet users.[7] Many of these mobile Internet users are young, with 27 percent between the ages of 20 and 29.[8] To service this young user base, Chinese companies have to innovate. Yes, Chinese companies have been protected from foreign competition, but the sheer scale of the market, the more than 200 million users under the age of 30, forces them to innovate. You gotta give the people what they want.

Similarly, China has gone all in on artificial intelligence. In 2017, China published a "Next Generation Artificial Intelligence Development Plan," which laid out its plans to be a leader in AI by 2030 (at which point presumably AI will write and publish its own development plans). China is spending more than $30 billion in research and development investments in artificial intelligence. Of course, it remains to be seen whether these are productive investments since many of them are in state-owned enterprises and it is difficult to differentiate between political and value investing in those cases. Chinese researchers now publish at least as many AI papers as American researchers, but as the Stanford-New America Digichina Project points out, "Numerous papers by Chinese researchers had zero citations, while the number of papers with over 1,000 citations by Chinese-only authors is also much smaller than that of papers

45

co-published by Chinese researchers together with U.S. researchers."[9] And the paper also notes that much of Chinese AI is still reliant on U.S. hardware and innovations.

Nonetheless, China is on the road to AI influence, or at least has great aims to do so. China has more and more talent working on AI, perhaps second only to the U.S. But, according to MarcoPolo.org, one-third of these researchers end up overseas. But if the U.S. cuts off Chinese researchers working in the U.S (more on that in a later chapter), that could add to and deepen China's AI talent pool.

China innovates in other ways too, including in biotechnology. Back in 2015 during a trip to Shenzhen, I ate genetically modified millet at the headquarters of the Chinese genomics company BGI. This millet is designed to grow in extreme weather with less water. BGI has one of the largest repositories of sequenced genomes in the world, operates in 100 countries (including in my hometown of Seattle), and works with more than 3000 medical institutions and more than 300 hospitals. BGI is providing testing equipment and capabilities to a number of countries during the Covid-19 pandemic.

China's life science sector is rapidly expanding. As of 2016, according to a report from The National Bureau of Asian Research, China is the second-largest market in the world for pharmaceuticals.[10] It is also developing more biologics, leading to a large increase in patent applications. Of course, there have been some famous ethical lapses in China's life science industry, including and especially He Jiankui's creating the first genetically edited babies. The Chinese government forced the suspension of his activities, placed him under surveillance in a university apartment, and eventually convicted and jailed him. He's activities are a testament to both the innovation that is happening in China and the need for a legal structure to deal with these new medical breakthroughs.

China becoming an innovative economy and continuing to grow economically is not in and of itself a problem. In fact, it should be welcomed. I often read about or see people advocating for trying to retard or damage China's economy. They want the United States to continue to be the number one economy in the world. This is unrealistic, immoral, and a misunderstanding of how economies work. China is a country of 1.3 billion people (give or take a few hundred million—there is some evidence that China is miscounting here, just as it does in so much other data[11]). Even with slower economic growth, China will eventually be the largest economy in the world, though as we'll discuss shortly, it is unlikely to be the largest per capita.

We should not be hoping for China's economy to crater. That would be harmful to the Chinese people, and their lives matter as much as the lives of Americans, Germans, Mexicans or any other people. Why should I wish for misery for people in China? A family in Yangzhou in Jiangsu Province is as important as one in Yazoo City, Mississippi. Remember the economy is a bakery, not a pie. If China continues to grow economically, it does not mean there are fewer slices for Americans or for the rest of the world. It means there are more pies for the rest of us to eat, or cakes, pastries, and torts for those not into pies (but get out of my sight, you pie haters).

When more genomic or biologic companies are created in China, that means additional medicines, treatments, and therapies for all of us. If China makes breakthroughs in artificial intelligence, we benefit from applications in self-driving cars, energy management and in other areas.

China's economic success is helping other countries. When people discuss China's activities in Africa, most of the attention focuses on large government-influenced projects such as loans that can't be paid back or China's taking control of ports or other worrying activities. But the 2017 book *The Next Factory of the World: How Chinese Investment is Reshaping Africa* focuses on the individual Chinese businesspeople who are opening factories throughout Africa. It is one of the most enlightening and important books of recent years. The author, Irene Yuan Sun, in the best way, melds individual stories of Chinese investors and Africans she has interviewed, with a broader macro data view to develop a current picture of Africa and a possible vision for its future. As she notes, these private Chinese investors are not part of the geopolitical games of the Chinese government. "They are instead driven by the economics of their individual businesses and the momentum of their own remarkable life trajectories. These are Chinese who rose from working in the early factories of China to developing their own in Africa." Sun's hope is that just as Japan begat Taiwan, which led to South Korea and China, a variety of African countries are now poised to become the next manufacturing powerhouses, with all the economic and social development that entails. Sun's glasses are not rose-tinted. She explains the trade-offs, challenges, and possible pitfalls of Chinese investment in Africa. The book may change how you view the ascent of China and the prospects for Africa. The book notes there are now more than 10,000 Chinese firms active in Africa (mostly privately owned), each transforming the localities in which they've set up shop. From flip-flop factories in Nigeria, to ceramics manufacturing in Lesotho, to drug capsules in Ethiopia. Sun's book notes the "confluence of rising labor costs in China, the relocation of Chinese factory owners with valuable life experiences to Africa, and how Africa's demographics make it possible for us to imagine that Africa might very well become the next factory of the world." China's heavy-handed, geopolitically driven state investment and loans are problematic. Individual Chinese investing and working in other lands are beneficial.

Other parts of Asia are also receiving investment. In the fall of 2019, I visited a shoe factory in Vietnam that had moved from southern China three years before. The factory employs hundreds of local Vietnamese to assemble these shoes. Some of them will rise to management level and eventually open their own factories and businesses, developing Vietnam's economy, know-how and experience. The U.S.–China trade war accelerated the trend of manufacturing moving from China to other countries, but the trend had already started, even before higher U.S. tariffs, due to rising labor costs in China. It is likely to accelerate due to Covid-19, which is illustrating the fragility of just-in-time supply chains that are centered too heavily in one country (and perhaps even in one region). In fact, I'd wager that supply chains will change more because of the pandemic than from any event since September 11th. The changing of the supply chain, the moving of manufacturing to other markets, are inevitable and helpful developments. But even as the world's economy continues to evolve, we should not lose sight of the fact that China's economic success is a good thing for the world.

China's Economic Development Did Not Lead to Political Liberalization

We should not be trying to stop China's economic progress. Instead, we should attempt to liberalize China, both politically and economically. This is, of course, easier said than done. Many people are understandably skeptical of this prospect because so many China experts, and people like me, thought that China's economic development would eventually lead to China opening up its economy and liberalizing politically. This was not merely wishful thinking, although it turned out to be wrong.

Economic growth leading to liberalization was the pattern for other Asian Tigers. Taiwan was originally a dictatorship under Chiang Kai-shek. In 1955, GDP per capita was under US$1000. By the late 1980s, it had reached $5000 per capita. There were other factors involved, including political pressure from the United States and from China's efforts to isolate Taiwan, but around that time Chiang Kai-shek's son and successor, Ching-Kuo, pledged political reform. In the early 1990s, Taiwan's GDP per capita reached US$10,000. The first full elections to Taiwan's parliament took place in 1992.

In the early 1960s, South Korea's economy was the same size as Ghana's. It was ruled under a military dictatorship. By 1984, South Korea's per capita GDP reached $5000. In 1987, as GDP per capita rose to above $7000 per capita, again with U.S. and international pressure, South Korea held its first free presidential election. By 1992, GDP per capita was at the US$10,000 level, and further political liberalization took place.

Cities and city-states have been resistant to democratization. In the case of Hong Kong, their British colonists resisted democratizing before the handover in 1997. Singapore is a city-state that has also seen constrained democratization as it grew economically.

But there is considerable academic literature linking economic development and tendencies towards democratization inside and out of Asia. UCLA Political Science professor Daniel Treisman, for example, has a paper titled "Economic Development and Democracy: Predispositions and Triggers."[12] In the paper, he asserts, "There is a strong and consistent relationship between higher income and both democratization and democratic survival in the medium term (10-20 years), but not necessarily in shorter time windows." The short term is difficult, Treisman says, because the incumbent dictators are adept at holding onto their power and economic development does not necessarily change that. In fact, "Vigorous growth—which boosts household incomes and government revenues—enhances the incumbent's survival odds. Thus, dictators have a personal interest in growth."

So it may be short-sighted to presume a growing economy will lead to the ouster of dictators in the short term. But, Treisman continues, "over time that same growth changes society and the ruling elite in ways that make it more likely the regime will collapse after the dictator is gone. What's good for the dictator is not so good for his dynasty."

The challenge in China is that once Xi is gone, and eventually he too will leave the scene, unless Silicon Valley techno-optimists succeed in their anti-aging dreams, the Communist Party of China has been very adept at peaceful succession. If we think of the CCP as the dictator, rather than the individual, the economic development leading to political liberalization model, is disrupted. Treisman in his paper notes, "The Soviet Union collapsed, yielding 15 new countries and liberating its East European allies. Almost all are more democratic today than 30 years ago." But as we saw in the previous chapter, Xi and his comrades have closely studied the fall of the Soviet Union and are taking active steps to ensure Communist China does not suffer the same fate.

So there were both many reasons to expect economic growth to lead to democratization in China and also reasons to not expect it too soon. And today we should understand the rulers of China are doing everything they can to prevent political liberalization coming to their land.

But regardless of political liberalization, it does not make sense to prevent China from growing economically. The U.S. should not aim to be the largest economy for eternity, we should not fear more innovators, and we should be happy that so many people have risen out of poverty. But, as we deliberate on how best to encourage a more liberalized China, we should view its economic future more clearly and recognize that the era of high economic growth in China is over.

China's Economic Challenges

Like the continuing question of whether Tony Soprano died or not (he did[13]), there are many mysteries in our world. But we find it strange that people continue to question whether China's economy is slowing no matter the official GDP figure (pre-Covid-19 pandemic). It has and is. But I think what people are really asking is whether the era of high GDP growth is over in China. The answer is also yes. GDP growth comes from increased productivity and/or an increase in the working age population. China's working age population is at best flat, and most experts believe it is actually falling. Caixin Global reports that a paper released by the Chinese Academy of Social Sciences (CASS) "said that China's working age population, defined as the number of people aged between 16 and 64, declined by 1.6 million in 2013, marking the beginning of a serious structural change to the population: a shrinking workforce." China's official productivity statistics still show strong growth of just over 6 percent, though this is lower than earlier in the decade. Total Factor Productivity growth has also been slowing since the Great Financial Recession.[14] As the great urban migration slows and its economy matures, China's productivity increases are likely to continue to slow. Oh, and if you examine China compared to other Asian Tigers, the end of rapid GDP growth is right on time, as the chart below shows.

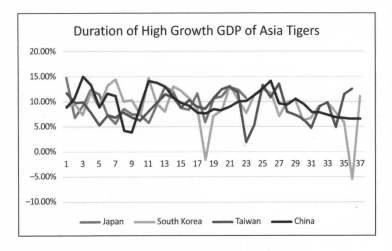

Analysts such as Nicholas Lardy point out that the economic growth histories of China and Taiwan, South Korea, Singapore, and Japan are not comparable. By the time the Asian Tigers ended their rapid economic growth they had reached GDP per capita growth levels much closer to that of the United States. In the cases of South Korea, Taiwan, and Singapore, they reached the level of half of U.S. GDP per capita. In the case of Japan, they made it all the way to two-thirds of U.S. GDP per capita. China is still only a little bit over one-quarter of U.S. GDP per capita. So, the Lardy argument goes, there is still plenty of room for China to grow at high rates. China extreme bulls don't stop believing.

Although Lardy and others know far more about China and are steeped more deeply in its economic data, we remain skeptical. Pushing through the weeds of unreliable official Chinese economic data, even the trees of its underlying, perhaps more reliable data, is one large forest of demography. China's aging demographics are too overwhelming to sustain high rates of growth.

In fact, China's overall demographics beyond its working age population are challenging. China is getting old fast—it's demographics currently are almost as old as that of the United States and if trends hold, its demographics will shortly be older than the U.S.'s The World Health Organization classifies a country's population as "aging" when the percentage of people over 65 reaches 7 percent. Currently, 11.4 percent of China's population is over the age of 65. One estimate, by the University of Washington's Institute for Health Metrics and Evaluation, projects a drastic fall in China's population by the year 2100, when the study projects China would only have 732 million people.[15]

Part of this demographic problem is due to the one-child policy, which China ditched in 2016. But, like other Asian countries, like developed countries, Chinese are still having fewer babies even after eliminating that policy. The latest World Bank figures show births per woman at 1.683. China recognizes this and is working to encourage its people to have more children, but many countries have tried and are trying to do this without much success. The latest figures from China's government in 2019 estimated new births at 11 million, down from 17 million two years prior.[16] This lower number of births is below projections and means China's overall population will peak in 2026, four years sooner than expected and projected by the UN population estimates. The relaxation of the one-child policy has not had the large effect on fertility rates that Chinese leaders hoped for (more evidence that they are not smarter or playing the long game better than everybody else, as so many argue). As you see in the table, within 20 years, China's population will be older than the U.S.'s. That is using projections for fertility levels that are actually higher than China's fertility levels were in 2019. If China is not able to raise fertility levels (although there may be a temporary coronavirus baby boom—people needed to do something while stuck in their apartments), and no other country has so far been successful in doing so, then China becomes grayer sooner and in ten years its demographics start to look like those of the Japan of today. And Japan's current population is old and a big challenge for its economy and society.

China's demographics will be a drag on economic growth and continued innovation.

Ratio of Population Aged 65+ per 100 population (15-64) Old-Age Dependency Ratio

Year	China	United States	Japan	South Korea	India
2020	17.0	25.6	48	22	9.8
2030	25.0	32.5	53.2	38.2	12.5
2040	38.3	35.4	65.5	57.8	15.7
2050	43.6	36.6	74.3	73.2	20.3
2060	53.1	40.4	76.3	83.1	26.1

United Nations, Department of Economic and Social Affairs, Population Division, World Population Prospects 2019, custom data acquired via website

Lardy and some others argue that China's aging demographics will not be as big a drag on its economy as one might ordinarily expect for a couple reasons. One is that China's labor participation is low among the 50 and older crowd and that this is due to the low retirement age in China. In addition, Lardy notes that "about half of all workers retire prior to reaching the low mandatory retirement age." [17] China is planning on gradually increasing the retirement age which currently is anywhere from 50-years-old to 60 depending on your occupation.[18] Lardy and others contend that by raising the retirement age, by encouraging oldsters to return to work, China will be able to mitigate its aging demographic challenge. We will be interested to see how successful China is in encouraging these older workers to return to the labor force, but we are also dubious that official statistics are capturing labor participation rates accurately. Yes, Chinese can retire early, but often they continue to work in other careers that may or may not be captured by official data. Pension benefits are not robust in China so there is already incentive for those reaching the young retirement age to keep working. In fact, China's labor participation rate of 67 percent (for those 15 and older) is higher than the global average and even the average of middle income countries (60 percent).[19] We're skeptical that China will be able to increase that percentage. Chinese in their 50s who have already retired but have not reentered the workforce are unlikely to do so unless their retirement benefits are cut. China's government is heavy-handed but is unlikely to do something that could cause social unrest. After all, the deal that China's leaders have made the last 40 years is in return for a growing economy and higher standards of living, they get to stay in power. Would these officials really lower the living standards of people 50 and older? Even if the decline in the working age population can be mitigated by raising the retirement age, the working age population will still decline, just not by as much. Aging demographics are a stiff headwind.

More workers is one way to increase GDP, increased productivity is another. But aging demographics retard that input as well. To cite a paper by the IMF, as one study among many, "workforce aging reduces growth in labor productivity..."[20] There has been a worldwide productivity slowdown. Productivity is increasing at a slower rate in Japan, South Korea, Germany, the U.K., and the United States. As with any phenomenon, there are probably multiple factors involved, but certainly aging demographics are one of them. China's productivity

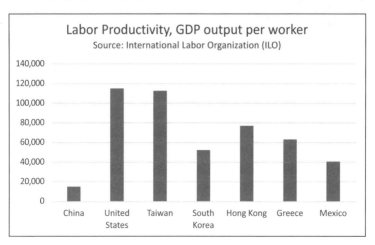

Labor Productivity, GDP output per worker
Source: International Labor Organization (ILO)

growth, while still above that of Europe, Japan, Korea, and the U.S., is also steadily decreasing, and is now down to 6.6 percent. It peaked at 13 percent in 2007 and has gone down ever since. More worrisome for China, though its productivity and economic growth have been extraordinary over the last 25 years, is that it had still not caught up to developed countries or even to the world average. Each Chinese worker is producing far less than a Japanese, European or American, even as the cost of Chinese labor rises. Some, including Lardy, would look at this optimistically and argue this means China has plenty of room for continued fast economic growth (coupled with certain economic reforms, Lardy would add). Maybe so, but we argue the aging demographics will make it increasingly hard to catch up.

Lardy and others also point to how few Chinese have a high school or college education as another way they can overcome demographics and again achieve rapid economic growth. Lardy cites a source that asserts less than 30 percent of the Chinese workforce had a high school education in 2015.[21] He notes "this is well below the level of educational attainment in some other upper middle-income countries such as Mexico (46 percent), South Africa (42 percent) and Malaysia (51 percent)…" Lardy concludes that China can easily increase its productivity, and thus its GDP growth, by providing a high school education to more of its people that will improve the quality of its workforce. But Lardy overestimates the importance of that 30 percent figure. Primary education is compulsory for all Chinese children up to the age of 15. At that age, school becomes voluntary, with some opting for a vocational track and some for a general academic track. China's Hukou system, a household registration system that categorizes every Chinese by where they live and their geographic origin, has certainly hampered the ability of rural Chinese to get a high school education. Education beyond age 15 is far more obtainable for urban residents than those classified as rural under the Hukou system. China has indicated it may reform this system and it would be good if high school was obtainable for more Chinese, but it is unlikely to improve worker productivity rates. China has improved the number of people getting a high school and college education over the last thirty years, but the low 30 percent figure is partly due to a large base of people to begin with. Remember China's aging demographics, which is older than Mexico's, South Africa's and even Malaysia's. As we move forward, as a percentage, there will be fewer younger people to be educated. Further, that source Lardy uses for the 30 percent figure? They too don't believe improvements in the percentage of people with a high school education will restore China to high GDP growth: "Using what we view as optimistic assumptions about the expansion of education in China, it seems almost impossible for China to grow at an annual rate of 7 percent for the next 20 years…" That's using "optimistic assumptions" I remind you. So even the authors of the paper Lardy cites for the low 30 percent of the Chinese workforce with a high school education to advance his argument that China can again achieve high GDP growth rates don't believe China can again achieve high economic growth.

China's economy will not grow as rapidly in the future as it has since the 1980s. It is probably not growing at the official rate of 6 percent currently (pre-coronavirus). This factor is important to remember as we develop strategies on how to encourage China to liberalize. But lower GDP growth is not China's only economic challenge.

China also has debt challenges. China has a total debt to GDP ratio of 310 percent. This includes households, non-financial corporate, government and the financial sector. This is higher than the U.S., France, Japan, U.K., and Germany. It is the highest indebted emerging market economy in the world. By far the biggest culprit in China's debt is non-financial corporations, which is 157 percent of GDP, which makes China's non-financial corporate debt one of the highest in the world.[22] China's government debt is not particularly high. Its household debt isn't either, though it has been rapidly rising in recent years. The Wall Street Journal reports, "For every dollar of gross domestic product generated in China last year, its households owed 54 cents, according to the International Monetary Fund."[23] This is compared to 78 cents per dollar in the U.S. And, of course, Chinese save much more than Americans. But that savings rate is going down, from 39 cents for every dollar earned in 2010 to 30 cents today. So the trend in household debt in China is increasing but still appears manageable.

It is private, non-financial corporate debt that is high in China. Of course, "private" is an interesting term to use here since much of this corporate debt is in state-owned enterprises. And even apparently private companies have many government ties, so determining what is public and private debt is difficult.

Corporate debt started increasing rapidly in China after the financial crisis as the Chinese government applied Keynesian-like policies to ward off recession/depression. It worked, with China appearing to suffer less economically than many other parts of the world. Compare China's relative economic success to the EU's sluggish recovery which practiced austerity during that time. Keynes might have been onto something.

But these policies did increase debt, and in recent years the return value for debt in China is lower. For each yuan of investment China makes, there has been a smaller increase in GDP growth. Many economists have been wondering about recent investment efficiency in China. The Mercator Institute for China Studies puts it this way: "One implication is that a decline in investment efficiency may contribute to a higher corporate debt/GDP ratio, since sustaining a given economic growth rate would require a higher investment rate."[24] The coronavirus crisis will likely make China's debt stress greater. The government is rightly infusing capital into the economy and lending more to companies that are under stress due to the economy shutting down as a result of the massive quarantine policy of the Chinese government. This is a necessary economic step to alleviate the effects of an unprecedented temporary economic shutdown, but it will add to China's debt problem.

China also has a high rate of inequality. Its GINI coefficient, a measure of inequality with zero being perfect equality and 1 complete inequality, is now one of the highest in Asia, the highest among industrialized Asia, and well above the OECD average.[25] If China had elections, presumably Bernie Sanders and Elizabeth Warren would do well there. China's inequality issues were growing so bad that for a number of years it refused to publish GINI coefficient data.[26]

Of course, one of the challenges in understanding what is going on in China is its unreliable data. Pre-Covid-19, China claimed a GDP growth rate of just over 6 percent. But not many people believe it. This leads analysts to look at underlying data—from car sales to imports to even beer sales (our favorite indicator). But even some of those figures may not be entirely reliable. China wants to be a leader of the world. Lack of transparency, including on economic data, will make that a challenge. So too will its coercive policies.

Coercive Economic policies

A few years ago, I was working with a Chinese company which was looking for investments in the U.S. The problem was they wanted me to find them investments but they didn't want to pay me to do so. It seemed an odd recipe for business. Or rather it was a great recipe for them, but a crap sandwich for me.

As time went on, I viewed it as a metaphor for the Chinese government's approach to economic policy. As has been written about often, testified to in Congress, complained about in various international fora, China forces technology transfer, closes large parts of its market to foreign competition, and installs selective boycotts on countries and companies that do not toe China's lengthy line.

Foreign companies wanting to do business in China in certain technology areas must transfer their intellectual property to Chinese partners. Often the foreign companies are required to set up a joint venture with a local firm. We once were in a meeting with an executive of a Seattle biotech firm that had developed a small medical device and a Chinese investor interested in investing in the company. The investor wanted to keep the small device and take it back with him to China. The local biotech company executive quickly snatched it back from the investor. He did not trust that his IP would not be stolen. He was almost certainly correct to be worried.

A Bloomberg article[27] provides a number of examples of companies that have dealt with forced technology transfer challenges, from Kawasaki in Japan to Dupont in the United States. China asserts that any technology transfer is done on a voluntary basis, as part of agreements between China and foreign companies. The Bloomberg article notes, "A 2018 report by the U.S. Trade Representative quoted one ex-White House official as saying the transfers are voluntary in the same way a business proposition from mob boss Vito Corleone in 'The Godfather' was."

The allure of China is its enormous market. The dream of selling to 1.4 billion people is a strong elixir for any business. But much of that market is closed for foreign businesses. China protects its industries like a bear eying a hiker near her cubs. There's a reason a hyper-successful company like Amazon is not successful in China and it has nothing to do with its business strategy. China decided it would grow its own online shopping platforms. Other tech companies such as Microsoft have had their China offices raided under flimsy pretext.[28] China is hostile to many foreign businesses, at least in certain industries. Of course, many foreign businesses do succeed there such as Starbucks Coffee, but even successful companies operate not under the rule of law but at the whim of the government. What if Xi Jinping wakes up one day and determines Luckin Coffee[29] is a strategic company? Starbucks would be forced out of China quicker than Howard Schultz forced the Sonics to move to Oklahoma City.

As the NBA discovered, if a single employee tweets something offensive to China policymakers (of course, Twitter is banned in China), their entire business is threatened in China. The NBA is not an isolated case. Other foreign companies have fired employees for similar so-called transgressions. Indeed, China has punished companies for acts by the country in which they're headquartered, regardless of the innocence of the company. When South Korea allowed the U.S. to install anti-missile defense systems in its country, China objected. But they also punished the South Korean supermarket chain, Lotte, citing "safety concerns," shutting down 23 stores across China. Or think back to when Norway awarded the Nobel Peace Prize to writer and human rights activist Liu Xiaobo. Suddenly Norway, which once was one of the largest exporters of salmon to China, was reduced to a piker, so to speak, with exports of its seafood crumbling. Eventually, Norway and China signed a bilateral seafood agreement that again allowed the flow of Norwegian salmon into China. But as part of that agreement, the two countries released a joint proclamation that reads like a hostage giving a statement with their kidnappers holding a gun to their head:[30]

> *The Norwegian Government fully respects China's development path and social system, and highly commends its historic and unparalleled development that has taken place. The Norwegian Government reiterates its commitment to the one-China policy, fully respects China's sovereignty and territorial integrity, attaches high importance to China's core interests and major concerns, will not support actions that undermine them, and will do its best to avoid any further damage to the bilateral relations.*

China has unquestionably been successful economically over the last forty years and deserves immense praise and credit for it. China's economic success has been a good thing for the world. But rapid economic growth in China has ended and is not coming back. And it faces many economic challenges going forward. But even a slower-growing China, one with economic challenges, is still very important. This is because it is big and even the economic development it has accomplished so far has created an enormous market. The size of China's economy and population means China, even the new, slower-growing China, is going to be important. And therein lies the challenge for the rest of the world, or at least for those who care about a rules-based world that respects human rights and freedom.

Many other countries throughout history have protected certain industries and advocated mercantile policies as they developed economically. If that was the only challenge China posed, we would not be writing this book and there would not be so much concern by people who know and work with China. But China, as we saw in chapter 1, now wants to export its model: the limited-rule-of-law economic model, the lack-of-trust business culture, and the repressive political policies. That is a problem. We will go into more detail in chapter 6 about the post-World War II/post-Cold War order that was built upon and was progressing to one of rule of law, even if imperfectly and not on a straight path. We will explain the many ways China is challenging that order and how the Trump administration undermined it. If the world tosses out a world order based on the rule of law and a business culture based on contracts, and instead moves towards a Chinese-ruled order and business culture, it will hinder future world economic growth and innovation, bring a new lawlessness to international business, and in the end will also harm China's economy, which is already facing headwinds.

The combination of an aggressive China in world affairs, a more authoritarian government, and one committed to continued economic warfare is an issue for all of the world. The U.S. needs new strategies to push back against China's coercive economic, investment, and trade policies and its political aggressiveness. We'll go into how best to do that later in the book, coupled with how the United States can again become a leader in promoting liberalization. But perhaps the most effective policy to counter China's pushing a new non-rules-based world order, unfriendly to democracy and human rights, is for the United States to become more successful itself.

CHAPTER 3

We Succeed in Changing China by Being Successful Ourselves

Some years ago, I stood in my hotel room in Shenzhen staring out the window at the city's glorious skyline. A tall high-rise across the way displayed a stream of LED lights that lit up in sequence going down the building and then flickering in different colors, from purple to red. A panoply of differently shaped skyscrapers, all unique, gave me the feeling of having stepped into the future. It was a beautiful sight, one that filled the senses and brightened the visage even on cloudy (or smoggy) days and nights.

I contrasted it to the town in which I usually lay my head on a pillow, Seattle. My city's skyline is full of dreary boxes, almost all colored gray, causing them to meld into the rainy-day gray weather of the town. They are boring, drab and look to the past, rather than to a bright, shiny glimmering future that Shenzhen and many other Chinese cities anticipate in their architecture.

China is the future, the United States is the past. We are in the Asian Century. The 20th Century may have been the American one, but that's already 20 years in the rearview mirror. It is China's economic success that empowers it to export its ruling values. China's economic success is why parts of the rest of the world seem willing to adopt the China way. After all, if China can sustain double-digit or high single-digit GDP growth, raise hundreds of millions of people out of poverty, and become an innovative economy creating cool mobile payment, entertainment, and informational systems, perhaps the rest of us should consider the virtues of its authoritarian governing system? Perhaps Churchill was wrong and democracy is not the worst governing system except for all the others. China offers a model for prosperity, safety, and stability.

That's the line China was able to start promoting out of the ashes of the Great Financial Crisis of 2008. When Lehman Brothers collapsed on September 15, 2008, it did not just bring down a 160-year-old company, trigger a loss of $10 trillion in market capitalization from global equity markets, and lead to a Great Recession in the United States and around many parts of the world, it also took a sledgehammer to American exceptionalism. Because you see, China recovered more robustly than the United States, the E.U. and other parts of the world damaged by the financial crisis. China, as we noted in the last chapter, went extreme Keynesian and kept its GDP growth rate above 9 percent through 2010. Even if China's official GDP numbers are as optimistic as my spring training hopes for the Seattle Mariners, it is still true that China weathered the financial crisis far better than the rest of the world.

In fact, post 2008, China became the single largest driver of the world economy. As Nicholas Lardy writes in his most recent book,[1] in 2015, China "accounted for about one-third of global growth." During that same time, the U.S. accounted for 17.9 percent, the EU 7.9 percent, and India 8.6 percent. The rest of the world became tied into China's growing economy in ways it increasingly was not with the United States. Again, Lardy notes that China "is a top ten export market for over 100 countries, accounting for about 80 percent of world GDP."

The economist Tyler Cowen captures the allure of a successful authoritarian China: "Individuals have a desire to copy or praise or affiliate what is perceived as successful, and a lot of our metrics of success have to do with power rather than freedom or prosperity. So if there is a powerful system on the world stage, many of us will be drawn to it and seek to emulate it, without always being conscious of the reasons for those attractions."[2]

At the same time that China avoided the worst consequences of the financial crisis, the U.S. went through a deep recession. The U.S. avoided a depression but experienced slow economic growth, and many years passed before the economy was restored to full employment. But the U.S. also experienced growing inequality (put aside for a moment that China's inequality has also risen substantially) and little to no real wage growth until 2017. The U.S., compared to glitzy, growing China, seemed like an old has-been. Meanwhile, much of the E.U. struggled in continued deep recession, with places like Spain and Greece suffering unemployment rates above 20 percent and youth unemployment near 50 percent. Europeans could easily be forgiven for believing that a Chinese future was rosier than a European.

Japan was in its third decade of low GDP growth, and its population, due to low birth rates, was actually decreasing. Japan is literally becoming smaller every year.[3] The democratic, economically liberal countries stretching from North America to Europe to Asia were in a funk.

And then came two political explosions: Brexit and the 2016 U.S. presidential election. On June 23, 2016, when 51.9 percent of U.K. voters pulled the Brexit lever, it sent a shockwave of angst through the democratic world. First, it was a surprise since pre-election polls showed Remainers would prevail. But it was also a blow to the post-World War II, post-Cold War order that had been built brick by brick out of the political, violent, and economic devastation of World War II. As much as anything, it shook the confidence of the democratic world, which since the end of the Cold War had been on a steady ascent around the world.

U.S. voters, never content to be outshined by the good people of the U.K., stretching back to a tea party in Boston, decided to send their own shockwave through the post-World War II, post-Cold War order by electing a man with no sense of order personally, politically or seemingly in any other way, Donald Trump.

The lessening of U.S. influence in the world was coming anyway, and there inevitably would have been an evolution of the post-World War II, post-Cold War order, but Trump, like a drunken arsonist in a stately, aging Frank Lloyd Wright structure, greatly accelerated it. On his first day in office, as he promised during the campaign, Trump withdrew from the Trans-Pacific Partnership (TPP) trade agreement, which had been negotiated by 12 Asia-Pacific countries, partly as a way to streamline trade with up-to-date environmental and labor protections and partly as a counter-weight to China's influence in the Asia-Pacific region. China was pointedly not a part of the TPP. This was by design. Of course, Trump's opponent in the 2016 election was also against the TPP, even though she was part of the Obama administration that negotiated the agreement. Many political/policy wags assumed that once she was elected, Clinton would find a way to reverse herself and keep the U.S. a part of the TPP. It was this kind of political dishonesty that helped make a Trump presidency possible.[4] Whether or not Clinton would have pulled out of the TPP, Trump did, setting afire a long-negotiated agreement among many U.S. allies and strategic partners. Pulling out of the TPP reduced trust in the U.S. as a negotiating partner and its influence in the Asia Pacific. It was a positive for China's geopolitical aims.

Early on, Trump also made clear his international trade policy would be based on trade deficits as the main issue of concern—not access to markets, not intellectual property protection, not market barriers, not labor or environmental concerns—just a strange transactional fixation on overall export and import balances between individual countries and the United States. In April of his first year in office, Trump signed an executive order implementing an overview of all trade agreements and trade relations with countries "with which the United States does not have free trade agreements but with which the United States runs significant trade deficits in goods."[5] Putting aside that the executive order does not include services trade, in which the U.S. usually runs a surplus, and that there are countless other measures more important than trade balances to indicate whether a trade relationship is "fair" and healthy, Trump was loudly announcing there was a new sheriff in town who knew he could shoot trade advocates dead on Fifth Avenue with no consequences.

In fact, 2017 was all prelude to Trump's placing tariffs on innumerable goods from dozens of countries: allies, competitors and foes alike faced tariffs and/or threats in 2018 and 2019. In March of 2018, Trump announced a 25 percent tax on steel and a 10 percent tax on aluminum that applied to any and all countries. As a host of countries threatened retaliation and blowback came from businesses within the United States, Trump soon exempted Canada and Mexico (with whom he was renegotiating NAFTA) and soon after that the EU, eventually exempting a variety of other countries. A year after the tariffs were implemented causing so much political disruption with countries who could have been allies in trying to force China to open up its economy, employment in the metals industry is slightly up but not by any more than the overall employment rate rose. Wages for steel workers are actually down in contrast to minor increases for workers overall. But production is up, although some are now worried about over-capacity in the steel industry (note that is, of course, all pre-Covid-19 pandemic).[6]

March of 2018 was also when Trump began placing tariffs on goods from China. In late March, Trump announced changes to the Korea-U.S. Free Trade Agreement. From then on there was a frenzy of tariffing, threatening and more, from Rwanda to Europe, Canada to Latin America, and especially, of course, to China. The trade Ides of March were abundant and loud. The trend of freer trade, or at least managed trade negotiated under multilateral trade agreements and some bilateral agreements, which abated in the Obama years, was now dead as Jacob Marley's doornail, a nail which we admit was probably imported from some far-flung country.

But, of course, it's more than the international trade component of the international world order that has been upturned by Trump. In June of his first year, Trump announced the U.S. would abandon the Paris Climate Change Accords. Whether or not one thinks the accords were effective, Trump, again following through on his campaign rhetoric, was abandoning U.S. leadership on climate change issues. Perhaps more surprising, or at least shocking if not surprising, was his overthrowing of traditional norms and long-standing security agreements.

During the 2016 presidential campaign, Trump called NATO "obsolete." After becoming president, he has often castigated NATO and its members and not just over their failure to live up to their commitments to pay 2 percent of their GDP to defense. In 2018, Trump repeatedly told aides he wanted to pull out of NATO.[7] Throughout his presidency, Trump maintained disdain for such institutional structures.

It is not Trump's actions, as dangerous and haphazard as they may be, that are the only damaging aspects of his presidency to the post-World War II order, norms and what was left of American leadership in the world, his words were often just as corrosive.

During the campaign, Trump first used the loaded term "America First," though also asserting this did not mean he was an isolationist. "I'm not isolationist, but I am 'America First.'"[8] Putting aside that the most prominent users of the term "America First" were often rife with anti-Semitic rhetoric and views[9], it was a powerful message, one that he repeated in his inaugural address.

> From this moment on, it's going to be America First. Every decision on trade, on taxes, on immigration, on foreign affairs, will be made to benefit American workers and American families. We must protect our borders from the ravages of other countries making our products, stealing our companies, and destroying our jobs. Protection will lead to great prosperity and strength.

This America First message resonated with the American public, with 65 percent of respondents to a Politico/Morning Consult poll liking the speech. Trump continued to use it, and it was a large theme of his speeches at the United Nations. In these speeches and elsewhere, Trump often talked sympathetically, sometimes even glowingly, of dictators around the world.

During the 2016 campaign, Trump said of Vladimir Putin, "It is always a great honor to be so nicely complimented by a man so highly respected within his own country and beyond." Trump has a bad habit of admiring the unconstrained power of authoritarian governments, as when he complimented Saddam Hussein: "He killed terrorists. He did that so good. They didn't read them the rights. They didn't talk. They were terrorists. It was over."

He has a strange affinity for Kim Jong Un, North Korea's leader. "I like him, he likes me. I guess that's okay. Am I allowed to say that?... We went back and forth, then we fell in love. He wrote me beautiful letters. And they are great letters. We fell in love."

After the murder ordered by Saudi Arabian Crown Prince Mohammed bin Salman of American permanent resident and journalist Jamal Khashoggi, Trump said of Salman, "He's a strong person. He has very good control. He's seen as a person who can keep things under check, I mean that in a positive way."

He even jokingly complimented Xi on his seemingly permanent grip on power: "He's now president for life. President for life. No, he's great. And look, he was able to do that. I think it's great. Maybe we'll have to give that a shot some day."[10]

In addition to displaying a strange fetish for the trappings of authoritarianism and the powers wielded by dictators, Trump has shown his disdain for countries with non-white populations, a manifestation of his deeply ingrained racism. Don't forget that he called African countries "shitholes." Or that he used a mock accent when talking about the leaders of key Asian allies, Japan and South Korea.[11]

To castigate Trump is not to say that the U.S. and China are moral equals. They are not. Trump and his like are constrained by a liberalized political system of checks and balances that mostly forced him to adhere to the Constitution and elections. Xi is constrained by none of that. There are certainly constraints on Xi from others in the politburo and even to a certain extent by a need to keep the people satisfied (although that is minimal as North Korea and dozens of other long-lasting dictatorships illustrate). But Xi has immense powers to do what he wants when he wants how he wants. The very opaqueness of party politic constraints in China is itself a sign of how unconstrained he is.

Trump is no Xi, the U.S. no China, but Trump has changed the world, even when Trump is no longer president. America and the world have been forever changed by the Trump presidency. America is no longer seen as nor acts as the leader of a liberalized order. As Trump said in his UN speech, "I honor the right of every nation in this room to pursue its own customs, beliefs, and traditions. The United States will not tell you how to live or work or worship." And in this Trump is right; the United States cannot force liberalization on other countries. There are many roads to prosperity and success, as economic systems as disparate as Sweden, South Korea, and Chile show.

But all these countries have something in common, even if their health care and social welfare systems are different. They are all democracies, and all utilize the market, even if they mitigate against the market's excesses and trade-offs by various, differing means. For all its faults, and they are many, the United States played the predominant role in the democratization and liberalization of the world. Even China's economic success was predicated on leveraging market forces and tapping into a post-World War II, post-Cold War, economic rule-based system that the United States was key to creating.

With China more influential and powerful around the world because of its economic success, one of the ways we can change China is by being more successful ourselves. There is much pessimism about America right now, understandable because of the Trump era, changes in the world, our country's sclerotic governing structures, a failure to contain Covid-19, and an uncertain technological future. But perhaps we need to remember how much we have improved to regain our optimism for what is possible for our future. Part of the challenge in doing this is the pervasive pessimism of Americans and their leading intellectuals.

An August 2019 poll found that a majority of Americans were worried about the economy.[12] But 69 percent of Americans were satisfied with their own financial situation. This same poll found Americans pessimistic about race relations in the future. This was well before the protests over the murder of George Floyd. Other surveys find Americans concerned about the future of the economy, the environment, America's stature in the world, and polarization in the country.[13] In fact, survey after survey shows Americans think the next generation will have it worse than we do. And this was all before the Covid-19 pandemic.

America's pessimism is goaded on by its commentators, intellectuals and opinion-makers, on both the right and the left.

Many on the right are pessimistic about immigrants, believing that today's immigrants are not assimilating as well as those in the past. This is not accurate, as we will show shortly. Others worry about crime, even though crime is at decades-long lows. While there are many challenges facing the country, many of the worries expressed today are not justified by the evidence. The Right focuses its concerns in areas where we are doing relatively well, while ignoring areas that are in need of improvement.

The left is also quite pessimistic about the future, including in regard to race. As we saw, polls reflect a pessimism about race relations. Concerns about racism are understandable given the election of Trump and systemic racism problems, made all the more clear by the protests after the killing of George Floyd. On most issues, Trump does not have an overarching, deeply felt philosophy. The only two issues on which Trump has deeply ingrained beliefs, in which he has been consistent throughout the years in his rhetoric and actions, are his hatred for trade deficits and his hatred for people of color, especially immigrants of color. Remember his campaign took off with an attack on immigrants and a call for building a wall on the U.S.–Mexico border. He was sued for housing discrimination against blacks back in the 1970s.[14] His election led to people feeling more comfortable believing and saying racist things in public. It's no wonder there is a newfound worry about racism.

Ta-Nehisi Coates has become a leading public intellectual on race issues over the last ten years, and for good reason. His blog posts at *The Atlantic* during the early part of the last decade were filled with reasoned arguments, research, and explorations on how America has treated blacks over the last 250 years. He educated millions on how housing redlining helped create a wealth gap between blacks and whites. He wrote achingly and eloquently on mass incarceration and the daily fear blacks experience living in a militarized police world. He even wrote a compelling case for reparations, although he did not tackle the practical challenges of how to implement such a policy. But Coates, as eloquent and wise as he is on these issues, was relentlessly pessimistic about the future.

On *The Late Show* a few years ago, Stephen Colbert asked Coates whether he had any hope for change, and Coates replied "No. But I'm not the person you should go to for that. You should go to your pastor. Your pastor provides you hope. Your friends provide you hope." Colbert, unsatisfied, followed up by saying, "I'm not asking you to make sh** up, I'm asking if you personally see any evidence for change in America." To which Coates replied, "But I would have to make sh** up to actually answer that question in a satisfying way."[15]

In a podcast, Ezra Klein asked Coates to describe what a good world would look like. Coates replied, "We have a 20-to-1 wealth gap. Every nickel of wealth the average black family has, the average white family has a dollar. What is the world in which that wealth gap is closed? What happens? What makes that possible? What does that look like? What is the process?"

The wealth gap between blacks and whites is longstanding and pernicious. It has gotten worse since the early 1980s. (it is difficult to find good data before then.) A number of studies have shown this is due to housing wealth, which points towards a solution.

So Coates is right to be concerned on this measurement, at least, and there is even cause for being pessimistic since having wealth makes it easier to beget more wealth, which speaks to the need for reparations or some sort of policy to rectify the wealth gap.

But as challenging as it might be to address this issue, there are also many positive signs of progress beyond the wealth gap. For example, the black poverty rate has continued to fall over time from crazy high numbers. In 1959, the black poverty rate was over 50 percent. Today, it is around 20 percent,[16] still far too high and a little more than twice the white poverty rate, but a remarkable amount of progress has taken place, including since the early 1990s when mass incarceration erupted, another issue Coates has rightly raised.

But there has been remarkable progress on incarceration too. As Kevin Drum reports, "the black imprisonment rate has dropped 40 percent from its peak in 2001."[17] Indeed, the black incarceration rate has been falling since 2001 and is at its lowest level since 1994. As Drum notes, "it is still 4.7 times the white incarceration rate, but that's down from 7.1 times in 2001." Incarceration rates are falling for everyone, but the rate of incarceration of blacks is falling faster than the incarceration rate of whites.

None of this is to invalidate Coates' points of continued pervasive racism and the importance and intractability of the black-white wealth gap. It is to say that there has been progress, even during the Trump years (at least pre-Covid-19), and there is the possibility of more progress in the future.

There is no reason to think things can't be better tomorrow, just as they are better today than they were yesterday. America can be and has been improved. An improved America is a tougher challenge for the authoritarian, anti-rule of law order that China would like to impose on the world.

Sometimes I feel our culture rewards pessimists. There is a sort of dark cool vibe to being pessimistic. Artists, musicians, movie and television creators are all rewarded by critics for creating works that illustrate the dark sides of our nature. I admire these works of art myself but as a matter of public policy, pessimism is misleading. A reflexive, pessimistic view is silly, immature and ignores data-based evidence. Coates himself is now being swayed by the evidence, as he revealed in a recent interview:

> I think I underestimated the left's response to Trump. I definitely underestimated the Democratic Party's response. Listen, I was in college during the Clinton era, in high school and college. That whole "super predator" thing that came up during Clinton's campaign, that wasn't — and is not — abstract to me. That was literally the folks I went to school with. It was well within the mainstream to say things like that. We're gonna see, but the kind of pressure that our activist groups, and the left wing of the Democratic Party has been able to exert … I get this rap for being pessimistic, but it's inspiring to see. It's really inspiring to see.

So if even Ta Nehisi Coates is inspired, perhaps we too can find solutions, if not utopia. Critics on the left and right play an important role in castigating America for its faults, which can help lead to improvements, but they have not earned the right to their pessimism. Even in the middle of a pandemic in which our political leadership and institutions have often failed us, there has been remarkable progress made, especially in areas of science and medicine. So even with this seismic failure, there is room for optimism about how we would do in a future outbreak.

There are big issues we must tackle, and many of the issues I lay out in the rest of this chapter are ones we all agree are important, but how we solve those issues is up for amiable debate (though I'm sure some/many would prefer vicious argument). Some of these issues are ignored by Republicans, some by Democrats, which is to again note that a post-Trump America is still one in need of fixing. Others I call out here may not be on your list. And your list may contain issues that I have either not thought of or I have a lower priority for. We can debate these as well. But, unlike in China, we do so in an open market of ideas with a political system, flawed as it might be (some people's list would include reforms to that political system), that ultimately makes the decisions and in which we can vote for new leaders when we don't like their decisions. But for now, here are some suggestions for how America can improve itself.

Infrastructure is too expensive; We are badly regulated

We live in north Seattle, but more than occasionally we travel south on Interstate 5 the 33 miles to Tacoma for work and pleasure (our in-laws live near Tacoma). Traffic in Seattle has become notoriously worse over the last ten years. But traffic on I-5 in Tacoma has become bad as well over the last half-decade or more. This is strange because Tacoma is much smaller than Seattle. One should not expect big-city traffic jams in a small city. But the rise of bad traffic on I-5 through Tacoma occurred because of the seemingly interminable construction to widen I-5 to add more HOV lanes. This is a worthy goal, but why does it take so long to do, as reported in this *Tacoma News Tribune* headline: "3 more years of I-5 construction before decade-old HOV project is finished."[18] A decade! Ten years??? Ten plus years to widen a freeway?????? I'm running out of question marks!!!

Much has been written about the infrastructure deficit in the United States, but too little attention is given to how expensive it is, how long it takes to build, and how inefficient it is to construct that infrastructure. Lots of attention is given to raising funds to build the infrastructure. Too little is focused on why such large funds are needed. It costs far more to build infrastructure in America than it does in Europe or Japan. People often make the excuse that this is because America protects the environment more or because of labor rules in public infrastructure. But Europe is just as conscientious about the environment as America, and many countries in Europe, such as France, have stronger labor unions than America.

Alan Levy, who has been comparing mass transit infrastructure costs for years, has compiled data showing how much more expensive it is to build mass transit in the U.S. than in other parts of the world. Real Clear Policy, using Levy's data, as well as their own, finds the following:

> New York's Second Avenue Subway will cost roughly eight times more than Tokyo's Koto Waterfront line and 36 times more than Madrid's Metrosur tunnels on a per-kilometer, purchasing power parity (PPP) basis. But this is not strictly a New York problem. Outside of New York, there are three more U.S. projects in the top 12: Boston's proposed Red-Blue Line Connector, San Francisco's Central Subway, and Los Angeles's Westside Subway Extension.[19]

It's not just mass transit. As Adam Tooze notes, "In Japan, giant sinkholes get fully repaired in one week. Even in the U.S. of a century ago, construction was pretty fast—the Empire State Building went up in 410 days. Yet today, it takes the U.S. many years to spend the money that Congress allocates for infrastructure. New buildings seem to linger half-built for months or years, with construction workers often nowhere to be found."[20]

This inefficiency has real-world consequences for America's infrastructure and is a big reason for the infrastructure deficit that everyone worries about. The public infrastructure system in the United States, at the federal, state, and local level, is broken. We are all for protecting the environment and ensuring safety and other issues protected by regulations, but today's regulatory system is doing so in a way that endangers and threatens the environment and the public's safety through its massive inefficiencies. After all, think how much better we could address climate change if it was not so expensive and didn't take so long to build mass transit or infrastructure such as charging stations?

The massive costs and long timelines to finish projects discourage taxpayers from supporting these projects. In the November 2019 Seattle area elections, voters repealed expensive car tab taxes that were paying for mass transit. Building the light rail lines is incredibly expensive and taking decades to do. If we solved our regulatory system and found more efficient ways to build the light rail systems, taxes on car tabs would be lower and perhaps there would not have been the tax revolt in the Seattle area. Ultimately, the environment is being hurt by our not providing mass transit options due to the overly expensive way we build infrastructure in the United States.

It appears to be both the byzantine environmental regulations and the non-competitive methods we use to build public infrastructure that are the main culprits causing costs to be higher in the United States than in other countries. Regulators have become so worried about protecting the public in public infrastructure projects that the rules actually reduce competition. Tooze writes about how this works in New York's subway system:

> *New York's legal system and procurement rules are not conducive to delivering high quality low cost projects on time. As one experienced observer put it: "In the private sector, if you rob your customer, you will suffer a hit to your reputation and possible losses in the courts," he said in an interview. "Not so if you rob an agency like the MTA. Then it's all rights and no responsibilities."*
>
> *As a result the MTA is forced into "writing longer and longer and longer contracts, expressly prohibiting every way it has been ripped off in the past." [quoting Brooklyn-based analyst Stephen Smith] The byzantine contracts that come out of this process drive entrants away, limiting competition and pushing up costs."*

Obviously we need to protect the environment, but Europe, which is equally concerned about the environment, is able to build infrastructure at much lower costs. In California, concerns about the lengthy delays and costs of building low-income housing have grown so much that legislation was introduced to exempt low-income housing from the California Environmental Quality Act.[21] The homeless problem is trumping concerns about the environment. Of course, a much better idea than exempting one category from the environmental law would be to reform the law so that it does not make building infrastructure so expensive and take so long to do.

But environmental regulations are likely not the only factor in America's inability to construct infrastructure efficiently. Levy, who mainly studies subways and rail, offers a number of suggestions to lower infrastructure building costs in the U.S., including building simpler stations, improving contracting practices, and relying on in-house expertise rather than consultants.[22] Many of these suggestions are enabled by better regulatory systems.

The U.S. has many challenges, almost all of which would be easier to address if it didn't cost far more to build infrastructure than it costs in other countries. The solution is not to simply attack regulations or to do what the Trump administration is doing by mandating for each new regulation written, two must be eliminated. It is not necessarily that we are over-regulated or under-regulated but that we are badly regulated. Comprehensive regulatory and bidding reform must be conducted at the federal, state and local level. At the least, local, state and federal policymakers need to examine the way we build infrastructure and look to other countries and locales for examples of how they do so at a lower cost while still protecting the environment and maintaining safety.

The problem of bad regulation plagues other parts of America's economy and public capacity-building beyond infrastructure. The lack of testing capability during the early stages of the Covid-19 pandemic was due to bad regulations of the CDC and FDA.[23] This led to difficulties handling the demand of too many patients. But our sclerotic regulatory systems also damaged our ability to address the supply part of the Covid-19 challenge—too few ventilators, masks, hospital beds and other needed medical equipment. America needs to regain its ability to be nimble. Doing so will help address nearly every other issue facing America. It takes too long and costs too much to do too many things in America.

Health Care Reform

"You need to see a doctor…right away," my physical therapist told me. Less than a month earlier I'd had knee replacement surgery in Los Angeles. Why in L.A. instead of Seattle where I lived? My insurance had a "center of excellence" program. Certain medical centers were deemed centers of excellence by my insurance because of the alleged better outcomes they had in certain procedures. If I went to one of those medical facilities, my insurance would cover all the costs, including flights, hotel rooms and food. I would save around $6000 in out-of-pocket costs by traveling to California to have the procedure rather than getting my knee replaced in Seattle. Crazy, right? But who wouldn't do this to save $6000? So I did. It was a mistake.

A week later, when we flew back to Seattle, things were not going well, and a few weeks after that my knee was doing terribly, unable to bend or straighten much at all. My general practitioner in Seattle was seeing me for follow-up, but I didn't have an orthopedic surgeon in Seattle. My surgeon in L.A., once he made the money off me, was impossible to get a hold of and not offering help. My physical therapist suggested an orthopedic doctor, and I made an appointment. When he examined me, he said, "This is really bad," but knee replacements turned out not to be his specialty and he referred me to another doctor in his practicing group whose offices were a few blocks away. He told me I needed to see that doctor as soon as possible and wrote this on the referral he gave me.

So I hobbled up to that office and showed the referral to the front desk person, who appeared to be a cross between Nurse Ratched and an old Soviet bureaucrat. She didn't even look up at me as I leaned against the desk in obvious pain. I tried to reinforce verbally what the other doctor's referral note said, that I needed to see a doctor as soon as possible. She typed on her computer and gave me a date a week later—which didn't seem like the definition of "as soon as possible." I tried to re-explain that the other doctor had said I needed to see someone faster than that. No deal, I was told.

So a week later I went to my appointment and after a while was ushered into a room. There I waited. And waited. And waited some more. I sat alone in the room for 45 minutes. Eventually I opened the door and asked a nurse if the doctor would be in soon. He said he would check. I left the door to the room open so I could see what was going on. The nurse didn't come back, but another one walking by told me I had to close the door because they didn't allow patients to sit in the rooms with the door open. I told him I preferred to keep the door open; I had been waiting for a long time and was trying to figure out when the doctor was coming to see me. The nurse insisted I had to close the door and asked whether I suffered anxiety from being in closed rooms. I looked at him and with perhaps a more un-kind tone than usual said, "No, what I'm anxious about is I've been waiting here for an hour for the doctor." He did not take to this well, and I limped out, using my cane, to the front desk, demanding to know what was going on.

Eventually, a third nurse talked to me and explained that when I made the appointment they hadn't realized I'd had knee replacement surgery in L.A. and the doctor wouldn't see someone who'd had sur-gery from another doctor. I asked whether they were just going to leave me in that room for eternity or whether the doctor or someone was eventually going to let me know? The nurse was apologetic but it was clear the doctor was too much of a coward to talk with me.

It took quite some time and a long struggle to find an orthope-dist who would see and treat me since very few doctors wanted to deal with another surgeon's patient—they would rather apparently just let someone suffer than help, even though helping humans is ostensibly the reason one becomes a doctor. Eventually I did find a wonderful surgeon who would care for me, and after a partial re-placement of the replacement, I now am more or less normal. (I eventually found a Seattle-area orthopedist who specializes in fixing screwed-up knee replacement surgeries—he's a hero.)

I tell this story not so you can know about my bad knee. I tell you this to reaffirm what you already know—the U.S. health care system is broken. I could go on and on about my personal experience with my knee, including receiving bills months and months after I had the surgeries, a provider trying to charge me $2000 that I didn't owe, and much more, but we have all had our own nightmares in the system and can tell similar tales of medical service woe.

We also all know, or should know, the comparative data on the U.S health care system to other countries. But just to remind you, the Organization of Economic Cooperation and Development (OECD) finds that America pays on average almost twice as much per capita on health care as other developed countries do.[24] The U.S. spends $10,224 per capita compared to an average of comparable countries of $5280 per capita. And we're not getting our money's worth—outcomes for Americans are not better than for these countries, and in some aspects they are worse.

Higher costs in the U.S. do not appear to be due to Americans using health care more than in other countries. The data doesn't show that. But our procedures are much more expensive. For example, a knee replacement is much more expensive in the U.S. than in other developed countries. (Maybe I should have traveled overseas instead of to California for my surgery.)

All this being said, I am not a health care expert. What are the best answers for reforming the broken health care system? I don't know (3!). But I do know our current system does not work and combines the worst aspects of socialism and capitalism. It is neither a market driven system—leveraging competition with smart regulations to protect people's safety—nor a purely government-run one, guaranteeing health care access for all that will not bankrupt patients with huge medical bills.

Democrats pine for a system similar to that of the European countries or Canada. Republicans…alas, Republicans have not offered any alternative to the current system at all. They defend the status quo, which is to say they defend a system that is not particularly market-driven. But then the modern-day Republican party departed from a love of markets long ago.

I am confused about why there is not more fondness on either the Democrat or Republican side for the Singapore health care system, even understanding Singapore is a quasi-democratic, city-state and it might be difficult to scale up to America's size. But one would think Singapore could still offer intriguing lessons. It is government-run but in a way that promotes competition. Perhaps that description of Singapore's system is the answer to why the two parties ignore it—it doesn't fit neatly in either ideology.

We noted that countries comparable to the United States have health care per capita expenditures half that of America's $5280. Singapore's health care expenditures is about half of that at around $2500 per capita. Their health care outcomes are every bit as good as or better than America's, Europe's or other advanced economies'. Singapore mandates health savings accounts and insurance. Workers contribute between 7 and 9 percent of their wages to their personal Medisave accounts, and those funds are matched by their employers. This covers most of Singaporeans' routine medical expenses. In addition, Singaporeans are also automatically enrolled in Medishield, the catastrophic insurance system. This system has high deductibles so individuals are paying some costs of their medical treatment out of pocket. Medifund pays for those individuals who fall through the cracks of the other two systems and is funded by the government. Singapore works to introduce the levers of the market into the system by making hospitals compete with each other and forcing individuals to act like consumers. At the same time, the Singapore government intervenes in the market, for example, by approving and creating a "standard drug list." Drugs on this list are subsidized for use by patients.

Again, we are no health care expert and certainly it would probably be difficult to scale up a health care system designed for a small city-state with a very different form of government from the United States. But it's high time for both parties to become constructive in building a new health care system, one that adopts important market principles of competition and socializes risks.

Atoning for the Original Sin

As so many have written over the years, slavery is America's original sin (Native Americans may have a bone to pick with this assertion). But it isn't just slavery that is the problem. After Reconstruction, until the civil rights era, America discriminated against black Americans in ways that affected them socially, psychologically, and economically. Earlier in this chapter, we discussed some of the economic impacts, including the wealth gap, much of which was caused by housing discrimination.

Of course, discrimination continues to this day, especially in the criminal system. Again, as pointed out earlier in the chapter, much progress has been made, but there is still much to do. Ferguson, Missouri offers a great example of this. No, not for the murder of Michael Brown. The Obama Justice Department found the officer who killed Brown shot "in self-defense" and thus his actions "were not objectively unreasonable under the Fourth Amendment," and did "not constitute prosecutable violations…" The Justice Department report found that the officer did not shoot Brown in the back as some claimed, and that Brown was moving towards the officer when he was shot.[25]

But that same day the Justice Department issued another report "finding a pattern of civil rights violations" by the Ferguson Police Department. This report found that the Ferguson Police Department "engaged in a pattern or practice of conduct that violates the First, Fourth and 14th Amendments of the Constitution" (three for three, congratulations, Ferguson). Ferguson routinely stopped blacks without "reasonable suspicion, arrested them without probable cause and using unreasonable force against them."[26]

Ferguson was emblematic of the problems in the American criminal system and Americans' misunderstanding of those problems. There have been some data studies that show blacks are not being killed by the police in numbers disproportionate to the rest of the population (This is not to say police in America aren't killing too many people; they are. For some reason Americans have difficulties applying to police what founders understood about rulers—power corrupts and thus checks and balances are needed) Most studies find blacks are killed disproportionately.[27] But all studies show that as in Ferguson, police stop blacks more often, arrest them more often, and use unreasonable force against them. This problem is perhaps not as sexy as calling out police for killing blacks, but it's just as pernicious and more important because it is more widespread.

It is high time that America atoned for its original sin by fixing our criminal system and making reparations in response to slavery, Jim Crow laws, redlining, and more. I wrote the previous paragraphs before the killing of George Floyd and the resulting widespread protests. There is, as of this time of writing, an ongoing, massive effort to reform the militarization of police forces and the disproportionate use of that force against blacks and people of color. These range from reducing the power of police unions to eliminating qualified immunity for police, to moving certain functions such as traffic stops to non-police entities to enacting more restrictive use of force policies. Tied into all of this is ensuring there is better data collection and coordination of data at the local, state and federal levels. This latter action will make it much easier to develop strategies and actions that can be measured on their effectiveness.

Reparations are problematic as a practical matter since it is difficult, if not impossible, to determine who qualifies for reparations, and reparations are expensive. There are approximately 40 million black people living in America. If we gave each black person in America $40,000, the total would come to $1.6 trillion. In fiscal year 2020, the discretionary part of the U.S. budget (i.e., the budget not including social security and Medicare) is about $4.75 trillion. Reparations would take up a quarter of the discretionary budget. But what if we spread it out over 8 years? Then spending on reparations would represent about 4 percent of the annual discretionary budget. Perhaps this lower amount would be more manageable budget-wise (though thanks to tax and spending policies of the Trump administration and past ones, we already have a sky-high deficit, one made far higher by the necessary fiscal response to the economic devastation wrought by Covid-19). I know some people will be outraged at the thought of providing any monetary amount in reparations. Others will think we are far too stingy with the $40,000 figure (In 1988, we paid Japanese-Americans interned during World War II $20,000. In today's dollars, that would be $40,000). Others will complain that some subset of the 40 million blacks in America are already wealthy and do not need or deserve money in reparations. Perhaps the reparations could be means-tested.

Providing $40,000 in reparations is a way of paying the present to fix the past. An alternative, more affordable and perhaps more politically palatable formulation would be to pay the future to fix the past. That's essentially the idea of baby bonds. The federal government would fund investment accounts for babies who could access these funds once they reach 18-years-old. There have been a number of baby bond proposals over the years, including by Hillary Clinton during her 2008 presidential campaign when she endorsed the idea of giving every baby $5000.[28] The problem with giving every baby $5000, no matter their circumstances, is that, as economist Alex Tabarrok writes, it is inefficient, "…instead of parents taking money out of their pocket and giving it to their children directly we have the government reaching into the pocket of the parents with one hand and giving to the children with the other. But taking a dollar from A and giving it to B typically costs a lot more than a dollar."[29]

But there are a number of proposals out there that would means test the baby bonds—babies in poorer families would receive more funds than babies in wealthier ones, regardless of their race or ethnicity. Naomi Zewde in a 2018 paper calculated such a sliding scale system that would cost around $80 billion annually and significantly reduce the black wealth age gap over the course of 18 years.[30] So it would be far less expensive than providing reparations in the present, even if we spread the $40,000 reparations over eight years and it would not be targeted only to blacks but to everyone and even so the result would be a significant reduction in the black-white wealth gap. One disadvantage of baby bonds is that if they turn out to be a bad idea in practice, it may be difficult to turn off the spigot. Once a spending program is in place, very rarely is it eliminated. We'd be stuck with baby bonds forever—the doddering 90-year-old first recipients of the bonds would be bouncing their well-bonded great-grand-children on their knees.

We do not live in a perfect world, and in making these recommendations we will not make the mistake of trying to create utopia. Providing $40,000 would go a long way towards reducing the wealth gap. So would a sliding scale baby bond system. Perhaps we could eliminate the federal income tax deduction for mortgages for everyone but blacks for a ten-year period. That would directly address the housing issue which is at the heart of the wealth gap. Whatever we do, it is high time we addressed our original sin.

Immigration

America is exceptional despite its flaws and sins. 1776 was a foundation of freedom in human history, setting the stage for so much of the progress the world has seen in the last 250 years. American democracy, its Constitution, its mostly market-driven economy are all important and amazing, but they are not what make us unique. Many other countries have developed democracies since then, often with different systems, including parliamentary ones. There are also many market-driven economies in the world. But what continues to make the U.S. unique is our relative success at assimilating immigrants.

It probably seems strange to write this given the backlash against immigrants that gave rise to Trump, who based much of his campaign and presidency on hating immigrants. In his first speech as a candidate for president, Trump said:

> *When Mexico sends its people, they're not sending their best. They're not sending you. They're not sending you. They're sending people that have lots of problems, and they're bringing those problems with us. They're bringing drugs. They're*

bringing crime. They're rapists. And some, I assume, are good people…It's coming from more than Mexico. It's coming from all over South and Latin America, and it's coming probably—probably—from the Middle East. But we don't know. Because we have no protection and we have no competence, we don't know what's happening. And it's got to stop and it's got to stop fast.[31]

As president, he tried to stop refugees, transform immigration and generally hated on anyone from another land who is not white. But this does not change the fact that America has been as successful at assimilating immigrants, including recent waves of immigrants, as any other country in the world. And, despite all the scare mongering, or maybe because of it, Americans continue to support immigration in large numbers. In a June 2018 Gallup poll, a record-high 75 percent of Americans said immigration was a good thing.[32]

Immigration is more popular than people realize. And for good reason. Immigration helps America. Immigrants are entrepreneurial and industrious, creating new businesses (even new industries) at rates much higher than non-immigrants. For example, 50 percent of CEOs in Silicon Valley are foreign-born. Across the entire United States, "from 2006 to 2012, about 25 percent of all engineering and technology companies had at least one immigrant cofounder," according to the Harvard Business Review.[33]

America is also going to need more working-age immigrants in the future because our fertility rates have fallen below replacement level. As of May 2019, it was 1.76. If we don't want to stretch our social security and Medicare systems to the point of breaking, we need more young people to move here from outside the country. In the short-term, increasing immigration is likely to be difficult due to the Covid-19 pandemic and anti-immigration and refugee policies instituted by the Trump Administration. But in the mid-to-long-term, increased immigration can continue its centuries-long role of refreshing and invigorating America.

Despite Trump's lies, immigrants commit crimes at a much lower rate than native-born Americans. They are also assimilating at least as well as, maybe even faster than, previous immigrants. The columnist Noah Smith reports that Hispanic-Americans have been learning English "just as quickly as earlier immigrant groups." He also notes that recent immigrant groups, Hispanic and Asian, are intermarrying at higher rates than previous immigrant groups and writes, "There's no act of integration deeper or more long-lasting than choosing to spend your life with someone from a different ethnic, racial or cultural group."[34]

Or course, much of the Trump immigration maelstrom is ostensibly about illegal immigration. But less remarked upon, certainly not by Trump, is that since 2009, there has been net migration to Mexico, not from it. This is because Mexico has become richer and, like the U.S., is having fewer babies (now down to 2.24 children per woman). So fewer Mexicans feel the need to leave their country seeking economic opportunity and more are returning home to take care of aging parents. The same pattern, as again Noah Smith shows, is emerging in Central American countries—El Salvador, Honduras, and Guatemala. In each of these countries, as in Mexico a generation earlier, fertility rates are falling rapidly. At the same time, GDP is rising rapidly and is crossing the $8000 per capita mark, a point at which populations' emigration levels usually start decreasing. Like most parts of the world, Central America is not static, it is ever-changing— and so too will the U.S. immigration debate ten years from now.

The U.S. should not be turning off the immigration spigot, it should be increasing it, including and especially from China, as we will argue in a later chapter. There are always going to be Americans who are anti-immigrant, often for racist reasons. Rather than returning the favor and hating these people, we should find ways to ameliorate their concerns. Fortunately, there is research pointing out how best to do that. *The Atlantic* magazine columnist Conor Friedersdorf, in a fascinating article, points to the research of Karen Stenner, who, using various experiments and double-blind studies, finds that at the root of "racist" people is a fear of differences. Many people are energized and heartened by new experiences, eating different types of food and exploring new cultures. But there are plenty of people who have the opposite experience. It is perhaps even a genetic disposition. Friedersdorf writes that such people's "intolerance is not a response to unfair accusations of racism. It likely stems from a perhaps innate predisposition to prize oneness and sameness that manifests most powerfully under conditions of perceived threat."[35]

Interestingly, such people best respond by emphasizing what we have in common rather than what separates us. Or as the article says:

> "All the available evidence indicates that exposure to difference, talking about difference, and applauding difference … are the surest way to aggravate those who are innately intolerant, and to guarantee the expression of their predispositions in manifestly intolerant attitudes and behaviors," she wrote. The appearance of sameness matters, and "apparent variance in beliefs, values, and culture seem to be more provocative of intolerant dispositions than racial and ethnic diversity," so "parading, talking about, and applauding our sameness" seems wise when possible.
>
> If you want an authoritarian neighbor to be maximally tolerant of the refugee family that moved in down the street, don't relate how cool it was to go to their house and discover food and music unlike anything you'd ever encountered. Relate that despite growing up half a world away, their dedication to their children shows how much we humans all have in common.

This reminds me of a story from the wonderful podcast *Dolly Parton's America* by Jad Abumrad, whose family came from Lebanon. In episode 4 of the podcast, Abumrad describes how his father, who is a doctor, became friends with Dolly Parton after he treated her for injuries she sustained in a car crash. But it's not the doctor–

patient relationship that is the reason they became friends. It is because, although Dolly grew up in the Smoky Mountains of Tennessee and Abumrad's dad grew up in the mountains of Lebanon, they had much in common. Their childhoods in these two mountainous areas half-way across the world from each other, with different languages and religions, were not dissimilar. And, believe it or not, the music of Appalachia has roots in Arabic music. As Dolly says on the podcast, "Two people who couldn't be more different, that we are so similar in so many ways, that is fascinating to us."[36] Abumrad's dad came to America in 1972, the same year Dolly wrote "Tennessee Mountain Home," even as he fled his Lebanese mountain home. Our differences, in the big picture, are much smaller than what unites us.

If we tackle these four big issues, we will improve America and provide a bigger contrast to those who are pulled into the allure of successful authoritarianism, including and especially China's. All four of these challenges pre-date the Trump Administration. Trump may not have addressed them and in certain cases exacerbated them, but they are issues that need to be addressed no matter who is president and they don't fall nicely in a Left-Right Venn Diagram so merely electing a president or congressional majority of the opposite party doesn't fix them. Of course, these are not the only challenges confronting America, and you undoubtedly rank other issues higher than the ones I list here. We could certainly talk about climate change. But that is an issue increasingly affected by countries outside of the United States, though that does not mean the U.S. should not be a leader in confronting the challenge. We could also discuss the treatment of women, but MeToo is also a worldwide phenomenon. Inequality is a large issue as is a system that favors large businesses over small in a myriad of ways, from regulations to patent law. We could discuss how innovation has slowed down in America or any number of other worrisome economic trends.

By all means, let's debate priorities, and within each of these issues, you will have different solutions than the ones I propose—some of them may even be better. Let's amiably but forcefully debate, take action, compromising, as America once did, and make the country better.

Making America more perfect is the most important thing we can do to counter China's propagating authoritarianism and imposing a China-led non-rule-of-law order on the world economy. But it is not the only thing we should be doing. Many of the tactics of the U.S.–Soviet Cold War will not be effective against China, which has studied that war, and, like all opponents, taken action to mitigate the mistakes they perceive the Soviet Union made. But one of the most effective tactics of the late stages of the Cold War can still be effective today—if only we reclaim its mantle.

CHAPTER 4

Promoting Human Rights
is Underrated

When Americans remember the Jimmy Carter presidency, it is usually with negative memories. People will bring up high inflation, the energy crisis, and, of course, the Iran hostage crisis. The Carter presidency certainly had its challenges, but Carter is not recognized enough for his policy of promoting human rights, which played an important part in the unraveling of the Soviet Union and the end of the Cold War.

Until the 1970s, U.S. foreign policy was dominated by the realist viewpoint, with human rights generally relegated to the background. Joe Renouard, in his book, *Human Rights in American Foreign Policy* sums up the two philosophies well:

> …*the classic struggle between the realist tradition in foreign affairs, which emphasizes the purist of power, stability, and the national interest, and the idealist tradition, which promotes multilateralism, humanitarianism, and international law. President Nixon crystallized the former sentiment with the mantra, "We deal with governments as they are, not as we would like them to be." Jimmy Carter articulated the latter tradition when he stated, "Human rights is the soul*

*of our foreign policy because human rights is the very soul
of our sense of nationhood."*[1]

Carter won the presidency in the wake of Watergate, the end of
the Vietnam War, and other such tumult (People claiming America
faces unprecedented turbulence and division have very short memories.) America's less savory tactics during the ongoing Cold War were
revealed and found wanting. The rise of TV and mass media made
such tactics less easy to pull off. It is one thing to have a realist policy
in which a country deals with unsavory governments and commits
troops in foreign lands or supports other countries' armies and police when those efforts are not well known or only written about. But
when they are broadcast on TV, when people see images of them or
hear eyewitnesses describe atrocities, it is much more difficult to say,
"Well, that's the cost of doing business."

It was in this political and cultural milieu that Carter became
president. He emphasized human rights from the beginning of his
presidency. In his inaugural speech in 1977, he said, "Because we are
free we can never be indifferent to the fate of freedom elsewhere. Our
moral sense dictates a clear-cut preference for these societies which
share with us an abiding respect for individual human rights. We do
not seek to intimidate, but it is clear that a world which others can
dominate with impunity would be inhospitable to decency and a
threat to the well-being of all people."[2]

He elaborated on this early in his presidency during a commencement speech at Notre Dame. First, he stated that democracies
had proven their success and could be used as an example to contra-
dict tyranny:

> *I have a quiet confidence in our own political system. Be-
> cause we know that democracy works, we can reject the
> arguments of those rulers who deny human rights to their
> people. We are confident that democracy's example will be*

compelling, and so we seek to bring that example closer to those from whom in the past few years we have been separated and who are not yet convinced about the advantages of our kind of life.

He then cautions against adopting our adversaries' tactics:

For too many years, we've been willing to adopt the flawed and erroneous principles and tactics of our adversaries, sometimes abandoning our own values for theirs. We've fought fire with fire, never thinking that fire is better quenched with water. This approach failed, with Vietnam the best example of its intellectual and moral poverty. But through failure we have now found our way back to our own principles and values, and we have regained our lost confidence.

But Carter in the speech also makes clear that we cannot be naïve about how the world works, that even in promoting human rights, we may have to take gray actions in a world that is not black and white.

This does not mean that we can conduct our foreign policy by rigid moral maxims. We live in a world that is imperfect and which will always be imperfect—a world that is complex and confused and which will always be complex and confused. I understand fully the limits of moral persuasion. We have no illusion that changes will come easily or soon.

But in the end, he reminds us that words are powerful and they frighten those in power in authoritarian and totalitarian countries.

But I also believe that it is a mistake to undervalue the power of words and of the ideas that words embody. In our own history, that power has ranged from Thomas Paine's "Common Sense" to Martin Luther King, Jr.'s "I Have a Dream."… In the life of the human spirit, words are action, much more so than many of us may realize who live in countries where freedom of expression is taken for granted. The leaders of totalitarian nations understand this very well. The proof is that words are precisely the action for which dissidents in those countries are being persecuted.[3]

It's a remarkable speech, an important departure from previous U.S. foreign policy. At the dawn of the information era, when it became more difficult to hide deeds and words, it was also a smart policy. Governments that denied freedoms were being revealed, more than ever before, due to the emerging information era, for the tyrannies they were. Pointing out the unconscionable human rights abuses of the Soviet Union and the everyday freedoms they repressed laid bare the fundamental lies of their existence.

Under Carter, the annual human rights report by the U.S. State Department was launched, analyzing human rights issues around the world. The report was presented to Congress each year, who would hold hearings on various aspects of the report. This ritual highlighted both other countries' shortcomings and the hypocrisies, or at least compromises, of U.S. foreign policy. Congress mandated the creation of a Human Rights Bureau at the State Department, which carried out this work.

In the late 1980s and early 1990s, I worked on foreign affairs issues for U.S. Representative John Miller, who served on the Foreign Affairs Committee. I remember witnessing vibrant debates about human rights in Latin America when these reports were issued and how this should affect U.S. foreign policy in those countries.

In fits and starts, with flaws and hypocrisy, the Reagan administration carried on the Carter human rights policy. Reagan, from the beginning, was outspoken about the human rights abuses in the Soviet Union and Eastern Europe. At the same time, he and his administration often turned a blind eye to human rights in other parts of the world, especially when they thought it would compromise their anti-communist efforts. During the 1980 campaign, Reagan was critical of Carter's human rights policy for criticizing U.S. allies for their abuses but at the same time trying to better relations "with the one nation in the world where there are no human rights at all—the Soviet Union."

The Reagan administration did not jettison the Carter human rights policy but applied it selectively. The administration called for "aligning ourselves with less than perfect nations (human rights wise) for national security reasons." Human rights groups and factions of Congress pushed back against this selectivity. Renouard's book, as well as Sarah Snyder's chapter in the book *Challenging U.S. Foreign Policy* detail the nomination of Ernest Lefever to be the head of the Human Rights Bureau. Lefever had been a strong critic of Carter's human rights policy.[4] During the hearings, Senator Alan Cranston complained that Lefever promoted "a diminished, muted role for American human rights advocacy." Lefever's nomination was defeated in the committee by a vote of 13-4, the first time in 31 years a Senate Committee had rejected a presidential nominee.

Although not applying human rights advocacy consistently, Reagan was eloquent and forceful when condemning the Soviet Union. Often the human rights he called for most were democratization and freedom of speech. In his 1982 speech to the British Parliament, he said:

> *It is the Soviet Union that runs against the tide of history by denying human freedom and human dignity to its citizens...We must be staunch in our conviction that freedom is not the sole prerogative of a lucky few, but the inalienable and universal right of all human beings. So states the United Nations Universal Declaration of Human Rights, which, among other things, guarantees free elections. The objective I propose is quite simple to state: to foster the infrastructure*

*of democracy, the system of a free press, unions, political
parties, universities, which allows a people to choose their
own way to develop their own culture, to reconcile their own
differences through peaceful means.*[5]

While Reagan was strong and assertive on human rights issues
in the Soviet Union and Eastern Europe, wielding it as a tool for
change there, he was muted regarding abuses in El Salvador, Indonesia and other places. As Renouard puts it in his book, "The
administration would challenge communist states and support
friendly, right-wing governments, often to the point of overlooking
blatant transgressions."

The Reagan administration eventually became more sympathetic
to applying human rights as a tool of foreign policy more broadly. As
one writer noted in the late 1980s after this pivot, "there had been a
change, a 150- if not a 180-degree change."[6] Our protractor does not
measure the change so precisely, but it is true the Reagan administration evolved to a more friendly human rights stance as reflected
in a State Department memo on the issue in the early 1980s: "We will
never maintain wide public support for our foreign policy unless we
can relate it to American ideals and to the defense of freedom." What
Carter launched, the Reagan administration continued: an emphasis
on human rights and the promotion of freedom and democracy in
U.S. foreign policy. This led to great foreign policy successes during
the Cold War era and its ending. Post-Cold War, the human rights
tool was sometimes used less effectively or even abused. In some
cases this was due to hubris as the W. Bush administration had more
confidence in its ability to influence events than it actually had. In
other cases, certain advocates and policy makers used human rights
abuses to make unwise policy choices. For example, although weapons of mass destruction were the main reason given for invading
Iraq, Saddam Hussein's human rights abuses were certainly part of
the argument for the "preemptive" war there. Even acknowledging
its occasional misapplication, human rights has been a useful tool

of American foreign policy in the past and can still be today when wielded smartly and humanely.

Reagan was certainly fixated on defeating the Soviet Union to the point of being willing to ignore other countries' human rights abuses if it helped him achieve his ultimate goal. But the important point for our purposes is that Reagan did use human rights as a tool for defeating the Soviet Union. He concentrated on democracy, freedom of expression, and religious rights. Like Carter, he used the Soviet Union's lack of human rights to pressure them in the court of public opinion, both in and outside the USSR.

China is vocal and strident in support of its political system, asserting loudly that it works for China, that China adapts to norms with Chinese characteristics. What works elsewhere, it repeatedly argues, is not for China. Further, it asserts that other countries have no right to interfere in China's internal affairs. What China does with the Internet, human rights lawyers, journalists, and other aspects of civil society, is a matter for China, not the rest of the world, and certainly not the United States. But as Reagan said in his speech to the British Parliament:

> *This is not cultural imperialism, it is providing the means for genuine self-determination and protection for diversity. Democracy already flourishes in countries with very different cultures and historical experiences. It would be cultural condescension, or worse, to say that any people prefer dictatorship to democracy. Who would voluntarily choose not to have the right to vote, decide to purchase government propaganda handouts instead of independent newspapers, prefer government to worker-controlled unions, opt for land to be owned by the state instead of those who till it, want government repression of religious liberty, a single political party instead of a free choice, a rigid cultural orthodoxy instead of democratic tolerance and diversity?[7]*

It is true that advocacy for human rights was not applied consistently by either Carter or Reagan. Carter cruised out of port strong and fast, and then as he ran into complications applying his human rights policy, there was tacking and even backsliding. Early on, Carter was very upfront about Soviet human rights abuses, even while trying to negotiate arms control treaties. Soviet leaders, unsurprisingly, were unamused (have we ever seen a photo of a Soviet leader looking amused?) and kept yammering about the "noninterference principle," as if it were some sacrosanct law of the universe that one cannot castigate a government for jailing dissidents, preventing free speech, and oppressing religions. China adopts the same theme when it tells governments, organizations, and individuals not to comment on China's human rights abuses or speak up for protestors in Hong Kong.

Nonetheless, Carter did modulate his public human rights pronouncements about the Soviet Union so as not to derail arms control negotiations. In other geographies, the Carter administration made compromises in order to continue military aid or trade with countries that had human rights problems. The Reagan administration also had blind spots on human rights, whether the Contras in Nicaragua or many other non-communist states around the world.

But both Carter and Reagan's conscious policies promoting human rights did help bring down the Soviet Union and free Eastern and Central Europe. I am not claiming it is the sole factor, maybe not even the most important factor, but it was an important component. Reagan devotees like to claim it was his military build-up that led to victory in the Cold War by bankrupting an economically feeble Soviet Union. Tech enthusiasts point to the information age making it impossible for a totalitarian to perpetuate itself. On the former argument, yes, by the 1980s, the Soviet Union was experiencing food and other goods shortages due to a command and control economy that did not work. But man does not live by bread alone. Strongly contrasting the oppression in the east with the openness of the west helped provide the tools for Poles, East Germans, Russians, and others to free themselves. Andrei Sakharov explained this in his speech accepting the Nobel Peace Prize (which his wife read since Sakharov remained in the Soviet Union). "But what made me particularly happy was to see that the Committee's decision stressed the link between defense of peace and defense of human rights, emphasizing that the defense of human rights guarantees a solid ground for genuine long-term international cooperation. Not only did you thus explain the meaning of my activity, but also granted it a powerful support." Whatever share of the credit we give to the U.S. military build-up in defeating the Soviet Union and freeing Eastern Europe, it could not do the job alone.

The same is true for those who solely credit the rise of the information age for causing the fall of the Soviet Union. It is easy to imagine that new technology made the persistence of the Soviet system more difficult. But giving sole credit to information technology ignores the "information" part, giving sole credit to the technology. Communicating the importance of human rights and the success of countries with self-determination, freedom of expression, and freedom of assembly was key. The medium, more powerful and pervasive through new technology, was not the message.

Of course, still others credit Mikhail Gorbachev for the demise of the Soviet Union and freeing of Eastern Europe. After all, he was the one in charge as it imploded and who did not, like in other states, including China in 1989, bring in the army to destroy the revolts. But, of course, why did Gorbachev institute perestroika and glasnost in the first place, which led to the possibility of revolt? Because of a struggling Soviet command economy in terms of perestroika, and the need to rein in a stultified bureaucracy in terms of glasnost. That was his stated reason for creating glasnost, or more transparency. Perestroika, economic restructuring, could not succeed without glasnost. In a 1988 speech at the opening of the 19th Party Conference, Gorbachev said, "One has to have the courage to admit today—if the political system remains immobile, unchanged, we shall not cope with the tasks of perestroika...We are learning democracy and glasnost (openness), learning to argue and debate and to tell each other the truth."[8] In an earlier speech, Gorbachev had urged the party "to speak to people in the language of truth."[9]

The consistent calls for democratization by both Carter and Reagan, their extolling the virtues of the democratic system, including its benefits for an economy, were a constant reminder to Russians and their leaders, or at least to Gorbachev, of their failings in this regard. Communications technology made it more and more difficult to hide the contrasts between a free west and a repressed Soviet Union, and the consequences of that to prosperity and freedom. The ideas of freedom and democratization communicated through that technology were the blasts of an information technology Jericho trumpet.

Almost every event has multiple, overlapping causes. The tyranny of narrative drives historians, economists, writers, playwrights, and others to simplify explanations to one overarching cause. But in truth probably all of the factors mentioned here—the military build-up, new communications technology, the rise of human rights in foreign policy, the fortune of Gorbachev's becoming the leader of the Soviet Union—and more contributed to the demise of the Soviet Union. And as we saw in Chapter 1, the Communist Party of China, including and especially Xi Jinping, has studied these causes intently and has worked to develop countermeasures.

After the end of the Cold War, followed by the prosperity of the 1990s, the West and the United States began to rest on their laurels. We began to think like a communist party, that history had an inevitable arc and it bends towards democratization. Political self-determination was self-determined, too many of us determined. Then came September 11th and the world changed. Fear became our driver and cockiness our co-pilot. The U.S. invaded Iraq, believing it could easily create a new democracy there. For some in the Bush administration, it was overconfidence in the sustaining wave of democratization to wash away the lack of civil society in Iraq, and the belief that America could easily forcibly compel a country to democratize.

Fear was perhaps what we should have been fearing in the wake of September 11th. For the first time, the U.S. adopted a policy of torture. Sure, at different times in different wars, Americans had committed torture, but the George W. Bush administration was the first to commit to a conscious policy of torture as a part of war, the so-called war on terror.[10] By doing so, the U.S. was violating international law and ceding moral ground, making it difficult to take United States persuasion on human rights seriously. It is one thing to apply human rights selectively in a challenging world, as did both Carter and Reagan. It is another to consciously commit human rights abuses oneself.

The Obama administration reversed the Bush administration's torture policies but did not prosecute or condemn its American practitioners. It also continued and expanded mass surveillance of the American public (and foreigners) in secret without public debate or Congressional approval. This provided a pretext for China and other countries to do the same. China would have done this anyway but now they could easily point to the United States and say, "We are only doing what you do."

And, of course, as we have discussed, the Trump administration showed no concern for human rights abuses at all. Indeed, Trump himself has a habit of lauding dictators around the world, seemingly wistful for their ability to oppress.

It is time to reclaim the tool of human rights. Yes, the United States is hypocritical in its extolling the virtues of human rights while not living up to them in name (aren't we all?), but human rights are universal, despite the flaws of the United States. And even with China studying the fall of the Soviet Union, taking measures to not suffer the same fate, having built a much stronger economy than the Soviet Union ever had, the universal truths and yearning for basic rights will still resonate.

Just as it was uncomfortable and unsustainable for the Soviet Union to be confronted by its not holding elections, imprisoning people for their beliefs and preventing the free movement of people, so too will China feel the same pressures if its human rights abuses become a more central part of the global conversation. This will be especially true now that China's economy no longer has high GDP growth.

China saw real world consequences for its proclivity to control information, to censor the Internet, during the coronavirus outbreak. As became well known around the world, when the virus was first discovered in Wuhan, China, in early December 2019, a group of doctors tried to spread the alarm about the new pathogen and urged taking action. Rather than laud them for their smart early warning and taking action to combat the virus, Chinese authorities arrested the doctors, punishing them for "spreading rumors" and "disturbing the social order." In the crucial early months of January and early February when containing the virus might have been easier, China's government worked to contain information about Covid-19, rather than the virus itself.[11] Information was deemed more dangerous than pathogens.

As of this writing, China contained the spread of Covid-19 within China as it spread more widely around the rest of the world, especially and notably in the United States. Some, including in the World Health Organization (WHO), are lauding the draconian steps China subsequently took to prevent further spread of the virus. It's too early to know what was and is the best approach to containing this pandemic (although test, trace, centrally isolate and wear masks sure seems like the winning bet[12]). Assessing China's approach is difficult because of the lack of transparency there. A delegation of WHO officials were in China for two weeks in February 2020 but were not given full access to facilities and cities. Regardless of whether China eventually reacted effectively, the initial approach was counterproductive, and this was due to China's ongoing abuse of human rights, in this case, freedom of information. It would have been better for China, and for the world, if the world had been more united in condemning China's human rights policies and, of course, if China had stopped practicing those policies years ago.

But advocating for human rights does not necessarily mean

cutting off aid, trade or other relations with China. American leaders, from the very top and down through the bureaucracy, can and should say the sky is blue—to note that it is a failing of China's that it censors free speech and does not allow free assembly, and oh by the way it shouldn't be imprisoning and torturing over one million Uyghurs. We can do that even when we are not perfect ourselves. It would be no problem, encouraged even, if the president of the United States prefaced every statement he or she made about human rights problems in China with an acknowledgement such as "America is not perfect and has a long way to go to improve our democracy, including race issues. But even as we are imperfect, your imprisoning human rights lawyers is wrong."

Humans are not consistent and are flawed. Better to have a flawed and hypocritical human rights advocacy policy than none at all. In the latter case, those that benefit are tyrannies. Just as Thomas Jefferson was right in his assertion, even as he was wrong in his personal life, that certain truths are self-evident, that all people are endowed with certain inalienable rights, that among these are life, liberty, and the pursuit of happiness, so too can countries and individuals note the crimes China is committing against its people.

Joe Renouard, in his book *Human Rights in American Foreign Policy* wrote, "Time and again, Americans were faced with a quandary: Should they stand up for liberal, democratic principles and human rights everywhere? Or should they follow a more pragmatic course in pursuit of a narrow set of national interests? Did superpower status oblige the United States to promote human rights around the world? Should America simply lead by example rather than "meddling" in other nations' affairs? Did moral concerns even belong in foreign policy?"

International Relations experts continue to debate this. But just as all events have multiple causes, foreign policy can grab from multiple theories. We do not have to be merely realists or idealists; a combination of the two is most effective. There has been some academic research on the effectiveness of using human rights to create change in countries. The research is a mixed bag, with different researchers coming to different conclusions.[13] One of the papers, which takes a negative view of human rights advocacy, does not attempt to quantify at all.[14] This paper also concentrates on human rights advocacy groups, rather than on a concerted, consistent foreign policy of a nation, the kind that Carter and Reagan practiced.[15]

All of these papers suffer from what sabermetricians in baseball would call small sample sizes, as well as from varying circumstances, perhaps the ballpark effect in this analogy. Hitting home runs might be easy in one ballpark because of its dimensions and the weather of the city but difficult to hit in another ballpark. Advocating for human rights might be effective in one country, more difficult in another given a different era, time, and circumstance. Or what works for one human rights abuse may not be as effective with another. It is difficult to reach definitive conclusions.

How and when we raise human rights issues is also complicated and will vary. In some cases and at some times it will make sense to publicly call out China for its human rights transgressions. The systemic repression of Uyghurs is a good example of this. The world cannot and should not sit by and let a crime against humanity go unnoted. The president should speak out on such transgressions, and legislation akin to the Uyghur Human Rights Policy Act is appropriate. In other cases, it may be better to advocate for human rights through quiet diplomacy. When U.S. officials meet with their Chinese counterparts, they can persistently and quietly advocate for political prisoners such as the journalist Gao Yu. The U.S. often did this in dealing with the Soviet Union during the Reagan administration. Secretary of State George Shultz, during meetings with Soviet leaders, often brought up prisoners of conscience. As a staffer for a member of Congress, I developed materials about such prisoners that my Congressman brought to Shultz, who in turn raised them with the Soviets. Sometimes we were even successful in gaining the release of the Soviet prisoners.

Similarly, the U.S. should work for human rights in a flexible way in other countries, including Vietnam, where a quiet diplomatic push would be the right formula. Vietnam is one of the five most important countries in the world today. Even before the U.S.–China trade war, manufacturing was moving to Vietnam as labor costs grew in China. The trade war accelerated that trend and concerns about undiversified supply chains arising from the Covid-19 pandemic may further accelerate the trend. Vietnam's economy is growing at a high rate, and its GDP per capita is now just under US$3000. If Vietnam's economy continues to grow and if it builds the necessary infrastructure and continues to reform economically, the big question is, will it also reform politically? Will Vietnam take the path created by South Korea and Taiwan? Or has China forged a new trail down which all non-democracies will now tread? Vietnam's Communist Party too could liberalize economically but use China's tactics to ensure continued control politically.

The U.S., for obvious historical reasons, is not positioned particularly well to help Vietnam glide into a more liberalized political future. But through our economic and political ties, this should be a goal. The U.S. should accept more Vietnamese students to study in our colleges. Under the Trump administration, 50 percent of Vietnamese applicants for student visas were denied. We should provide more assistance to Vietnam as it deals with the consequences of climate change—it is one of the countries likely to be most affected. The U.S. should generally be a good ally and help infuse the culture of Vietnam with liberalized notions.

Both Carter and Reagan deployed, at different times public and private diplomacy. A flexible policy should also be applied to China and other countries in ways that will encourage further liberalization.

As China's economy slows (irrevocably, as we argued in chapter 2) and as its repression is revealed more and more with each step it takes towards the center of the world stage, there is a chance for the United States, in concert with other democratic states, to remind the world (including the Chinese people) that indeed, flawed as we all are, like any human institution, a liberalized democracy is the worst system except for all the others, including China's socialism with Chinese characteristics.

Even better than the United States consistently and strongly calling out China for its human rights abuses, would be to do so in concert with allies. Just about all policies—human rights, trade pressure, and others—will be more effective when done jointly with other countries around the world which have similar concerns.

CHAPTER 5

Better To Hang Together: Multilateralism

In November, 2019, the Swedish Minister of Culture, Amanda Lind, was to present the PEN Tucholsky Prize in honor of the Chinese-born Swedish citizen Gui Minhai at a ceremony in Stockholm. The Tucholsky Prize is given annually to a writer or publisher and is named after the German writer Kurt Tucholsky who fled Nazi Germany as a refugee. The award has been presented in the past to Salman Rushdie, Svetlana Alexevich, and other writers who have braved reprisals and repression. Gui Minhai was a worthy successor to receive the award, having published and written books and articles critical of the Chinese government.

Minister Lind would be presenting the award to an empty chair during the ceremony. That's because Gui, the Hong Kong bookseller we mentioned in Chapter 1, is currently in prison in China. While on vacation in Thailand in 2015, he disappeared and resurfaced in jail in China where he remains today. You and I wouldn't know about Gui receiving this award from the Swedish chapter of PEN except for the fact that China's government was so upset about the award being given to Gui that they threatened the Swedish Minister of Culture with reprisals for presenting the award to him. The Chinese Ambassador to Sweden Cui Congyou, in a Swedish radio interview said, "We firmly oppose representatives of the Swedish government attending such an event, and if they decide to stick to what they are doing, we will have no choice but to take countermeasures...I believe some individuals in Sweden should not expect that when they hurt the interests and sentiments of China, things will just move on naturally."[1] China continually cries out the mantra "internal matters in China" any time anyone even dares to mutter discontent about a human rights abuse in China, but the Chinese government has no compunction about interfering with an awards ceremony inside another country. China's government believes it is fine for it to interfere in other countries' internal affairs, whether opposing Sweden's giving an award to one of its own citizens' writers or threatening other countries who don't agree to buy a Chinese telecommunications company's products. This is a one-way street the world needs to drive away from.

It is now starting to do just that, or at least Sweden is. China overreached. Sweden's government did not put up with China's interfering in their internal matters. The Swedish prime minister said forthrightly, "We have no intention of yielding to these sorts of threats. Ever. We have freedom of expression in Sweden and that is what applies here. Full stop." Minister Lind also pushed back against China: "We have conveyed to the Chinese ambassador that our view remains that Gui should be released and that freedom of expression applies in Sweden...This means that Swedish PEN should of course be able to give out this prize to whoever they like, without any pressure on them."[2]

Sweden is not alone in receiving threats from China, far from it. Luke Patey, a senior researcher at the Danish Institute for International Studies, writes, "The importance Denmark attaches to trade and investment opportunities in China has also come at the cost of upholding Danish democratic values at home. But economic engagement with China is both an opportunity and a vulnerability. China regularly employs trade as an economic weapon to advance its industrial, geopolitical, and security aims."[3] Patey notes that Danish protestors against China have been restricted, all out of the Danish government's fear of losing out on the large China market.

China threatened the Czech Republic with economic retaliation after Prague mayor Zdenek Hrib welcomed Taiwanese and Tibetan delegations. China insisted Prague, which is a sister city of Shanghai, respect the "One China" policy. Instead, Hrib doubled down and signed a sister city agreement with Taipei, after which Shanghai terminated its sister city relationship with Prague. In a statement, the Shanghai city government asserted Prague "repeatedly made wrongful moves on the Taiwan question" and that their actions "constituted a blatant interference in China."[4] But, of course, China's actions in the Czech Republic, where they have invested over $1 billion, aren't merely restricted to complaining about a renegade sister city. It turns out the richest man in the Czech Republic, Petr Kellner, who made a good portion of his money from Chinese consumers, paid a PR firm to place local stories favorable to China in the Czech media. His company also formed a thinktank to pitch a pro-China line.

The United States has economic and geopolitical concerns with China and should have human rights concerns as well, but so too does much of the rest of the world. The Trump administration deserves credit for forthrightly raising the issue of China's counterproductive and unfair economic policies. The way it did so was typically Trumpian-foolish, short-sighted, and un-strategic. First, it almost exclusively concentrated on the trade deficit to the exclusion of other far more important economic matters and, at the same time, mostly ignored geopolitical and human rights concerns. Worse still, it tackled China unilaterally, which, to continue the American football metaphor while trying not to give ourselves a concussion, is not effective. China is big, it is powerful and it will not go down easily. Gang tackling the CCP, utilizing our safeties, cornerbacks, and linebacker teammates, is the only way the world can effectively deal with China. This will not always be easy, and on certain issues regarding China, the U.S. and the world will not always agree in principle or on method. But in many regions of the world, there are common interests and concerns when it comes to China. After the last four years of U.S. policies designed to tear the world apart, it's time to explore these commonalities for possible joint action.

The EU as Ally

The European Union and its member states have at least as many concerns with and interests in China as the U.S. does. A European Council Policy Brief from July 2019 asserts, "The rise of authoritarian China, the increasing penetration of European domestic affairs by Russia, and the growing self-absorption of the U.S. all mean that the old model looks unlikely to endure."[5] China is the E.U.'s second-largest trading partner—its top trading partner is the United States. Like most of China's trade partners, it has the same concerns about market access, intellectual property theft, and other protectionist policies. The European Commission specifically calls out China for its "lack of transparency, industrial policies and non-tariff measures that discriminate against foreign companies, strong government intervention in the economy, resulting in a dominant position of state-owned firms, unequal access to subsidies and cheap financing and poor protection and enforcement of intellectual property rights."[6] Europe, like the United States, calls for a level playing field.

In a July 2019 interview with *Der Spiegel*, European Trade Commissioner Cecelia Malmstrom said, "With regard to China, we see many things in the same way as the U.S. does. We are defending ourselves against state-subsidized companies buying up our most creative companies, we are fighting against intellectual property theft and for greater transparency."[7] The EU Chamber of Commerce also calls for reforms in China and says if they are not forthcoming, then "…such measures will be necessary to protect the EU market; not from competition but from distortions caused by entities that do not conform to the multilateral trade and investment system."[8]

There could have been a ready and willing ally in the E.U., the largest market in the world. But instead of leveraging this natural alliance, the U.S. instead prosecuted a trade war against the E.U., as it has against so many other countries in the world. The Trump focus on trade deficits has led to a rebuffing of potential allies around the world, all of whom have concerns about China's unfair trade practices, closed economy, authoritarian government, and new expansionist tendencies. The U.S. has squandered a golden opportunity. Of course, creating alliances would not have been easy. Even if Trump had not been elected in 2016, there would have been differences of opinion between Europe and the U.S. on how to work with and deal with China. Those differences remain no matter who is president. Another European Union analyst states, "Despite its best efforts, the EU has failed to realize that it shares with the US a common interest in addressing the China challenge and to find a way to form a united front or, even better, use their mutual problem to ease tension between Washington and European capitals."[9] The most economically powerful country in Europe, Germany, has so far been reluctant to be forceful on China issues, whether on economic issues or human rights. Angel Merkel, who will soon exit the stage, is in favor of continued dialogue with China and eschews firmly calling out China on just about any issue. She prefers mild talk. As she puts it, "We also need to talk about topics where we are of different opinions. That includes things that are happening in Hong Kong at the moment."[10] Germany has vested economic interests in China, including its auto makers. Forty percent of Volkswagen cars are sold in China, and thirty percent of BMWs and Mercedes.[11] At least under Merkel, Germany is unlikely to speak up robustly on human rights issues or take meaningful actions on China's closed economy. It was certainly even less likely to do so with a United States unstably managed by Trump.

And, of course, China has worked to split the EU with its economic leverage. Hungary and Greece worked against the EU's effort to counter China in the South China Sea in 2016 because of their economic ties to China which they did not want jeopardized. Angela Merkel in Germany and Boris Johnson in the U.K. were both resistant to U.S. calls to eschew Huawei technology in building their countries' telecommunications networks. Johnson eventually relented under much pressure from people in his own party and additional information about the security risks of using Huawei to build its 5G network.

Former Portugal government minister now political analyst Bruno Maçães who wrote a book about the Belt and Road to which we previously referred, has also written about Europe and China's common continent in his book, *The Dawn of Eurasia*. In it, he posits that China and Europe will find areas of mutual agreement and will in some ways be separate from the United States. He describes Europe and Asia "as a unified political space," one that is not organized. "The question of our time," Maçães asserts, "is how this unified space should be organized." Maçães has also noted that the EU in its current structure has difficulties developing a coherent foreign policy. So yes, it will be difficult for the U.S. to work consistently with the EU in dealing with China, but essentially we haven't even tried. In fact, under Trump, the United States has practiced transactional foreign policy, treating the E.U. and China virtually the same, certainly in terms of trade policy. But the E.U. and U.S. have many common concerns. As the EU analyst noted, the U.S. and the EU do have a common interest in addressing a challenging China . Going forward, U.S. presidents must grasp this opportunity and work to organize that political space in a way that is conducive to a rules-based world order, one predicated on liberal values.

Asia as Ally

Possibilities for alliances to counter China are as true in Asia as they are in Europe. Japan has many concerns about China, of course. One of the main reasons for Japan's participation in the Trans-Pacific Partnership (TPP) trade agreement that the U.S. abandoned under Trump (and which Clinton also said she would renegotiate) was the need to create a rules-based economic order in Asia. After the U.S. pulled out of the TPP, the former Economic Minister of Japan, Akira Amari, who was the main negotiator for Japan on TPP negotiations, worried about the possibility of China setting the rules on trade and investment in the region without the existence of the TPP. "China is trying very hard to get its own rules recognized as the standard." China's rules are, Amari said, "a bit different from what Japan, the U.S. and Europe see as fair."[12] "A bit different" was diplomatic speak for a gaping chasm.

Of course, Japan has non-economic concerns about China as well, including and especially China's ambitions in the South China Sea. Japan does not claim any territory in the South China Sea—its territorial disputes with China are to the north, over the Senkaku Islands. But Japan's commercial and resource life blood flows through the South China Sea, so they are keenly interested in and worried about China's increasingly aggressive maneuvers there. So much so that for the first time since World War II, Japan sent a submarine into the South China Sea as part of a U.S. military exercise. Japan has criticized China for its growing naval presence in these waters. These are key shipping lines for Japan, which as an island country, is dependent on energy and other goods that are transported through these waters.

Such is Japan's interest that it has developed a new alliance with Vietnam. In May of 2019, Japan and Vietnam's Defense Ministers met in Hanoi and announced the two countries "will work together to peacefully resolve the issue of China's rapid expansion in the South China Sea."[13] The two countries are deepening their alliance more generally to address a host of security and policy issues. They signed a Memorandum of Understanding to cooperate on "maritime security, humanitarian assistance, disaster relief and cybersecurity."

Vietnam, of course, has a long and contentious history with China. When I traveled to Vietnam in the early 2000s, I traveled with some older American men who were of age during the U.S.–Vietnam War. They were wondering how the Vietnamese would react given this history. But when they asked Vietnamese about "the war," inevitably the reply they received was "Which war?" That's because Vietnam and China fought a war in the late 1970s. The U.S.–Vietnam war is in some ways ancient history to Vietnam, most of whose population was not even born at the time of that war. Today, Vietnam is quite concerned about China's expansionist tendencies. I was in Vietnam twice in 2019 and often heard Vietnamese complain about China's aggressiveness. During one of my trips, China towed a large crane ship into Vietnamese territory. So Vietnam is keenly interested in working with the rest of the world to counter China. Indeed, as we noted earlier, Vietnam is one of the five most important countries in the world.

Indonesia is important, too, of course, and it's often forgotten that it's the fourth-most populous country in the world. It has tried to leverage China's economic development for its own interests. China is Indonesia's largest trading partner, as is the case for most Asian countries. China has also been a large investor into Indonesia in recent years, both through loans as part of its Belt and Road initiative and through individual Chinese businesses investing in the country. Indonesia is carefully managing its foreign policy between the U.S. and China. In June of 2019, the former foreign minister, Marty Natalegawa, said, "Indonesia is not unique in the sense of having very close and substantive economic relations with China but at the same time having friendly relations, not only economic but also political, security relations with the United States."[14] It's a smart realpolitik move for Indonesia to straddle the two countries. But Indonesians themselves do not hold fond feelings for China, some of which is rooted in historical discriminatory tendencies against Chinese living in Indonesia. Nonetheless, a Pew Research Center survey finds that while 53 percent of Indonesians view China in a positive light, that's down from 66 percent in 2014. The survey also asked how confident Indonesians are in President Xi Jinping. Not very. Only 36 percent are confident President Xi will "do the right thing regarding world affairs."[15]

Indonesia has been a target for China's Belt and Road projects since nearly the beginning of the initiative. In April of 2019, Indonesia agreed to 28 Belt and Road projects with China. But Indonesia is at risk to the same debt trap problems of the initiative as other countries and return on investment of many of the projects in Indonesia have been questioned. Plus, of course, these projects can be seen as benefitting China more than Indonesia because of the projects' requirements that 70 percent of the project materials must be purchased from China and that Chinese workers must be allowed to work on the projects.[16] Maybe that's why the same Pew Global survey found that more than 40 percent of Indonesians said "China's power and influence is a major threat to their country."

Those theoretical concerns expressed in the survey manifested themselves in early 2020 when a Chinese coast guard vessel traveled into Indonesia's exclusive economic zone near the northern islands of Natuna. To orient you geographically, these islands are closer to Vietnam and Malaysia than mainland China. In fact, from these waters, just off the coast of Indonesia, the distance to mainland China is over 1000 miles away. China justifies its claim to these waters by claiming sovereignty over "the Spratly Islands and their waters which are nearer to Indonesia's northern islands."[17] Of course, China's claims over the Spratly Islands are much disputed by Malaysia, the Philippines, Vietnam and Taiwan. Putting aside whether China's claims over Spratly are legitimate or not, the Spratly Islands are still nearly 700 miles away from Indonesia's exclusive economic zone which China's coast guard vessel sailed into. China's exaggerated sense of distance is a bit like mine when someone asks me how long it takes to drive somewhere and I say ten minutes when really it will take at least half an hour. My optimistic sense of distance may help in getting through a long drive, but it is not so helpful if you're a sovereign country within 1000 miles of China.

Indonesia dismissed China's claims and called out China for its provocative move: "China's claims to the exclusive economic zone on the grounds that its fishermen have long been active there… have no legal basis and have never been recognized by the UNCLOS 1982." The exclusive economic zones are geographic areas extending out from shores of countries and were designated by the United Nations Convention on the Law of the Sea (UNCLOS). In disputing China's actions in the South China Sea, the Indonesian government noted that China had already lost a legal case to the Philippines over disputed South China Sea claims (more about these post-World War II order legal structures in the next chapter). At any rate, while Indonesia has important economic interests with China and hopes to partner with it on much-needed infrastructure-building efforts in its country, it is also fully aware of the China challenge, as are Indonesians at large, as measured in that survey.

Like that of most countries, Indonesia's relationship with China is complicated and important. It will be neither simple nor easy for the United States and other countries to ally with Indonesia on issues of concern over China. But it is crucial to try, given Indonesia is the third-largest democracy in the world, with an economy of great potential. Again, working together to counter China's expansionist, aggressive behavior has a far better chance of success than working alone. A large and growing Indonesia could be a key ally.

Of course, India is the largest democracy in the world, with an economic potential greater even than Indonesia's. The China–India relationship is also complicated but more consistently strife-ridden than Indonesia's. India is the second-most populous country in the world (if China's census counts are accurate—even here China's data is questioned) and likely to be more populous than China sometime in the next half-decade.[18] In addition, India's demographics are younger than China's. India and Africa are essentially the only two regions of the world where the working age population is growing, with all the economic and social ramifications that entails. In India's case, this will be true for at least another decade.

You may be surprised to learn that until 2019, India's economy grew faster than China's for a decade. When considering that China's official GDP growth rates have been inflated, India's growth rates are even more impressive compared to China's (with the caveat there are also accusations that India's official GDP growth rates have been exaggerated). A Brookings Institution study determined that China was inflating its GDP growth rate by an average of 1.7 percent each year from 2008 to 2016 (China's government economists also work closely with Tom Brady).[19] That's not a huge surprise. Most analysts believe that China has been overstating its economic growth, but it's interesting to see someone try to put a number to it. If Brookings' numbers are accurate, this has ramifications for understanding China, including its comparison to India's economy. As you see in the chart below, using the new GDP numbers for China, on average India's economy grew faster than China's from 2008 to 2016. In fact, in six of the eight years, India's economy had higher growth rates. People often ask me how an authoritarian government can be more successful economically than a democratic one. Well, for the last decade, India's democracy has outperformed China's increasingly repressive government in GDP growth rates. Of course, China's economy outperformed India's before that, and demographics play a huge role in economic development and growth; nonetheless, the story has become more complicated with Brookings' calculations.

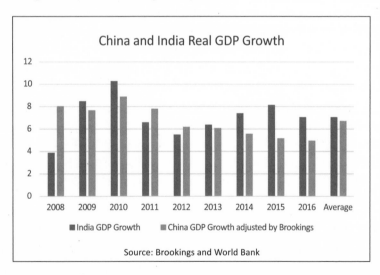

But what if India was also inflating its official GDP growth figures? A paper published in Harvard's Center for International Development by Arvind Subramanian, a former economic advisor to the Indian government, claims, "A change in the method used to calculate India's GDP led to a significant overestimation of growth." How much? The report claims instead of an average of 7 percent growth from 2011 to 2017, the average was actually 4.5 percent.[20] This changes our chart considerably. Who else has been inflating GDP growth around the world? And how much grade inflation is there at Harvard? We don't know (4). But we do know even official Indian GDP numbers have decreased in the last year down to 5 percent or lower. That's less than the official China GDP of 6.3 percent growth, but lots of analysts believe China significantly overstated its GDP in 2019, perhaps by much more than Brookings' 1.7 percent number. Of course, the Covid-19 pandemic has further depressed both China and India's economies.

How much faster India has grown economically than China in recent years, if at all, is hard to say, but all of this points to how important India is to the world's future, one that China increasingly wants to shape in its own image. I have not worked with India nearly as much as with China and other countries, but when I have, it's amazing how long it takes to get something done. In my experience, it is just as difficult to do business in India as in China, but for very different reasons. Backing up my personal experience, India and China have an identical corruption score in Transparency International's Corruptions Perception Index.[21] The chief problem in India is a broken bureaucracy. Indians themselves recognize this, with "corruption/bureaucracy" listed as the biggest challenge facing startups and small businesses, according to a survey of Indian business people.[22] A variety of independent studies ranks India's bureaucracy among the worst in Asia. In fact, you are more likely to have to pay a bribe in democratic India than in authoritarian China, according to Transparency International's Global Corruption Barometer.[23] Remember the book, China's Gilded Age by Yuen Yuen Ang we referred to in chapter 2? Ang created her own corruption index and found that India is more prone to what she calls "speed money" corruption, the kind where a businessperson or customer has to pay small bribes to local bureaucrats. Remember that China's corruption is more about what she dubs "access money" where a business can gain access to projects, monopoly powers or other privileges through cultivating relationships with Chinese officials. As she puts it, "…in India, people pay bribes to override obstacles; in China, graft buys lucrative business deals."[24] So, yeah, India definitely has its challenges.

While much attention has focused on pollution in China over the last decade, today 22 of the most polluted cities in the world are in India, including seven of the top ten. With what we now know about air pollution's effect on cognitive ability,[25] India's air pollution problem becomes even more problematic.

At the end of 2019, India became mired in controversy as Modi's ruling Hindu party pushed for a citizenship bill that critics say is discriminatory to Muslims. The legislation allows for six religious immigrant communities—Hindu, Sikh, Buddhist, Jain, Parsi, and Christian—to be able to apply for Indian citizenship if they have lived in India for six years. Notably absent on that list are Muslims (Uyghurs attempting to escape Xinjiang may not make India their first choice of destination). India's trajectory in recent years, both economically and politically, is worrisome.

So why an alliance with India? It may have a host of challenges, but like China, its size requires the world's attention. A few years ago, the McKinsey Global Institute calculated the economic center of gravity of the world. They did this by "using Gross National Product (GDP) as a measure of the mass or weight of a country and using the world map as a physical object."[26] They calculated the economic center of gravity dating back to the year 1000. At that time, the center of gravity was in eastern India. As the Ottoman Empire arose, the economic center of gravity moved west, and then, with the industrial revolution, it kept going west through Europe towards the U.K. Then, as America's mighty economy soared, the economic center of gravity continued shifting west until in 1950 it was located smack dab in the middle of the Atlantic. As the London School of Economics noted, "By 1950, Europe and the United States combined GDP accounted for more than 50 percent of the world's production, and China and

India combined GDP had fallen to less than 8 percent of world's GDP."[27] But then Asia began to rise again with Japan's economic resurgence after World War II and then the emergence of the Asian Tigers. The economic center of gravity began moving back to the east. When China started taking off again in the 1980s, the center of gravity continued to move east, so that today it is smack dab in Asia. But the big question is will the economic center of gravity continue to move into the center of China or will it turn south towards India where it resided 1100 years ago? This is one of the most important questions of the coming decades. Is the world round…economically?

Unlike China, India is a democracy, with all the slowness, bureaucracy and everything else that makes it the Churchillian worst form of government, except for all the others. It is a natural ally in working to prevent China's corruption of the liberal world order and its increasing expansionist tendencies. If India continues on a nationalist Hindu track, it will make an alliance dealing with China more difficult but still necessary. India's recent jaunt down nationalism road makes it all the more important for the U.S. to do all the things we call for in chapter 3. Democracies, America's democracy especially, must continue to be successful and act as a model for others.

India and China have been rivals and competitors for decades, with border disputes that erupted into military skirmishes in the 1960s and 1980s. In 2017, China and India clashed over the building of a road in Doklam in the north of India, southwest of China. In 2020, a larger, more deadly dispute erupted in the Galwan Valley. Some 20 Indian soldiers were killed. India has also opposed China's Belt and Road initiative. This is partly due to the Belt and Road project dubbed the China-Pakistan Economic Corridor (CPEC), which goes through the Pakistan-controlled part of Kashmir, something India very much disputes territorially. India has not participated in the annual Belt and Road gatherings in China and has even begun its own infrastructure initiative in response to the Belt and Road, which maybe shows the Belt and Road can be helpful after all, given the woeful state of Indian infrastructure.

India has been proactive in the wake of the border disputes and the Covid-19 pandemic in proactively contending with China. As countries looked to diversify their supply chains out of China due to its higher labor costs, its increasing economic nationalisms and the Covid-19 pandemic revelation that too much concentration of supply chains can make them vulnerable, India offered itself as a place to diversify. Bloomberg reported that India "reached out to more than 1,000 companies in the U.S. and through overseas missions to offer incentives for manufacturers seeking to move out of China."[28] Of course, it's not just India looking to convince companies to move to their country. Japan began offering subsidies to its companies to move back to Japan from China or to other countries in Asia. Europe looked to encourage diversification out of China too.[29]

In fact, Japan, which has already created an alliance with Vietnam to deal with China's South China Sea aggressions, also is talking to India and Australia about a Supply Chain Resilience Initiative (SCRI). The idea is to build up their supply networks with each other and further diversify from China.

At the same time, it is important to remember that China is India's largest trading partner. Like all the countries we have discussed, China is important to India but also of concern. Creating productive alliances to push back on China's unproductive power will not be easy. Under Trump, America generally tried to build closer relations with India. But overall, building alliances was made more difficult by the Trump administration abandoning American leadership in the world while at the same time fighting with allies and foes alike over trade and other issues. Trump treats countries like he has treated all relationships in his life—contentiously, boorishly, and ladled in spittle invective.

China's Relative Unpopularity

But Trump is no longer president. And the world is more wary of China and Xi Jinping than it is of the United States, even one that for four years was ruled by an unpopular president. Again, the Pew

Research Center finds that most Europeans (57 percent) have an unfavorable view of China (Greece is a notable exception). Asian countries' populations have a similarly unfavorable view of China, especially the Japanese, 85 percent of whom hold an unfavorable view of China. In Korea, it is 57 percent, and even in the Philippines, where Duterte has often courted China's favor, 54 percent of Filipinos have an unfavorable view of China. Canadians, who have seen China arrest and hold incommunicado two Canadians in retaliation for Canada's legally arresting Huawei's CFO and allowing her to live confined in one of her Vancouver, B.C. mansions, also take a dim view of China, with 67 percent viewing China unfavorably.

President Xi himself is also not popular around the world. In 2018, Pew Global asked, "How much confidence do you have in Chinese President Xi Jinping to do the right thing regarding world affairs?" This was before the Hong Kong protests and greater publicity on the atrocities in Xinjiang, as well as before China's high-and-heavy handedness on the NBA and other organizations and companies. But even without all those negative China incidents, confidence in Xi was low, with 62 percent of Europeans having no confidence Xi would do the right thing. And even with the world unnerved by the Trump administration, they still prefer America to China. Pew finds that "63 percent say they prefer a world in which the U.S. is the leading power, while just 19 percent would favor one in which China leads." Many of the countries most inclined to favor the U.S over China are in Asia, with "81 percent of Japanese, 77 percent of Filipinos, 73 percent of South Koreans and 72 percent of Australians."[30] A big part of the concern of the world regarding China is its human rights abuses. The more someone is concerned about China's not respecting personal freedoms, the more likely they are to have an unfavorable view of China.[31] Again, as we pointed out in chapter 4, human rights promotion is a powerful tool in working against China's expansionist efforts.

A separate survey by Singapore's ASEAN Studies Centre of professionals—from business, government, and media—throughout Southeast Asia found increasing worries of China's influence in the world. A little over 60 percent of these respondents had little or no confidence in China to do the right thing. Of those who responded that China was the most influential economic power in the world, 72 percent were worried about its expanding influence. Of those respondents who deemed China the most influential country politically and strategically, 85 percent were concerned about China's rising influence.[32]

The World Moves On

The world is rightly concerned about China and the direction it wants to take the world. China is a big challenge because it is a big country and the second-largest economy in the world, perhaps soon to be the largest. But with alliances, this size can be countered. The U.S. and the E.U. combined are a larger market than China, with nearly twice the GDP. When factoring in ease of doing business in these markets, the two have even greater leverage in combatting China's unfair trade practices and desire to push its economic model on the world. Then add in Japan, India, South Korea, Vietnam, Indonesia, and other economies—that becomes real leverage. This should not be an EU-U.S.-led effort. The countries of Asia have the most to lose and are often the most concerned about China's rising expansionist efforts.

And it should certainly not be just a U.S.–led effort. In fact, with America's abandonment of global leadership under the Trump administration, we are already seeing alliances formed and initiatives launched to fill the vacuum and to deal with the China challenge. In the fall of 2019, Japan and the EU signed an infrastructure deal designed in part to combat China's Belt and Road Initiative. At the signing ceremony, Japan's then Prime Minister Shinzo Abe said, "Whether it be a single road or a single port, when the EU and Japan undertake something, we are able to build sustainable, rules-based connectivity from the Indo-Pacific to the Western Balkans and Africa."[33] The rest of the world is not content to just let China act like a bull in a China shop (China in a bull shop?). imposing its own plans of how the world should be ordered.

Indeed, Japan has been developing its own belt and road, much more quietly and without the fancy branding and fanfare of Xi's. In fact, as warontherocks.com reports, "At the end of 2016, Japan's stock of foreign direct investment in major Asian economies (excluding China and Hong Kong) was nearly $260 billion, exceeding China's $58.3 billion."[34] And Japan is working to increase its investments in infrastructure projects in Asia, nearly doubling its infrastructure exports since 2017. At the same time, Japan is cooperating when it can in the Belt and Road Initiative, with Prime Minister Abe saying, "Under this Free and Open Indo-Pacific Strategy, we believe that we can cooperate greatly with the Belt and Road plan touted by China." But Japan is also distinguishing itself from the Belt and Road by emphasizing "quality" and environmental concerns.

It will not be easy to build a coalition, and even if we do, it will certainly break down at certain times and over certain issues. Each country will act in its own interests. The key will be to create institutions and alliances that help those self-interests rather than fighting them.

For decades, the post-World War II, post-Cold War liberal world order acted to help the world economy flourish and develop and to help maintain a general stability so that regional skirmishes, great power ambitions, occasional U.S military overreach, and other issues did not blow up into full world wars or global catastrophes. Thanks to the Trump administration's change to America First and Xi Jinping's global ambitions, that order has been wrecked. It needs to be rebuilt with 21st Century characteristics.

CHAPTER 6

A New World Order with Chinese Characteristics

Twenty years ago, in a room on the 37th floor of the Sheraton Hotel during the World Trade Organization (WTO) meetings in Seattle, I looked down at Donald Trump supporters running rampant on the streets of Seattle as the then Governor of Washington State, later to become U.S. Ambassador to China, Gary Locke, announced a state of emergency on the television. It was a surreal moment. Earlier that morning, with our seven-months-pregnant colleague, we'd braved the line of protesters who had taken over the streets as we attempted to get to one of the WTO meetings. The protesters, who were violent from the beginning, despite how they were depicted in the media at the time and in books and movies since, shoved our pregnant colleague as she tried to cross the street.

I was one of the staff of the local host committee helping to organize the WTO meetings. At one point just a few days before the meetings, I caused a U.S. State Department official to cry. Ordinarily, I would feel bad about causing someone to weep openly, but if you knew what the State Department official had done, you might weep yourself. Trump supporters controlled the streets that day and have set the agenda for trade policy ever since. It took the protesters 17 years to gain complete control of the levers of power when they elected Donald Trump and made their dreams and wishes official

U.S. trade policy. Pulling out of trade agreements, increasing tariffs on foe and ally alike, trashing the WTO, and tearing down the post-World War II, post-Cold War liberal economic order have all been accomplished. Donald Trump won in 1999 and cashed in his policy winnings after his election, thus opening the door for China to remake the world order with Chinese characteristics. It is not clear that a successor administration will rebuild and evolve it.

Are You Down with TPP?

As discussed earlier, Trump pulled out of the Trans-Pacific Partnership (TPP) agreement, but it wasn't like he was alone in his disdain for it. The Democratic Party was against it, and their presidential candidate forthrightly opposed the deal during her campaign, even though she was part of the administration that negotiated the agreement. In fact, TPP was a tool of the Obama Administration to counter China's efforts to impose its economic system on the world. Yes, the ostensible purpose of the TPP is to bring together Asia-Pacific countries with the hope of increasing trade and instilling labor and environmental standards into such trade, but China was pointedly not a part of the TPP. It was not invited to be a part of the TPP. This was not an accident.

President Obama explained the reason for the TPP in his 2015 State of the Union Address. He said, "…China wants to write the rules for the world's fastest-growing region. That would put our workers and our businesses at a disadvantage."[1] He then went on to ask for trade promotion authority so he could negotiate trade deals in Asia and Europe (the Transatlantic Trade and Investment Partnership—TTIP).

The TPP was to write the rules of trade for Asia and the TTIP for Europe and America. These trade agreements would maintain a rules-based economic order and evolve it with stronger environmental and labor provisions. The idea, as Harvard Law Professor Mark Wu has written, is "China would then need to choose whether to embrace these rules eventually or risk displacement from the new preferential trade arrangements."[2]

But the Donald Trump supporters on the streets of Seattle that day in November 1999 prevailed and have held sway on trade agreements since, or rather in opposing trade agreements until the recently negotiated USMCA. The U.S. pulled out of the TPP, TTIP negotiations were ended, and the Trump administration undercut the WTO during its time in office.

While Democrats often took the lead in the anti-free trade agreement crusade, it became a bi-partisan cause, perhaps one of the last issues that large swathes of Democrats and Republicans could come together on. For many, it became a litmus test. For those on the left, there were no provisions that could be added that would make trade agreements palatable. In Seattle, union members marched in the streets by the thousands, crying out into the soggy gray day that the WTO and trade agreements in general ignored labor issues. Environmentalists, meanwhile, shouted that trade agreements threw the environment to the wind, a foul and polluted one, thanks to multinational corporate control of the negotiations. All well and good, but when the Obama administration negotiated the TPP, it included a range of measures to ensure labor rights were advanced and the environment protected and enhanced. But the Obama administration might as well have been the Bush administration, or, for that matter the Trump administration, given the distrust those who oppose trade agreements had for their provisions. It seemed there was no labor provision tough enough, no environmental one precise enough, to satisfy.

On the environment, the TPP contained a variety of provisions designed to protect the environment even as it lowered tariffs and other barriers that would encourage more trade between participating countries. Among the provisions were ones on endangered species and wildlife conservation, sustainable fishing practices, marine conservation, and illegal logging. Perhaps most important for concerns about fighting climate change, the TPP eliminated tariffs completely on a variety of clean technology products such as wind turbines and solar panels. As you will see in Chapter 7, this is a policy that needs to be expanded. There were also enforcement provisions, including a dispute settlement mechanism.

Despite all of this, many environmental organizations, including the Sierra Club, opposed the TPP. Among their concerns was the dispute mechanism which they felt corporations would be able to game. Of course, with no TPP, there is nothing for the U.S. to dispute at all should other countries not live up to environmental promises. Having America outside of the TPP opened the door for China to have more influence on how the rules would work in Asia. The Sierra Club and others may have noticed that China is not all they dream of when it comes to environmental protection and regulations. Opposition to the TPP is part of an ongoing trend in American political life to eschew compromise, to allow the perfect to be the enemy of the good. Rather than obtain 40 percent of something, political movements all too often prefer 100 percent of nothing, without calculating the trade-offs. Is the environment, the movement to combat climate change, in better shape with the U.S. outside the TPP, or would it have been better served with an imperfect agreement (as every agreement in the history of the world is) that included the U.S.? I don't know—in this case, I do know, but we'll let you make up your own mind.

On labor, the TPP mandated that all workers have the right to unionize and bargain collectively, required each participating country to eliminate exploitive labor practices such as forced labor, stipulated that countries must maintain acceptable work standards, including minimum wages, and a whole host of other protective measures. These were all new and strengthened from past trade agreements. Organized labor rushed to support the TPP, right? Er... no. They for the most part opposed it. Even labor unions such as the International Longshore and Warehouse Union, which are dependent on international trade for their jobs, opposed the TPP. One of their arguments in opposition was they didn't trust that the labor provisions in the agreement would be enforced; multinational corporations controlled the world and would control the enforcement process of the TPP.

It is a fair point that regulations are too often written in a way that favors big business in America, or are written in a way that large companies, with access to lawyers and money (but at least not guns!), can navigate to the detriment of small businesses. America certainly does have what the libertarian-leaning economist Brink Lindsey and the politically liberal Steve Teles call in their book a captured economy. A few years ago, for a client, we interviewed a variety of small companies regarding their challenges and opportunities in doing business. It was remarkable how many of them commented on the difficulties they faced in competing with large companies. And not natural differences stemming from economies of scale but rather from rent-seeking that has been unfairly built into our regulatory and legal systems. Lindsey and Teles's book *The Captured Economy* details–using data, case studies, and anecdotes–how rent-seeking is out of control in the United States, at all levels of government–federal, state, and local. It explains how and why the finance industry has become too large a part of our economy, why doctors, lawyers, and dentists are so expensive and why it costs too much to buy a house or rent an apartment. It explains how rent-seeking is a large reason for the increasing income inequality in our country. The book notes that rent-seeking is one of the reasons, though not the only one, for the slowdown in the formation of new businesses, which "has fallen from 12 percent in the late 1980s to 8 percent as of 2010."[3] Yuen Yuen Ang's book *China's Gilded Age* that we referred to earlier regarding corruption in China and India, contains an index of corruption that finds the U.S., in the category of "access money," scores above average for corruption. Remember that "access money" means businesses are able to gain influence through cultivated ties to public officials. In the case of the U.S., this does not mean paying bribes to government officials but rather refers to regulatory capture by companies through lobbying, as well as revolving door practices where officials go back and forth from business to government.[4] None of this is illegal, but it does distort the economy and many would argue leads to equity issues and rising inequality.

So we can understand concerns over rent-seeking in the negotiations of the TPP and in the final agreement that the U.S. Congress never voted on. But, again, too often in policy and political debates each side holds off for the perfect rather than compromising. Too many interest groups are satisfied to torpedo legislation, which does not let them so much fight for another day, but instead go out and continue to fundraise against the evil other. Because the truth is that preventing the passage of the TPP has not strengthened labor conditions in the participating countries; it has merely ceded the market to China, which the ILWU and all other unions might have noticed is not too helpful on workers' rights, in their country or elsewhere.

Of course, for years labor unions and others have been blaming trade agreements for the hollowing out of the American manufacturing workforce, and sometimes it feels for nearly every other economic ill afflicting the United States. But data does not support this argument, at least not entirely. Yes, the United States has lost manufacturing jobs over the last forty years. But so too has every other developed country in the world. If you graph the loss of manufacturing jobs in Germany, the U.K., France, and every other developed country, the slope of the rate of decrease in manufacturing jobs since 1970 is the same. Some countries, such as Germany, started with a larger number of manufacturing jobs as a share of total jobs, but they have lost them at the same rate as the United States.[5] Even China is losing manufacturing jobs though its data is too byzantine to graph it accurately. Manufacturing, like agriculture before it, has become more productive, and become a smaller share of jobs as countries develop economically.

Now it does appear to be true, according to several recent economic research papers, that in the early 2000s up through perhaps 2010 or so, that China's rise as a manufacturing and assembly hub did cause a loss of jobs in discrete geographic locations of the United States (Other studies dispute this but currently the momentum of the research is in the China-caused job loss side). This certainly had negative consequences for these U.S. geographic locations. But even the studies showing China caused job losses, indicate a net job gain for the United States as a whole, and for the economy, too, when factoring in gains for the consumer.[6]

In the renegotiated trade agreement between the U.S., Mexico, and Canada, re-branded from NAFTA to USMCA, stricter enforcement provisions on labor were put in place. These were insisted upon by Democrats and organized labor in the U.S., chiefly the AFL-CIO. These provisions put the burden of proof on those being accused of violating the labor provisions, mandate labor attachés who will travel to Mexico to monitor compliance, and establish a set of panels to adjudicate labor disputes. Whether these provisions will be effective, I do not know (5). Was jettisoning the TPP by electing Trump and the anti-trade crowd in order to get these types of labor provisions in USMCA worth it? I doubt it. Even if the TPP would have lowered wages in the U.S. or caused a loss of jobs, something that is hard to argue, ceding Asia to China's larger influence on labor standards and other issues seems like a bad trade-off.

WTO

Of course, even accepting that China caused job losses, the U.S. had no trade agreement with China. What it did do was work to include China in the WTO. (I can hear the angry shouts on the streets of Seattle already.) Many people now view this as a mistake. Entry into the WTO did not transform China into a law-abiding economy and has not tamed its non-tariff barriers or its mercantile excesses. This is true. And perhaps in a contrafactual world in which China was not allowed to enter the WTO, those jobs in certain geographic locations of the U.S. would not have been lost. Or maybe China would have found ways to still be the manufacturing/assembly hub of the world even without acceding into WTO. I don't know (6). It is true that China's exports grew faster after accession to the WTO, increasing from $266 billion to $1.4 trillion between 2001 and 2008 for a five-fold increase. But even before China entered the WTO, it was not exactly an export slacker. Between 1990 and 2001, China's exports increased more than four times from $62 billion to $266 billion. And as Arthur Kroeber notes, special circumstances helped amplify China's exports post-joining the WTO. China benefitted "…from the explosion in global demand for computers and cell phones; and the world economy grew by 5 percent a year in 2003-2007, well above the long-run average."[7]

In weighing the pros and cons of China's entrance into the WTO, it is important to remember that the rules and enforcement provisions did temper China's behavior though it did not transform it. Between 2006 and 2015, more than 40 cases were brought against China in the WTO. As Harvard law professor Mark Wu notes in a seminal paper on China's challenge to the WTO system, that was more than 25 percent of the WTO's caseload during that time period. When it comes to cases involving the largest economies of the WTO, the percentage is even larger: "Between 2009 and 2015, China-related cases accounted for 90 percent of the cases brought by the four largest economies against each other." China lost many of these cases, and as Wu notes, "On the numerous occasions when the WTO has ruled against China, the Chinese government has willingly complied with the judgement and usually altered its laws or regulations to comply with WTO rules."[8] The cases brought against China focused on a variety of issues, including intellectual property, its penchant for subsidies, restrictions on exports and discriminatory taxes.

The WTO has constrained China's behavior but has certainly not transformed it. When China loses a case in the WTO, it does take steps, as Wu writes, to address the issues. But many times those steps are for show. It is easy for China to say the right thing or even to pass laws that on paper seem to address the issues raised. But often, in practice, the issues are not addressed. We have seen this in the U.S –China trade war initiated by the Trump administration. China does not have to put in place retaliatory tariffs, although it has done that, to combat U.S. tariffs. It can up the already considerable non-tariff barriers it has in place. Talk to any U.S. agricultural exporter to China, as we have done, and they will tell stories of their perishable fruit suddenly being held up in customs until it is too late to be sold. What Wu calls "China Inc."—the "networked hierarchies and embedded relationships...of the state, the Party, and firms with links to one or both actors" is a powerful mechanism of China policy to continue a closed domestic market, even as it has expanded export markets for China.

There are also a number of trade issues that the WTO does not address, or at least does not address sufficiently, given changes in technology and in China since it joined in 2001. Among these are factors around subsidies to state owned companies (these types of issues were addressed in the U.S-abandoned TPP), the forced localization of computer servers, the forced transfer of technology and sharing of trade secrets, a whole range of issues surrounding services trade, and many issues around intellectual property. Some of these issues were to be addressed in the negotiations that never took place in Seattle.

Nonetheless, while the WTO has not transformed China, it has mitigated a few of its excesses. The Trump administration abandoned the WTO as a tool. Since Trump became president, the U.S. has only brought one complaint against China. The Trump administration abandoned the WTO with Trump ranting and raving like a protester in the Seattle streets. We half expected him to don a Mutant Ninja Turtle costume like some of the 1999 protestors did.

The U.S. Trade Representative's January 2018 report lays out the Trump administration's view clearly: "The notion that our problems with China can be solved by bringing more cases at the WTO alone is naïve at best, and at its worst distracts policymakers from facing the gravity of the challenge presented by China's non-market policies."

The WTO is not sufficient to counter China's business practices, that is true. But that is not a reason to abandon the organization and cede the field of international institutions to China, which would likely either bend the WTO to its own aims or create a substitute that would be far worse. We are in worse shape without the WTO. And the issues the WTO doesn't cover, or doesn't cover sufficiently? Some of those issues were originally to be negotiated in Seattle and since, but the anti-WTO, anti-trade agreements, anti-capitalist, anti-rules-based sentiments won the streets in 1999 and now rule the U.S. Not much has been proposed to replace this world order other than a return to major power bilateral confrontations. That's likely to turn out as well as it did earlier in the 20th Century.

A paper by the libertarian Cato Institute frames the issue well: "The understandable frustrations of the United States and other WTO Members with the statist, mercantilist, and clearly protectionist aspects of a great many of China's trade policies should not cause us to discard the rules-based trading system we have endeavored so long to establish as a crucial part of the liberal international order. Rather, it should cause us to redouble our efforts to reinvigorate the rules-based trading system by negotiating new rules to discipline protectionist actions and encourage China to adopt the market-based approaches that alone can secure long-term economic success for the Chinese people."[9] We could also redouble our efforts to include stronger environmental and labor provisions as well. Instead, activists on both the right and left would rather take their ball and go home, abandoning a rules-based world order.

Creating a rules-based international order, and sustaining it, are, as we are finding today, difficult. We should be under no illusion that utilizing the WTO will be the key to changing China. But tearing down the rules-based order not only does not change China but exacerbates the problem. It is far better for the world to operate under an imperfect rules-based order than under none at all, or, as will likely be the case if we continue our current America First policies, one increasingly written and influenced by China. Even if the U.S. again utilizes, sustains, and if possible, improves the WTO, that does not mean we cannot use other economic tools as well, such as TPP-like agreements or alliances with like-minded countries, to influence and pressure China.

If the U.S. succeeds in aiding and abetting China in the destruction of the international rules-based order, world GDP and trade will likely slow as corruption and confusion reign. The world economy will be less efficient, with corresponding hits on economic growth and innovation. In fact, despite worries about globalization, in terms of international trade, it has already slowed down. After growing faster than GDP for many years, global trade has often grown at a slower rate than GDP over the last decade.[10] The protesters in Seattle, and the anti-globalists since, are seeing their dreams come true.[11] And yet the world does not look better for it; it appears worse.

U.S.–China Trade Agreement

But what about the Phase 1 trade agreement signed by China and the U.S. in early 2020? The agreement focuses on intellectual property protection, technology transfer, agriculture, financial services, currency manipulation, commitments by China to import more U.S. goods and services, and dispute resolutions designed to address the effective implementation of these agreements. On issues such as intellectual property and technology transfer, the agreement contains promises that China has made previously and not lived up to. China had already agreed to allow foreign financial firms access to their domestic market, though there too the proof will be in the banking pudding. Foreign firms can now wholly own life insurers, futures, and mutual fund companies in China. They can also own Chinese banks. But how this turns out in practice as foreign companies navigate state-owned companies' turf and the relationships they maintain, as well as how they navigate the opaque application process, remains to be seen. But if I owned a financial firm (and the FDIC is surely glad I don't), I would not have high hopes. Currency manipulation is a big topic but is not currently a problem. If anything, China is propping up its currency, not artificially lowering it to make Chinese products cheaper and thus theoretically easier to export.

Much of the agreement comes down to China's agreeing to import more U.S. goods and services. The commitment is to buy goods worth no less than $200 billion more than the 2017 baseline through 2021. The agreement calls out a variety of goods to be imported, from manufactured products to agricultural products, energy and services. This has thus far been difficult to achieve in light of depressed demand due to the Covid-19 pandemic.

If we analyze the agreement merely from an economics standpoint, it is difficult to defend the agreement as a major victory. It will apparently guarantee more U.S. exports to China, for at least two years, but it keeps in place $360 billion in tariffs on Chinese goods, which is a cost to the American consumer. It does not make substantive changes to China's closed market, subsidies, and other features of China Inc. Of course, those are very difficult nuts to crack, and castigating Trump's nutcrackers for not yet succeeding is not entirely fair. It is fair, however, to ask if the strategy utilized by the Trump administration is the most effective one for cracking the hard shell that is the Chinese economy: that of a bilateral negotiation that does not leverage other markets with similar interests in opening China.

But what about possible geopolitical and negotiating benefits of the agreement? A number of analysts, including the economists Tyler Cowen and Christopher Balding, argue that the negotiations and agreement have productively reset the nature of the U.S.–China relationship, set helpful precedents, and provided strong leverage for additional negotiations. They note that previous administrations gave too much leeway to China's flexing its authoritarian muscles around the world. As Cowen puts it, "The U.S. has established its seriousness as a counterweight to China, something lacking since it largely overlooked China's various territorial encroachments in the 2010s. Whether in economics or foreign policy, China now can expect the U.S. to push back."[12] There is something to this, whatever my concerns about the Trump administration as a whole and its wrecking of norms and the international order. For the first time, China faced a United States that pushed back with tangible threats and with the knowledge that America still has large tariffs in place and might instill new ones. Again, as Cowen states, "This trade deal takes Xi down a notch, not only because it imposes a lot of requirements on China, such as buying American goods, but because it shows China is susceptible to foreign threats."

But, of course, there is a cost to all of this. If China fulfills the agreement and purchases no less than $200 billion worth of U.S. goods and services, there is a good chance that comes at the expense of other countries' exports. This may all be well and good from a narrow let's-increase-U.S.-exports perspective, but it could make it more difficult to create an alliance of countries pushing back against China, with all the market leverage that creates (and that the U.S. lacks, as large as we are economically). We have not succeeded in the ultimate goal of opening up the China market, and we may have made it more difficult to do so. Perhaps Trump in an imagined second term would have been successful in Phase 2 negotiations, in which case all credit would have been due him. But if he had not been, then it would have been doubly difficult to deal with China in a world where it's every country for itself. Further, how do we know, once Phase 1 was complete, that Trump would not have turned his trade guns on other countries that are crucial to dealing with China, such as Vietnam? Those pointing out the potential geopolitical, future negotiating advantages of the agreement are not incorrect. But we worry they underrate the costs and future risks in accomplishing this agreement.

Of course, Trump may be defeated in his reelection bid. What will the Democratic candidate, Joe Biden, do with the new playing field created by the U.S–China Phase 1 trade agreement? Most of the Democratic candidates ran on tough on China, even more so, tough on free trade agendas. This is especially true of Elizabeth Warren and Bernie Sanders, the latter of whom has been very anti-trade over the years and would likely have been almost as norm-breaking as Trump (policy-wise not ethically or personality-wise) although from a different angle. Even Joe Biden, who was not overtly tough on China while vice president, spoke more harshly on China as a candidate. Undoubtedly Biden will implement a different policy on China than the Trump administration, but it is easy to imagine him leveraging the U.S. – China trade agreement. With Biden as president, the question is how much anti-trade influence the Sanders-Warren wing of the party will have on him. At one point during the campaign, Biden said he would remove the tariffs Trump imposed but soon thereafter a campaign aide said Biden "would reevaluate the tariffs upon taking office."[13] During the campaign, Biden stressed "Buy American" policy proposals so it's easy to imagine a Biden Administration at the least attempting to leverage the Trump trade agreement with China to gain concessions in its trade negotiations. After Biden won the nomination, Elizabeth Warren emerged as a key advisor to the Biden campaign. During her presidential campaign, instead of advocating a Trump America First policy, she substituted an Economic Patriotism policy. She asserted that "tariffs are an important tool" but that "they are not by themselves a long-term solution to our failed trade agenda…" She would "use our leverage to force other countries to raise the bar on everything from labor and environmental standards to anti-corruption rules to access to medicine to tax enforcement."[14] If Biden is persuaded by Warren to adopt this unilateralist approach, I will hazard a guess that he will find his leverage with other countries on such issues is just as strong as Trump's was in trying to reduce trade deficits. Such a heavy-handed, America-imposes-its-values-on-the-world attitude is perhaps a fun-house mirror image of Trump policies and approaches.

The most effective way to face China's counterproductive economic policies would be to bring other countries into the fold in an alliance to attempt to open up the China market. This would mean changing the Buy American provisions in the China trade agreement, which only last through 2022 anyway, and at least early in the pandemic, will be difficult for China to achieve. But there will be great pressure on a Biden administration to maintain those provisions and perhaps even expand on them.

The new trade agreement does reset the relationship. The most effective way forward would be to expand the circle that the Trump administration believed they created around China with the agreement, by creating alliances with other countries, joining the TPP, which would provide additional leverage, and rebuilding institutions like the WTO. But economic organizations are not the only ones the

U.S. is abandoning and that China is trying to remake in its image.

China's Subversion of Other Institutions

China is increasingly assertive and working to change a wide range of multilateral institutions to give them Chinese characteristics. Again, it is natural for a new global power to want to have more influence on the world's organizations. This would be fine if China were a liberalized democracy. But it is not, and it is working to bend institutions to its authoritarian bent. Take the United Nations, as one example. If you think about the UN at all, it's probably with the Security Council or peacekeeping missions in mind. But the UN is a multilateral institution involved in a whole host of global rule-making institutions that also work to facilitate connections. UN bodies create standards and compatibility on postal policies worldwide, the global use of the radio spectrum, for international aviation, maritime and other sectors, and in technological areas.

China is actively working to transform these institutions. It is now the second-largest contributor, after the U.S., to the UN general fund and to its peacekeeping operations. All well and good, and we're sure it pleased Trump that China is pulling its financial weight, but China is using its influence to negate UN efforts to persuade China on human rights and on other matters of Chinese interest. *The Economist* reported that a UN Security Council diplomat said China is trying to "make Chinese policies UN policies."[15] China is also working to place its officials in positions of authority in various UN departments and agencies. As *The Economist* article notes, "The senior jobs being taken by China's diplomats are mostly boring ones in institutions that few countries care much about. But each post gives China control of tiny levers of bureaucratic power as well as the ability to dispense favors." It uses the posts to persuade other countries to vote China's way. China's UN officials are also working to get the UN to speak the language of Xi, "using his catchphrases" such as "a community with a shared future for mankind," which is China propaganda talk for "don't interfere in our internal matters such as imprisoning

1.8 million Uyghurs, er, we mean reeducating terrorists." China prevented the UN from funding a position with responsibility for ensuring the UN agencies and departments promote human rights.

The United Nations International Telecommunications Union (ITU) sounds like the kind of organization created to help insomniacs. But, China is actively using this organization to propagate facial recognition technology standards on the world. You see, the ITU, which is the oldest global international organization, originally called the International Telegraph Union, has responsibility for creating standards for global telecommunications technology. As a *Financial Times* article based on leaked documents about China's efforts notes, "Standards ratified in the ITU, which comprised nearly 200 member states, are commonly adopted as policy by developing nations in Africa, the Middle East and Asia, where the Chinese government has agreed to supply infrastructure and surveillance tech…"[16] China *should* have a role in standard making in technology. But, do we want to cede facial recognition technology standards, of all things, to China? Human rights activists are concerned. In the article, one of them notes, "When it comes to facial recognition [these standards are] extremely dangerous from a human rights perspective." Some of the uses the draft standards of the ITU on facial recognition technology advocate include police observation and inspection of people in public areas, confirming people show up for work, and the implementation of a "smart street light service" that would use video monitoring to track and identify people. You're thinking: "Great! Now we can keep track of criminals in my neighborhood or maybe that darn cat who keeps digging up my garden." But more likely the usage China has in mind, and that would be used in the developing countries in which these standards would be applied, would be the tracking of activists and protesters. You may want to rethink your willingness to ignore the admittedly boring-sounding United Nations International Telecommunications Union. The U.S., Europe, Japan, and other countries certainly should not be ignoring it. The rules-based order matters, and we should not cede it to China. Their attempts to remake it is another example of China's new expansionist tendencies.

The coronavirus crisis exposed the ways China controls the World Health Organization (WHO)—China is the second-largest funder of the WHO, after the U.S. (though at a much lower level). For weeks, the WHO did not have any access to China as the virus spread inside and outside of Hubei Province. Eventually, for two weeks in February, a WHO delegation was allowed into the country but did not gain access to "dirty sites" or other areas that one would expect the leading world health organization would be allowed to inspect and give advice on. The WHO's report out of that trip was completely silent on China's negligent approach to the virus in the early stages when China not only did not sufficiently attack the virus but instead spent most of its energy, time, and resources on controlling information. In fact, at times the WHO seemed like a cheerleader for China, including recommending the use of 5G technology to combat the spread of the virus—which appears to be more propaganda to help Huawei than a sensible measure to defeat a potential pandemic. WHO applauded China's quarantine methods for effectively dealing with the Covid-19 outbreak. China's efforts were effective, but liberalized countries, such as South Korea, Taiwan, and New Zealand, appear to be just as effective, if not more so, without the authoritarian trappings of China's. America's response, as we'll discuss shortly, was disastrous, but it was an outlier among liberalized, democratic countries, at least in mid-2020. Early on in the pandemic in March 2020, we wrote in our weekly newsletter *International Need to Know* about the Covid-19 pandemic, "we are willing to wager that much of what we think we know will turn out to be wrong in the light of longitudinal studies and time." It is difficult to discern, as of this time of writing, how much T-Cell immunity, more infectious strains of Covid-19 and other variables play in the success of various countries containing Covid-19. Undoubtedly science will unravel this over time.

No matter which countries are judged best in show in combatting the coronavirus, if China gains more control over crucial world organizations such as the WHO, with all the information controls and propaganda that comes with that, the world will be less safe. In fact, in early March, China floated some trial balloons on replacing the WHO with a new China-led organization. Axios reported that a state-run think tank explored "the possibility of a Beijing-led global health organization that would rival WHO."[17] This was part of China's efforts to rebrand itself as a successful leader in the fight against the coronavirus rather than the place from which it originated and spread. It is also, of course, another example of China's working to recast the world order. Trump continued to make such a recasting easier with his tactics, including withholding funding from the WHO. The WHO certainly needs reform and performed very badly in the earlier stages of the pandemic, but does withholding funding in the middle of a pandemic make reform more likely or instead give China even greater leverage over the organization? Arguably the pandemic wreaked more harm than it would have if the U.S. had not ceded its global leadership in the three years preceding. Organizations such as the WTO, UN and others were all weakened and corrupted by China in the lead-up to the pandemic.

China's new-found aggressiveness and expansionist tendencies can also be found at the World Bank. In December 2019, the World Bank informed Taiwanese staff they needed passports from China to continue working there.[18] This was due to pressure from China. Current and prospective Taiwanese wanting to work at the World Bank would either have to give up their citizenship or their job. After pushback, the World Bank revised its rule, saying they would give preference to citizens of member states (Taiwan is not a member of the World Bank, because, well, China says it is not a country) but not ban the hiring of non-member state citizens. Regardless, it's another example of China's working to either change, destroy or bend the world order to its less than savory aims.

Trading American for Chinese Business Mores

Interestingly, as global trade slows down, as the Trump administration battled ally and foe alike on trade issues, American support for "free trade" is at an all-time high according to polls. An August 2019 NBC/Wall Street Journal poll, for instance, finds that "…64 percent of Americans—including majorities of Democrats and Republicans—agree with the statement that free trade is good for America, because it opens up new markets, and the country can't avoid the fact of a global economy."[19]

Maybe Americans are more supportive of free trade because there was a president in Trump they perceived trying to make it more fair. Or maybe Democrats became more favorable to trade because a Republican president is against it and policy positions are more akin to rooting for a favorite sports team than considered policy judgments. I loved Richard Sherman when he played for the Seahawks, but now I root against him when he plays for the San Francisco 49ers. But I hope I don't change my position on policy issues based on which party is currently supporting them. Or maybe in addition to tribal tendencies, Americans are internalizing the intrinsic benefits of trade now that it is under siege.

Occasionally I am asked to speak to college students about international trade. When I do so, I often start with an exercise I long ago ripped off from some economist—so long ago I don't remember who it was, so excuse my not giving them credit (Feel free to file a complaint against me at the WTO.) At any rate, during the class, I give each student a small bag of candy. Each bag has two to three pieces of candy in it. One bag might contain Skittles, a Mars Bar and a Kit Kat, another a Three Musketeers, a Twix and a Reese's Peanut Butter Cup, and so on. At the beginning of the class, I ask the students to write a dollar value down for the bag of candy. I also ask them not to eat the candy yet—it's amazing how many students, upon getting their bag of candy, will immediately open it up and start eating unless told not to do so. Then I tell them to take five or ten minutes and trade with their classmates. One student who loves Twix bars will trade their Skittles for it. Another, admittedly misguided student, will trade their Reese's for a Three Musketeers.

After the students finish trading, I ask them to again write down the value of the bag of candy in front of them. Every time I have conducted this exercise, over 90 percent of the students write down values higher than that of their original bag, thus illustrating what economists and two-thirds of the American public understand: trade adds value. Sometimes I'll add a twist and have sealed pieces of paper affixed to some of the pieces of candy. I ask a student with one of those pieces of paper to read it out loud. The piece of paper will say something like "This candy bar was made by child labor," or "This piece of chocolate was grown by tearing down five hectares of rain forest," or some other sentence that allows us to discuss some of the other complications of international trade.

With the current trend of American abandonment of world leadership and Chinese ascendance, I may soon need to add different messages to these pieces of paper that deal with issues of bribery, corruption, and increasingly closed markets.

When I conduct business in America, Europe, Japan, and other developed countries, I can be assured of contracts being honored and I am less likely to have to deal with bribes. It is a rules-based order. It is not perfect. Corruption continues to happen but is less likely than in the past. But that is not necessarily the case for the future if China is increasingly in charge of the new world order. A lawyer friend who often works with Chinese businesses told me a story of counseling an American client who was about to work for a Chinese company. He negotiated an employment contract with many protections. The worker told the lawyer many years later it allowed him to avoid breaking a variety of corruption and bribery laws the Chinese company wanted him to commit. This is not an uncommon story. It will become even more common if China's rules of order and business culture sweep through the world.

After World War II, the American way of doing business was ascendant. It was not just the institutions created but the American way of business, the culture, that was rooted in the rule of law, contracts, and trust gained from those factors. The American way of business was, of course, also not perfect, but a culture based on the rule of law is far better than the modus operandi of Chinese business dealing that has risen out of the murky soup of commerce mixed with CCP/ state meddling, and the general civil society challenges of a still-developing country. The China Law Blog relates many difficult China business experiences, including the challenge of protecting your intellectual property, which in the last year has become more problematic. "If your manufacturer in Shenzhen wants to secure 'your' trademark in China it will not go off and register it under its name as it knows that cannot work. So instead of registering the trademark under its own Shenzhen company name, it will ask a cousin or a nephew in Xi'an to register it under its company name, making it nearly impossible for you to invalidate the trademark."[20] These kinds of issues are not unique to China. They are often found in developing countries. But China, unlike other developing countries, because of its economic size and increased ambitions, is now starting to influence international business culture and policy.

Welcome to the new world of global business if the U.S. continues to abandon world leadership. Indeed, the Trump administration admired the transactional, anything-goes business culture endemic to doing business with and in China.

The post-World War II/ post-Cold War international order was not perfect. Far from it. But it did offer order and a process for improvements. A wild, wild Chinese east offers neither. A new world order shaped by China will be one favorable to authoritarianism, unwelcoming to a free exchange of ideas, and less efficient economically. Various studies show that democracies grow faster economically than authoritarian countries. As one academic paper puts it, "Our estimates imply that a country that transitions from nondemocracy to democracy achieves about 20 percent higher GDP per capita in the next 25 years than a country that remains a nondemocracy."[21] That's not a huge number, but who wouldn't want to live in a country with slightly higher economic growth *and* freedom of speech, assembly, elections and all the rest? Xi, Putin, and your crazy Uncle perhaps, but most other people would choose the democracy door.

It could be argued that China is not trying to transform the post-World War II, post-Cold War liberalized world order with some overarching ideology. It could instead be merely trying to make the world an easier place for China to navigate. This could be true. This is certainly not mile 63 of Michael Pillsbury's 100-year marathon. But even if there is not an overarching ideology, if many of the steps taken by China to change the world order are rooted in practicality to make Chinese navigation easier, we need to remind ourselves of the characteristics of the China ship. It is not a yacht of drunken frat bros partying on the seven seas. It is not a sailboat of earnest do-gooders wanting to explore the world without carbon emissions. It is a large authoritarian ship intent on protecting its authoritarianism and making the waters more hospitable for the like-minded.

What does this new world look like? The coronavirus makes it easier to imagine. The sun's corona is usually only visible during a total solar eclipse. Covid-19 is the global pandemic eclipse that allows us to view a new world order re-made by China.

Corona Illuminates the New World Order with Chinese Characteristics

On January 14, 2020, the World Health Organization (WHO), which had not yet been allowed to travel to Wuhan, China, tweeted, "Preliminary investigations conducted by the Chinese authorities have found no clear evidence of human-to-human transmission of the novel #coronavirus (2019-nCoV) identified in #Wuhan, China." Nobody knew it yet, but the new world order was arriving…and it would abet the deaths of tens of thousands of people around the globe.

On December 27, nearly three weeks before the WHO tweet, Wuhan health officials were informed that a new coronavirus was infecting patients. Three days later, on the eve of New Year's Eve, December 30, Wuhan doctor Li Wenliang posted to WeChat with seven other doctors about this mysterious new SARS-like virus at his hospital in Wuhan. He warned his fellow doctors that "seven people were in quarantine, the symptoms were similar to SARS, and doctors should consider wearing protective equipment to prevent infection."[22] He was quickly called in for questioning by authorities—not about the virus and for advice about how to contain it, and not about how to treat the increasing number of patients sickened by it. No, instead they castigated him for spreading fearful rumors on the Internet. He was accused of making false statements and acting illegally to disturb the social order. Li was forced to sign a statement that he would no longer talk about the virus. In just over a month, Li would be dead, a victim of the novel virus he had been trying to warn authorities about.

On December 31, China informed the WHO about the mysterious illness. It would not, however, allow WHO experts to travel to China to help with the investigation. It was not until the second week of February that they were allowed to enter China. Even then, WHO officials were not permitted to view "dirty sites," hospitals where the sickest victims were being treated and parts of the city where the real action was taking place. Instead, they were taken on a hand-held tour of what Chinese officials wanted them to see.

Axios reported that on January 1 "An official at the Hubei Provincial Health Commission orders labs, which had already determined that the novel virus was similar to SARS, to stop testing samples and to destroy existing samples."[23] The next day, on January 2, Chinese scientists mapped the complete genetic information of the new virus, a testament to their scientific know-how and diligence. Unfortunately, in a testament to the China government's shortsightedness and stubborn authoritarianism, this information was not made public until January 9, 2020.

One day later, the WHO announced there was no clear evidence of human-to-human transmission of the novel virus, even though it had been transmitting from Wuhanian to Wuhanian since at least October.

An individual from Wuhan traveled from there to Washington State—where I live—and eventually, on January 21, this person became confirmed as the first U.S. case of Covid-19. Washington state would become the first epicenter of Covid-19 in the United States. On January 19, China's central government sent epidemiologists to Wuhan. On January 20, the day of the first confirmed case of Covid-19 in South Korea, one of China's top doctors confirmed that the new coronavirus could be transmitted from human to human. The WHO did not announce that the novel virus could be transmitted from person to person until January 24.

By the time China started to open up about the coronavirus, millions had left Wuhan and thousands had left China to other parts of the world.[24] Throughout, the WHO either acted to protect China, which is the second-largest funder of the organization, or diminished the seriousness of the disease. For another example of the WHO's ineffectiveness influenced by China, on January 10th, 2020, the WHO tweeted, "WHO does not recommend any specific health measures for travelers to and from Wuhan, China." The WHO, whose mission is to "build a better, healthier future for people all over the world" was doing the exact opposite.

Even as China was still digging out from the epidemic in its country, as I wrote about earlier, it was seeking to replace the WHO with a new health organization based on China's successfully combatting the coronavirus. The Covid-19 pandemic (the WHO finally called it such in March) is accelerating the death of the old world order and showing us what a China-led one could look like: lack of cooperation between countries, bare-knuckles competition, an aura of national braggadocio rather than countries helping each other, and the use of a global health crisis for a country's own benefit.

China engaged in a worldwide propaganda effort to convince people that the virus did not start in China. China's Foreign Ministry spokesperson tweeted, "It might be the U.S. Army who brought the epidemic to Wuhan."[25] They are also propagating the line that China "bought the world time" and the world is increasingly thankful for it. They did not buy the world time.[26] And many of the world's governments, especially in Europe and parts of Asia, are not only not thankful but blaming China for the world's predicament. Meanwhile, a China government spokesperson retweeted fake videos of Italian citizens clapping along to the PRC national anthem, as if Italians believe China is their savior.[27]

As has been consistently the case the last three years, Xi and China were abetted in tearing down global cooperative capacity by Trump and his minions. Early in the epidemic in China, Trump's Commerce Secretary, Wilbur Ross, told Fox News, the coronavirus "...will help to accelerate the return of jobs to North America, some to U.S., probably some to Mexico as well."[28] This might be true as global supply chains are likely to change more because of this pandemic than because of any event since September 11, but it was a counterproductive and provocative thing to say. The U.S. should have been sympathetic to China's plight, even if China was not allowing outside experts in. There was no need for the U.S. to pile on with unnecessary rhetoric. Of course, the United States should have also been preparing itself for the virus spreading throughout America. It did not.

China erred badly in its initial response, but so too has the United States. Trump's repeatedly calling Covid-19 the "Chinese virus" gained nothing in the effort to liberalize China politically and economically, but it did enable racism within the United States, as too many Americans irrationally blamed their fellow Americans of Asian descent for a virus that infects people of all ethnicities. In January and February, the U.S. federal government messed up testing protocols due to our sclerotic regulatory regimes, did not increase supplies of needed medical equipment, and otherwise did not prepare for the coming pandemic. Trump himself downplayed the virus and spread false information through speeches and press conferences.[29]

The Covid-19 pandemic wrote large what has been happening the last three years: the United States tearing down international structures and areas of global cooperation, and China stepping in to finish the job. In fact, as China recovered and the rest of the world began combatting massive outbreaks of their own, China began crowing about its success and the rest of the world's failure, exuberantly trumpeting to the world the day that global cases of Covid-19 outnumbered total China cases. They also began spreading conspiracy theories that the novel virus did not originate in Wuhan but in other countries. They claimed, as we noted, it was created by the U.S. Army.[30] At another point, Chinese officials stated it originated in Italy.[31]

The post-World War II, post-Cold War liberal world order has now been replaced with the model of every sick patient for themselves. We started this book in October, 2019 when the world order was already in disarray; by March the world order had been nearly completely upturned. If you want a glimpse of a rules-based, cooperative world order replaced by one that has China's authoritarian interests top of mind, the pandemic is a glimpse into that future. The WHO was complicit in making mistakes. The WHO has continued to completely ignore the so far successful system Taiwan has implemented to contain the spread of Covid-19. That, of course, is because of China. This is what happens when an authoritarian culture infuses our global institutions. Welcome to the future.

What else will this future look like? Let's assume country A starts subsidizing what it deems an essential industry. Country B can complain, but there is no mechanism to bring a complaint to the WTO, which no longer has an adjudication panel. Such disputes will be decided by whatever leverage each market is able to bring to bear on the equation. Businesses that once adhered to anti-bribery statutes, or at least were constrained somewhat by them, when seeing Chinese companies and developing countries' companies using nefarious means, will now feel no constraints. Indeed, to compete, they will feel compelled to throw off all legal shackles. The practice of Chinese companies, and other developing countries' companies, to not adhere to contracts, will start to infuse the international business culture. Trust will begin to erode in international markets, and international trade efficiencies will begin to wane, making goods and services more expensive. This will become even more so as, rather than working through existing multilateral trade agreements, regions and countries create multiple often contradictory trade agreements with each other. Companies will have to navigate these differing trade regimes, further creating operational inefficiencies, and providing even more advantages to large companies with resources to deal with a more complicated world, all at the expense of small businesses. Rather than a world slowly, hesitantly, certainly imperfectly, moving towards one set of trade rules, there will be multiple trade regimes. China, through its market power, will be able to influence many of these regimes. Labor and environmental protections will become less influential in these regimes.

Standards on new technologies and their uses will reflect an authoritarian government's perspective. Surveillance technology will run rampant in developing countries and perhaps in developed countries as well, with little constraint on how it is used and how data extracted from it is utilized. The UN peacekeeping missions, although already flawed, will increasingly reflect the geopolitical interests of countries. We will revert to a pre-World War I era of Great Game geopolitics, in which instability and the threat of war continually looms. The weak mechanisms that currently exist for dealing with large, transnational threats, such as climate change, will disappear completely.

When the next transnational threat arises, such as another coronavirus pandemic, there will be no global structural means to confront it. Such a crisis could also take the form of another financial crisis or some other threat we are not anticipating that is connected to multiple countries and geographic regions. The structures to deal with it will no longer be there or will be structured in a way favorable to an authoritarian China, not to solving the global problem.

The U.S., for all its many faults, was a better fit for world leadership than an authoritarian China. A March, 2020 article *in Foreign Affairs* by Kurt Campbell and Rush Doshi articulates the situation well:

> *The status of the United States as a global leader over the past seven decades has been built not just on wealth and power but also, and just as important, on the legitimacy that flows from the United States' domestic governance, provision*

*of global public goods, and ability and willingness to muster
and coordinate a global response to crises. The coronavirus
pandemic is testing all three elements of U.S. leadership. So
far, Washington is failing the test.*

In failing the test, the U.S. opened up room for China to continue transforming the global order. One of the many symptoms of Covid-19 is a fevered glimpse into the future. It is a worrisome one. But the future we describe above does not have to be the world's future.

Think what the future could look like with a politically and economically liberalized China. Let's take the present crisis as an example. Information is freely shared, the WHO acts responsibly, and the rest of the world takes prudent steps not only to help China but to protect their own citizens. There are coordination and response on medical supplies, medicines, doctors, and nurses, as well as throughout the complicated global food supply chain. These assets are deployed where they are most needed, as often happens in other natural disasters such as earthquakes and hurricanes. From the beginning of the crisis, there is coordination on an economic response to avert a financial crisis, as well as cooperative efforts to help refugees.

Beyond responding to global crises such as pandemics, a successful, liberalized China will make for a more open, efficient global economy with all the benefits that brings to people around the world—from the alleviation of poverty to higher standards of living. A more open China will lead to more innovation and more treats for all of us from the global bakery. It will make for a much better world and a much better United States.

China's efforts to shape the new world order to favor its ways, means, and culture are yet another example of its new expansionist tendencies. China has changed over the last decade. It is more authoritarian, its economy is much larger but will no longer grow rapidly, and it is becoming expansionist. So how does America deal with this challenge and these circumstances? We have answers.

CHAPTER 7

Dealing with China

To recap, the People's Republic of China, although always authoritarian, has changed for the worse under President Xi. It is more repressive, censors free speech more stringently, has committed atrocities against Uyghurs, and has committed other gross human rights abuses. It continues to maintain a closed economic market even as it seeks to expand its markets overseas and as its own economy irrevocably turns downwards from high GDP growth. There are many authoritarian regimes committing human rights abuses while maintaining closed economies. But what sets China apart, in addition to its sheer size, are its new efforts to supplant the imperfect liberal order developed post-World War II and post-Cold War with a new order with Chinese characteristics, or more accurately with Communist Party of China characteristics. Xi is the bizarro Woodrow Wilson, determined to make the world safe for authoritarianism. China has become increasingly aggressive in doing so even as, and partly because of, America's retreat from world leadership and our own undermining of the rules-based liberal world order by the Trump administration.

What to do about it? The previous chapters foreshadowed our ideas, but we'll state them more concretely and specifically here. But first, let's give a little context, discuss some well-traveled analogies, and give a few cautions. We should note that while it is easy to fall prey to a Cold War analogy in analyzing how to deal with China, there are important differences between the long confrontation of the Soviet Union by the West and today's situation, as many have explained in articles, tweets and punditry. China is, of course, far more powerful economically than the Soviet Union ever was. China accounts for somewhere between 15 and 20 percent of world GDP depending on how you count. The Soviet Union, after World War II, accounted for a similar share of GDP, when most of the rest of the developed world's economies had been ravaged by war, but by the late 1980s, its share of the world economy was down to less than ten percent.[1] China is also far, far more integrated into the world economy than the Soviet bloc ever was. China is the largest trader in the world, accounting for 12.4 percent of global trade compared to the U.S.'s of 11.9 percent. Unlike the Soviet Union and Eastern Bloc, it has many unicorn companies—a private company with a valuation of over $1 billion—conducting business around the world. While it is true many of these companies are probably not truly private, even so they are global businesses, something that the Soviet Union did not have. There were no Soviet Alibabas or Tencents or Huaweis. China's economy and technology is far more enmeshed in the world than the Soviet Union ever was. Take fiber optic cables buried under the sea, for example. These are the arteries of modern day communications carrying 95 percent of data and voice traffic. European, American and Japanese companies are still the leaders in installing and maintaining these cables but Huawei's marine division (yes, that Huawei), is fourth. Between 2015 and 2020, Huawei was expected to complete 25 percent of the all underwater cables built. China is not the Soviet Union.[2]

It is also true that China is not as territorially ambitious as the Soviet Union was. China has been aggressive in the South and East China Seas but has not indicated any geographic ambitions in, for example, Latin America (though its fishing fleet aggressively catches fish in Ecuadoran waters).[3] China does, however, want to gain influence around the world and, as discussed, is interested in spreading a China-friendly world order to supplant the liberal rules-based order.

So the current and future challenge of China is not the same as the one that lasted from after World War II to 1991. And, even if it were, it would be good to avoid the mistakes the United States made during the Cold War. We do not need a neo-McCarthyism or to fight proxy wars around the globe. If a Hollywood writer wants to espouse the virtues of the Chinese Communist Party, have at it, we won't haul you in front of a congressional committee and deny you the right to write screenplays. In the United States, you have the right to believe whatever you want, however misguided, or however much money from Chinese financiers you are receiving. We, of course, reserve the right to make fun of you and your beliefs, but we won't take away your job or cancel you from society.

The push back against China should also not be about preserving America as the preeminent power in the world. If China were a democratic country that respected the rule of law and protected human rights, we should have no problem with its gaining more power and sway in the world. China is three times larger than the United States and should naturally gain more influence, as long as it came within a rules-based, liberalized world order. There are officials in the Trump administration and in certain corners of the military-industrial complex who are creating strategies and policies based on keeping America preeminent no matter what. This idea of preeminence generally means both militarily and economically. This is a wrong-headed policy morally—again, a liberalized China should not be constrained—and strategically. The Chinese people are rightly proud of what they have accomplished in the last 40 years. If the Chinese people believe America is constraining China because we want to remain top dog, they will be justifiably angry and less likely to pressure their government to liberalize. But if America works to help China continue to succeed and to liberalize, then we will be on the right side of history and the Chinese people.

That is the aim of the policies we will recommend here. We hope to encourage China to transform itself into a liberalized country. Until that happens, we should work to counter China's efforts to transform the rules-based liberalized order into a China-based one. We will be called naïve and short-sighted by some for doing so, but those calling us that are the ones in need of better eyesight and a more realistic bent to their thinking. We don't argue that our policy recommendations will lead to China's changing overnight and admit there is a risk our recommendations won't work. But we do argue they have a better chance of succeeding than current policies and many of the policies being advocated by China experts, foreign policy strategists, and others that you can read in your neighborhood international journals. Our approach is certainly a smarter and more moral course than trying to keep America number one for all time.

It also does not revert to the pre-Trump policy of too often turning a blind eye to China's aggressions and transgressions. The Trump administration tore apart alliances, abetted the destruction of the post-World War II, post-Cold War liberalized order and implemented counterproductive policies to confront China. But the answer to the Trump administration approach is not to return to pre-Trump policies. China has become more authoritarian and expansionist and the world has changed over the last four years. The policies we recommend are likely to be more effective than continuing the policy course of the last 40 years of engaging with China while ignoring its human rights abuses, excessive mercantilism, and new-found attempts to reshape the world in its authoritarian image. There is a smarter path than the radical trek of those arguing for complete disengagement with China, the nationalist march to keep America always above China, and the well-trodden trail of complete engagement with China, ignoring its human rights abuses, closed economy, and expansionist policies.

If the world can help China change, America, China, and the world will benefit. A liberalized China with a flourishing economy? Sign me up. I'll look forward to benefitting from the products and services they create, to being healed by breakthroughs they make in health care, to watching their basketball players succeed in the NBA, to listening to new musical genres they create, and all the rest of the technological, cultural, and sociological potpourri of an ascending, successful, liberalizing country.

But none of this is likely to happen on its own. In the last 40 years, the U.S. and the world have continued to engage with China with very little pushback on its closed economy, authoritarian ways, and now its efforts to export its political system onto international structures. It is time for a more proactive policy, not one meant to destroy China, or to ensure America's preeminence but rather one with a greater chance of successfully encouraging China to transform itself into a country the world will be the better for its leadership.

Although we are not in any way a fan of Donald Trump, it should be noted that his administration more forthrightly confronted China than its predecessors. The Trump administration eschewed the last 40 years of always looking the other way when it came to China's transgressions. However, Trump himself did so with a lens on the bilateral trade deficit and approached the China challenge not only unilaterally, but while attacking allies as much as he confronted foes, including China. Of course, in typical Trump fashion, he cared not a whit about human rights policy in China, and, as he had with authoritarians around the world, had a strange affinity for Xi himself.

The Obama administration did not ignore the China challenge. The TPP was designed and launched as a way to counter-balance China. The so-called Asia pivot was also a response to the China challenge. The Obama administration brought many complaints against China at the WTO. But the cool, non-confrontational approach of Obama, perhaps playing the long game, did not address overtly enough the human rights abuses in China nor China's new-found efforts to transform the world system into one with Chinese characteristics. The Obama administration mostly looked the other way on China's human rights abuses even as the country became more repressive under Xi. It was also meek in calling out and countering China's newly expansionist tendencies. The Obama administration was too quiet on China's aggressiveness in the South China Sea. That is not to say the U.S. should have confronted China militarily in these waters, with all the risks that entails, but the U.S. should have raised a bigger fuss about this on the world stage. We get the speak softly and carry a big stick philosophy. Certainly, the Trump administration, which does essentially the exact opposite, illustrates the utility of that philosophy. But the Obama administration didn't speak softly, they spoke not at all. Theirs was more of a mute and twig foreign policy.

Just removing Trump from office will not remedy a challenging China. A new administration does not erase China's rising authoritarianism, increasing expansionist policies or its aggressive economic approach. The Trump administration, for all its numerous and deep faults, did raise the visibility of a challenging China. That it did so ham-handedly, in a unilateral manner, while offending allies and strategic partners was par for the course. But rectifying the faults of the Trump administration in dealing with China will be not be accomplished merely by replacing him with Biden. Both American political parties have become more concerned and more willing to confront China. What is needed are smart strategies to encourage China's liberalization, strategies that both Republicans and Democrats should embrace.

There is the possibility of a new approach, one that enhances the Obama approach, institutes new efforts, and avoids the ham-handedness of the Trump administration. This approach will be more assertive on human rights and liberalization issues, will not try to punish China's economy but instead work forthrightly on places where it needs to open up hand-in-hand with other countries concerned about and effected by these issues. This approach does not try to retard technological progress in China and does not try to stop U.S. companies from collaborating with China, but it does make sensible suggestions on preventing China's technology from spying on us. Our policy suggestions even call for cooperation with China where it makes sense.

Human Rights

If China still stole intellectual property, subsidized industries and state-owned enterprises, and closed its market to outside products and services, but respected human rights, protected civil liberties, provided free speech, and democratized, we might be annoyed but we wouldn't need to worry from a grand geopolitical perspective. China would merely be annoying and economically counterproductive, a larger version of Brazil. Encouraging the civil and eventual political liberalizing of China is perhaps the most important policy endeavor of the still-young 21st Century. It is admittedly a tough task and presumably won't happen anytime soon. But we must act in line with the mythical long-term thinking that so many ascribe to Chinese leaders.

The U.S., along with other liberalized countries, should not be shy in calling on China to initiate civil reforms and respect human rights. The United States should bring up human rights in bilateral meetings, during relevant speeches and in international forums. The president should raise China's human rights abuses in speeches. Congress should continue to pass resolutions and legislation addressing specific human rights issues such as the Uyghurs in Xinjiang or the protests for freedom in Hong Kong. The annual U.S. State Department report on human rights should continue to be clear and evidence-based in its analysis of human rights problems in China.

Now China's reaction is easily predictable. They'll do two things. First, they'll bring up all the problems we have in the United States, going back to our founding and the injustices we perpetrated on indigenous people, all the way up to present-day challenges around race and other issues. The response to this rhetorical tactic is easy. As we mentioned in our human rights chapter, it's fine to preface every statement about China's human rights abuses with a mea culpa that we have made mistakes, that we continue to have problems. But, regardless of what we may have done wrong, that does not exculpate China's imprisoning and torturing 1.8 million Uyghurs, persecuting the Falun Gong, censoring free speech, and imprisoning human rights activists, to name just a few of their many and deep transgressions. This is not a two-wrongs-make-a-right situation. There are enough room and time in the world to both work on our own issues and to call out the gargantuan, systemic abuses of the unelected, at-tempted-perpetual-power-motion machine of the CCP.

China will also scream that we have no right to interfere in Chi-na's internal affairs. Massive human rights abuses are never, in any place at any time, an internal affair. A political prisoner is a matter for the whole world. Nelson Mandela was not just a prisoner of the apartheid regime of South Africa, he was a prisoner of conscience for the whole world. Andrei Sakharov was not a mere prisoner of the Soviet system, he was a beacon for freedom of expression. Gao Zhisheng is not merely being held incommunicado somewhere in China, he is a voice silenced for worker and religious freedom.

These are universal rights. They are self-evident as a certain American founder so eloquently wrote over 200 years ago. That they were written by a slaveholder does not diminish the truth of the words, just as whatever hypocrisies of those today holding China accountable—and every man, woman, and child on this planet is a hypocrite in one way or another, to be alive is to be cruel—do not negate the alarming truth of China's policies. The scale and depth of China's human rights abuses make them impossible to ignore. De-termining the rate of a capital gains tax is an internal affair. Debating the best route for a new high-speed rail line is an internal matter. The torture of Zumuret Dawut is a matter for the whole world.[4]

Sometimes I hear people make the argument that Chinese cul-ture is not compatible with so-called Western ideas of liberalization. Free speech, democracy, the right to assemble—these are somehow antithetical to Chinese culture. People making this argument often invoke Confucianism to claim that Chinese have different values than Westerners. To this, I have a one-word answer: Taiwan. Last I checked, Taiwan is full of Chinese people. In fact, the CCP claims Taiwan is part of China. And yet the Chinese there have embraced liberalization. They have free elections, a free press and all the rest of the attributes of a free and successful society. In fact, Taiwan became the first country in Asia to legalize gay marriage. Claiming Chinese culture somehow cannot embrace freedom is the last refuge of authoritarians and their enablers.

The U.S. and its allies need to forthrightly call out China's closed society. WeChat, the ubiquitous Chinese social media platform, can be used in America and Europe, but Twitter and Facebook are banned in China. It's important to remember that China began decoupling from America long before some U.S. policymakers and advocates embraced the idea. In the summer of 2020, the Trump administration, through an executive order, called for the banning of TikTok and WeChat in America. The United States should be confident enough in its society to not ban foreign platforms, even ones originating from authoritarian countries, from its shores. It is true, however, that TikTok and WeChat hoover up data far more comprehensively than do other social media platforms, including American ones such as Facebook and Twitter. A software engineer posted on Reddit that they reversed engineered TikTok and claimed "TikTok is a data collection service that is thinly-veiled as a social network.... For what it's worth, I've reversed the Instagram, Facebook, Reddit, and Twitter apps. They don't collect anywhere near the same amount of data that TikTok does..."[5] Meanwhile, WeChat is very much monitored by the Chinese government. Posts offensive to the government, and they are easily offended, are routinely taken down. Plus, any data collected by Chinese platforms is ultimately used and seen by China's authoritarian government. American companies do collect information on users but however much you dislike Mark Zuckerberg, there is a difference between Facebook and the rulers of China, in terms of power, reach and intentions. The U.S. government must go to court to collect data from these companies and U.S. companies usually actively oppose those attempts. So, to be clear, there is no comparison between China social media platforms and American ones and one can understand the impulse to ban them in America. But it's an urge we should resist. However, it would be appropriate to enact laws restricting what kind of data these platforms can collect. There is no reason at all for TikTok or WeChat to be able to grab our personal information and spy on our devices.

In late 2019, Chinese officials increasingly took to Twitter to defend its policies and attack those pointing out China's transgressions. We should continue to welcome Chinese officials on American social media platforms—I am not for censorship, even of Chinese officials. But we should loudly and forcefully call for China to break down its firewall and allow outsiders to post on their platforms, without censorship, on all these important issues. China will not comply, but the longer we point out the differences between freedom and authoritarianism, the more the message will imbed in people's psyches, whether in China or elsewhere, of China's foolish, repressive censorship regime.

Now we know there are lots of concerns about social media here in America. Former presidential candidate Elizabeth Warren has even called for breaking up Facebook, for example. There are certainly aspects of social media that I don't care for. I much preferred Facebook when it was a platform for my friends and family to post photos of their kids, their meals, and their pets rather than learning of their political opinions, however informed or ignorant I found them. But there has been a rush to blame social media for all sorts of society's ills that in many cases are not backed by evidence. Pundits and politicians often blame social media for the increase in depression among our youth. But an eight-year-long longitudinal study found that, "time spent using social media was not related to individual changes in depression or anxiety over eight years."[6] Social media also does not appear to affect the life satisfaction of youth, according to another report: "In this study, we used large-scale representative panel data to disentangle the between-person and within-person relations linking adolescent social media use and well-being. We found that social media use is not, in and of itself, a strong predictor of life satisfaction across the adolescent population."[7] Nor is social media the reason for the rise of right-wing populism as so many people assert, including so many of my friends on various social media platforms. A study analyzing data from France, the U.K., and the U.S. did "not find evidence that online/social media explain support for right-wing populist candidates and parties. Instead, in the USA, the use of online media decreases support for right-wing populism."[8] Clearly, you need to get your crazy uncle away from Fox News and onto Facebook, Twitter, and Instagram stat.[9]

So please, *Global China Times*, various Chinese government officials, and propogandists, have at it on Facebook, tweet to your hearts' content, post your favorite torture photos on Instagram. We won't and shouldn't ban you. But we will, at every turn, remind you that you prevent your own citizens from accessing these platforms and you prevent the conversation the world is having about Xinjiang from taking place on WeChat and other services in China. This, you realize, is evidence of weakness. If the party-state concoction of China cannot withstand information about its internal policies from being transmitted to the people, then perhaps it's not such a strong regime after all. Elizabeth Warren and her chattering allies should remember that about the United States as well. Certainly, social media, like everything in this world, has its drawbacks. It can be problematic, and, as we will see later in this chapter, it has the ability to organize large masses, for good and ill. But we should welcome China on our platforms even as we demand international social media platforms be allowed in China and that Chinese be allowed to speak freely on platforms indigenous to China and on ones that are based outside of the country.

For the worst, most pervasive human rights abuses committed by China, such as the cultural genocide of Uyghurs in Xinjiang, the U.S. and the world should do more than call out China in words. The U.S. Congress passed the Uyghur Human Rights Policy Act and it was signed into law by Trump. The law calls for further investigations of China's abuses in Xinjiang, the protection of Uyghurs in the United States from harassment by China, and the imposition of travel sanctions on Xinjiang Communist Party Secretary Chen Quanguo. This is a good start, and it is important that other countries take similar actions. The U.S. should work with like-minded countries to do so and to continue to urge the U.N Security Council to open an investigation and to denounce the human rights abuses in Xinjiang. China, being a Security Council member, will veto any resolution condemning their acts in Xinjiang, but the U.S. and other countries should continue to place China under pressure on this issue.

There should also be serious consideration of bringing China's actions in Xinjiang to the International Criminal Court as a "crime against humanity." In the fall of 2019, the bipartisan Congressional-Executive Commission on China (CECC) issued a report asserting that a good case could be made that China's repression in Xinjiang meets one of the 11 acts defined by the Court as a crime against humanity "when committed against a widespread or systematic attack directed against any civilian population."[10] This report was completed before evidence emerged of forced sterilization of Uyghurs so if anything the case for genocide is now stronger. Going to the International Court would be a big step and certainly seen as provocative by China's government. But as we saw in chapter 4, sustained continued pressure on these issues will in the long-term help induce change in China. It is important for the U.S. president to speak forthrightly on these particular human rights issues. The bully pulpit has been sorely missing as a tool for human rights during the Trump Administration but also under the Obama Administration. As we saw earlier, Carter and Reagan were often at their most eloquent and effective when standing up for human rights around the world. And, of course, we should work with our allies to speak up on these issues, including in formal forums such as the G-7. Certain countries, or at least their leaders, are sometimes reluctant to speak up on human rights with China (we're looking at you, Germany), but the U.S. should work to try to change that.

Businesses are continually placed in difficult positions when it comes to China's problematic policies and practices. We have some sympathy for them. If you are producing a product or service that makes sense for the Chinese market—putting aside for the moment the various non-tariff barriers China erects to prevent companies from succeeding in the Chinese market—given the size of the market, it is much to ask of a business person to not do business in China. It is easy for you and me, who may be able to ignore the China market in our employment—we can easily say no to billions of dollars of imaginary revenue. But for someone for whom such revenue is a concrete possibility, most of us would try to tap into the market. I do not believe the United States should cut off American companies from doing business with China except in specific situations and circumstances, which we will detail shortly. But perhaps a code of conduct could be created for companies doing business in China.

You may remember the Sullivan Principles launched in the late 1970s to confront the apartheid regime of South Africa. They dealt specifically with the discriminatory policies of the South African government. More than 100 companies adopted the principles, which included provisions such as "Increasing the number of blacks and other nonwhites in management and supervisory positions" and "non-segregation of the races in all eating, comfort and work facilities." They were targeted at specific issues taking place in South Africa. Sullivan tried to launch a global set of principles on more general human rights issues such as equal opportunities for all employees and providing a safe workplace. The fact that you have never heard of the Global Sullivan Principles speaks to their ineffectiveness.

Even the Sullivan Principles for companies conducting business in South Africa were eventually overtaken by numerous countries instead instituting sanctions against South Africa and many companies ultimately pulling out of the country due to political pressure and protests by consumers and shareholders. But the Sullivan Principles helped elevate the issue of the anti-apartheid movement and provided guideposts for companies doing business in a problematic regime. We were involved with a nascent effort towards the end of the Cold War to develop principles for companies doing business in the Soviet Union. The Slepak Principles, as they were dubbed, urged companies conducting business in the Soviet Union to not use goods produced by forced labor, protect the safety of their employees, and other such conditions. Before the Slepak Principles were adopted, the Soviet

Union fell (Just the mere threat of the Slepak Principles brought the regime down!...Or, uh, er, perhaps there were other factors.)

A set of principles for companies conducting business in and with China could also provide a modest boost for pressuring China on human rights (We're in this for the long game.) They would need to be focused on the challenges particular to China. One of the principles could be to not allow a company's technology, product or service to be used in the campaign against Uyghurs. Or to not use forced labor, including by Uyghurs. In March 2020, the Australian Strategic Policy Institute documented the forced transfer of Uyghurs to factories throughout China where they are forced to work. These factories supply companies such as Apple, BMW, Nike, and Huawei.[11] Another principle could focus on protecting workplace safety. Yet another could be a commitment by companies not to allow the use of their technology to censor online speech.

The principles should not be a U.S.-focused effort; that would unduly disadvantage American businesses (though many of these principles such as use of forced labor, are already against the law). It needs to be a multilateral effort of the EU, Japan, and other countries. At the least, there should be a concerted effort to have companies live up to the United Nations Global Compact, a voluntary set of principles on how businesses should operate. They are somewhat vague, and there are no enforcement provisions. There are around 13,000 corporate participants in the Compact from countries all over the world. For example, both Microsoft and Starbucks are participants in the Compact. There are even Chinese company participants, including Baidu and the real estate development company, Vanke. Clearly, the Compact is not having a large effect on how business is conducted by Chinese companies, but we need to start somewhere. A sustained effort that elevates the visibility of these principles would go a long way to increasing pressure on China on these issues.

A Short Sidebar on Lebron James and How Businesses Should Not Act with China

Lebron James is one of the three greatest basketball players in the history of the game (We have him ranked just behind Michael Jordan and probably just ahead of the underrated Kareem Abdul Jabbar). He also has many great achievements outside of basketball, from speaking out on civil rights issues in the United States, to starting his own public school for youth in Akron, Ohio. So we don't mean to pick on him and greatly admire his efforts to create a better America (full disclosure, we sports hate the Los Angeles Lakers and actively root against James and the Lakers), but he provides a text-book case on how a business should not act when dealing with the admittedly difficult geopolitics of doing business in China.

Lebron James makes many millions of dollars because of China. Just as we have sympathy for other businesses who risk losing revenue by speaking out against Chinese abuses, so too do we for LeBron James. But while it is understandable for a company to be quiet about those abuses, or at least to eschew speaking out forthrightly against them, how LeBron James handled the NBA China controversy is the exact opposite of how a U.S. business should handle the complicated issues of China.

Let's remind ourselves what happened. In the fall of 2019, Houston Rockets General Manager Daryl Morey tweeted an image that read, "Fight for Freedom, Stand with Hong Kong." The Chinese government, fighting against freedom, and trampling all over Hong Kong, swiftly denounced the tweet. CCTV—the state-run broadcasting service— suspended televising all NBA games. China generally threw their usual hissy fit about people commenting on its lack of respect for freedom of speech, assembly and other basic human rights. The NBA, after an initial misstep in its Chinese language response to Morey's tweet, mostly acted as responsibly as any company with significant business interests in

China ever has. The Commissioner of the NBA, Adam Silver, repeatedly defended Morey's right to free speech, if not the contents of the tweet. Morey himself deleted the tweet and backtracked. The Houston Rockets, because Yao Ming had played for them, had more to lose in China than probably any other NBA team.

LeBron James was in China at the time of Morey's tweet, with his Los Angeles Lakers preparing to play an exhibition game there. Other prominent players, such as Stephen Curry, were asked about the imbroglio and mostly pleaded ignorance. They were not profiles in courage to be sure but given they also have significant business interests in China, their responses were understandable.

But LeBron James, when he finally weighed in more than a week later, and presumably after giving the issue much thought, did not take the route some of these other players did of merely saying he didn't know enough about the situation in Hong Kong and deferring to speak out about the situation. Instead, he attacked Daryl Morey. For commenting on Hong Kongers striving for freedom. Not China for abusing human rights. Let's annotate Lebron's statement to the media to explain just how wrong-headed his response was and how it is a model for how a business should not deal with China's problematic policies.

"We all talk about freedom of speech—yes, we do have freedom of speech." Lebron is getting ready to criticize someone for using their free speech to defend others' right to free speech. "But at times, there are ramifications for the negative that can happen when you're not thinking about others and you're only thinking about yourself." So he's upset at Morey, not China or the Hong Kong government. Morey, you see, wasn't thinking about Hong Kongers, he was only thinking about himself apparently, and he should have been thinking about LeBron James. "I don't believe—I don't

want to get into a ... feud with Daryl Morey but I believe he wasn't educated on the situation at hand." Is "at hand" the Hong Kong protests? If so, then is LeBron asserting that there should not be freedom for Hong Kongers? And if he doesn't want to get into a feud with Daryl Morey, then why is he making this statement? "And he spoke. And so many people could have been harmed, not only financially but emotionally, physically and spiritually." By "so many people could have been harmed financially, emotionally, physically and spiritually" he's referring to the down-trodden million-aire NBA players—most especially himself—who could lose money by Morey angering the Chinese. If, as LeBron later asserted, he means Morey was putting him and the other players in jeopardy because they were in China at the time of the tweets, doesn't that mean he is aware of just how au-thoritarian China is? In other words, even though LeBron James is one of the most famous people in the world, and probably in the richest 1 percent in the world, he realizes China is so corrupt and repressive that it is possible they would do something even to him while he is in China over a mere tweet. If so, shouldn't he be welcoming, in fact backing, the sentiment of Morey's tweet? If China is that bad, isn't it incumbent on him to speak out? Or if that's not what he thinks, if he's just pissed that Morey's tweet could cost him money, rather than attacking Morey shouldn't he just use the tried and true line that he doesn't know enough about the Hong Kong issue, collect his money, and not attack someone for speaking up for freedom? Either way, it's a bad look for Lebron. "So just be careful with what we tweet and what we say and what we do, even though, yes, we do have freedom of speech. But there can be a lot of negative that comes from that speech." Perhaps LeBron should take his own words to heart. There is a lot of negative that can come from speech, as his words to the media so amply illustrated.

To sum up, instead of saying nothing, or also speaking up for people demanding their basic human rights as Hong Kongers were doing, LeBron James forcefully attacked the person using their free speech to speak up for free speech. It was the worst approach a business could take. He was helping China achieve what they wanted with their attack on Morey and the NBA—creating a chilling effect so nobody else would speak up on human rights issues in China. LeBron couldn't have spoken more usefully for tyrants.

Later, LeBron tried to clarify a bit after his original statement was so roundly and justifiably attacked, but those clarifications only helped China more. Again, we do not bring this up to detract from the many good actions LeBron has taken off the court, which should be commended. We are merely using his actions and words regarding China to illustrate what not to do. We cannot expect everyone to be as courageous, accurate (and funny) as the creators of South Park[12] in dealing with China. And we realize that businesses like LeBron James are giving up lots of money to speak out against China. We shouldn't expect them to give up that money. It's a bit like the scene in the classic movie Chinatown when Jack Nicholson's character Jake Gittes asks John Houston's wealthy, corrupt character Noah Cross how much more money he needs: "Why are you doing it? How much better can you eat? What could you buy that you can't already afford?" Noah Cross replies, "The Future, Mr. Gittes. The Future." LeBron James and other businesses see a very lucrative future in China. We don't begrudge them that future, only call for them to act with a minimum of decorum and decency.

Democracies everywhere must support each other when China's heavy-handed tactics are used against them. For nearly two years, China has held incommunicado two Canadians in retaliation for the arrest of Huawei's CFO, Meng Wanzhou. While Meng is out on bail, living in one of her two mansions in Vancouver, B.C. with full access to lawyers, as well as all the luxuries wealth and power bring, Michael Kovrig, a former Canadian diplomat and employee of a nonprofit working on conflict issues, was held incommunicado for six months, has not been allowed to meet with Canadian officials or a lawyer and is held in severe conditions. The Globe and Mail reports, "Mr. Kovrig can possess only three books at a time. He can write letters for only a few hours on a single day each month; the remainder of the time, he is barred from using pen and paper. He cannot hold on to the letters he receives from family." He is also subject to repeated harsh interrogations. In June, 2020, his family revealed letters they received from Kovrig, where he wrote, "If there's one faint silver lining to this Hell, it's this: trauma carved caverns of psychological pain through my mind. As I strive to heal and recover, I find myself filling those gulfs with a love for you and for life that is vast, deep and more profound and comforting than what I've ever experienced before." Canadian business executive Michael Spavor is also being held in such conditions. As of the time of this writing, both have been charged with spying and both have been held for over 600 days. As Kovrig's wife said in the Globe and Mail article, "I truly believe that by doing this, China sends a message to the rest of the world that is chilling – that basically says, 'nobody is safe here.' That even folks that are genuinely trying to understand, to build bridges, to improve relations, can be arbitrarily detained because of a geopolitical struggle that they had nothing to do with."[13] Meng is enjoying all the rights and regulations of the rule of law society that is Canada. Spavor and Kovrig are suffering under the usual cruel artifices of an authoritarian regime.

The world is far too quiet about this and other intimidation by China against foreigners. While there are, of course, diplomatic complications for Canada, and they presumably are trying to be careful in their approach to protect their two citizens, the rest of the world needs to take a more active, more vociferous approach. Kovrig and Spavor should be causes célèbre, there should be benefit concerts for them, Hollywood stars should be calling out their names while thanking their agents at award shows. The U.S. must work to elevate these issues at the UN, in meetings with China, and work with allies in Europe and Asia to do the same. China gets away with such behavior in part because the world has been too reticent to call them on it. If the U.S. and its allies are more vocal in concert about these egregious transgressions, perhaps China will be more reticent to come down hard on Sweden the next time it gives an award to a Chinese-Swedish citizen who has been arrested for doing his job as a journalist.

China acts very much the bully on these types of issues. China often pressures smaller countries to bend to its will. These countries often give in to the pressure, or if they don't, they have a more difficult time dealing with the consequences. The U.S. and its allies must be willing to help such countries, perhaps even financially when needed. For example, the next time Norway awards a Nobel prize to a Chinese dissident and China cuts off their salmon exports, the rest of the world should buy that salmon. When China attacks Sweden for presenting a PEN award to a Swedish-Chinese journalist, the rest of the world must rise up to denounce China and defend Sweden.

Keeping human rights in the forefront, speaking up for the benefits of freedom of expression and the positives of liberalization are the key to pushing back on China as it works to gain prominence and power in the world. China loses on that playing field. A mere struggle between two great powers such as the U.S. and China puts China on an equal footing. Besides being a morally dubious proposition, the U.S. aiming to be top dog of the world forever is unrealistic and makes the field of combat advantageous to China. We should not care that the U.S. is the most powerful nation in the world, but it is in our interests that the great powers of the world are ones that respect human rights, the rule of law, and liberalization.

Build trade regimes with other countries and regions

Chapter 5 explained how various multilateral trade agreements were meant to help the world continue a rules-based trade regime and counter China's efforts to undermine that rule of law order. I won't belabor it in this section. Suffice it to say the U.S. should work to re-join the TPP if they'll have us. Creating an Asia-Pacific trade agreement that includes the United States, but does not include China, will help undermine China's undermining. As China looks from the outside in, perhaps it will feel compelled to join as it did the WTO back in 2001. If it is brought in, it will have to be with adequate enforcement provisions that will make China a more constructive player in the world economy. It is likely there would be some renegotiation necessary of the TPP for the United States to join in the fun. Certainly labor interests in the United States will want to add the labor enforcement provisions included in the new U.S. -Mexico -Canada Free Trade Agreement, such as labor attachés and the creation of panels to adjudicate labor disputes. Since both Mexico and Canada are already part of the TPP, perhaps it will be easier to include these provisions.

There is lots of talk of the U.S. and China's economies decoupling because of the U.S.–China trade war. But China has been decoupling from the world economy in certain ways for a long time. The creation of the Great Firewall over a decade ago separated China from the Internet. In recent years it has stepped back from engagement by concentrating on building its own industries in sectors it considers strategic. Even in the trade war, we have seen China decoupling, not the United States. Imports to the U.S. from Asia have not decreased, merely shifted from China to other parts of Asia. Chinese imports are decreasing, partly due to its slowing economy, partly due to supply chains moving to other parts of Asia, and partly due to trying to build up its own companies at the expense of foreign goods. The rest of the Asia-Pacific countries trading with each other more robustly, with the rule of law in place, will make China's decoupling more painful to its own economy. Yes, China can build up tech industries and other strategic sectors, and yes, they have a large internal market to sell to, but the larger world market will be more expensive for them to access. China is big, the rest of the world is bigger. Plus, if current demographic trends hold, in the not too distant future, China's population will begin shrinking. Their large market will become smaller. If they try to become a self-contained bakery, apart from the world's much larger bakeshop, they will miss out on lots of treats.

For similar reasons, the U.S. should re-engage with the European Union on the now-dead TTIP negotiations. The EU and U.S. economies combined still dwarf China's. Drawing them closer together, as with the TPP, will force China to either try to be an isolated success or to make changes and more easily access markets that will make its own economy stronger.

Similarly, the U.S. needs to again work within the WTO. That means bringing cases against China when warranted which the Trump administration has declined to do. To do that, however, the U.S. must allow the appointment of judges to the WTO's Appellate Body which adjudicates disputes brought to the WTO. The Trump administration did not allow new judges to be appointed as current judges' terms expired. There is no longer a quorum of judges available to adjudicate. This was due to the Trump administration's dim view of the WTO. Rather than trying to reform it, the Trump administration instead destroyed it, taking down the rules-based world order like, well, like China's government. The WTO has its faults, but it can continue to be a useful tool in reckoning with China's unfair economic practices. Reform and evolve, don't destroy. Some critics propose creating a new trade organization from scratch. They don't believe it is possible to reform the WTO. Evolving WTO will be difficult, but I am deeply skeptical creating a new organization will be easier. Those calling for developing completely new organizations and the destruction of the old are prone to the fallacy of utopian thinking. They only see the faults of the existing structure and not any of the benefits, while only envisioning the perfect gleaming house they hope to build and not any of the faulty piping, wiring and chipped wood it will undoubtedly have. Plus, we are doubtful they will find it any easier to find cooperation in building the new home than in remodeling the old one.

The U.S. should look at other regions and countries for possible trade agreements, including India. The Trump administration indicated interest in negotiating a free trade agreement with India. As of this writing, it is still working on a smaller trade deal with India that could prepare the way for a more comprehensive agreement in the future. India's small steps towards populism are troubling, but the U.S.–India relationship is one of the key assets in a world restraining authoritarianism. The relationship must continue to be nurtured. As noted in Chapter 5, the U.S. should help Vietnam continue to develop economically, perhaps by omission more than commission— do not place tariffs on their goods, do not try to bar their imports even if we are worried about competing with them economically. Do softly encourage their liberalization by accepting more Vietnamese students, providing assistance to their efforts to adjust to climate change, sharing helpful technology, and in other ways. This same approach can be adopted with other Asian countries such as Indonesia. The U.S. should also encourage intra-Asian defense, economic and other alliances such as the ones between Japan and Vietnam we described in chapter 5. We live in a more multi-polar world than that of the Cold War era and the U.S. should accept and encourage productive, positive poles coming together.

Since the WTO protests in Seattle in 1999, the trade agenda and globalism have been under attack. Since the 2008 financial crisis, and especially with the election of Donald Trump, they have been in retreat. I understand a newly reinvigorated trade agenda is neither popular nor, under the Trump administration or a Biden administration, likely, but enacting all of these trade-related policies would be helpful both for the world economy and for working to hedge China's economic ambitions.

Be forceful on China's closed market

China continues to have a closed economy. In fact, there is evidence that the trend is towards more protectionism, not less. While China's exports continue to be robust during the U.S.–China trade war, as we have noted, imports have decreased. This is partly due to China's wanting to build more stuff within China, to substitute domestic industries for imports. In 2015, China announced its Made in China 2025 initiative, as part of its 13th five-year plan. The initiative aims to reduce China's reliance on foreign suppliers and build up its own key industries such as aerospace, semiconductors and biotech. Recently, China has been quieter about its Made in China 2025 initiative, but that does not mean it is not continuing to implement it, it is merely ratcheting down the PR for the initiative. If anything, China is accelerating its efforts to build up those industries and decrease its imports. It's their speak softly and carry a Chinese-built, high-tech stick approach.

All of this may mean that we should have applauded Trump's desire to get tough with China regarding its economy. The Trump administration deserved credit for raising the prominence of China's closed market policies. But the Trump administration concentrated on transactional gains not systemic ones. Trump, and too often his trade negotiators, focused on reducing the trade deficit and requiring China to buy a certain dollar amount of U.S. goods, as evidenced by the trade agreement they negotiated with China. His administration should have kept a laser focus on the non-tariff barriers of China, which have effectively prohibited foreign companies, including American, from successfully entering the China market. Further, tariffs are not a particularly effective tool to open the China market. It is fair to note that U.S. tariffs helped accelerate an ongoing trend of manufacturing moving to cheaper labor markets from China, but they have thus far had no effect on opening China's market. That they were done unilaterally, rather than with allies, further reduced their effectiveness. Plus, though the tariffs may reduce the U.S. trade deficit with China (which really has nothing to do with the health of either economy), studies show they are not helping increase jobs, and, of course, they hurt the American consumer. Industries for which tariffs have been imposed, have seen employment go down, while prices for their products have gone up.[14] Trump's trade war has been lose-lose economically and has thus far had zero impact in opening up China's closed markets.

The U.S. should take both multilateral steps and, when necessary, unilateral measures as well. First, the U.S. should bring cases against China at the WTO, as we noted above. But the U.S. should also work with the E.U. and Japan and other countries to create an equal playing field with China. This includes dealing with theft of intellectual property, disallowing companies to compete in certain industries, the use of their cybersecurity law to see all data of foreign companies, the use of the new company tracking system to unfairly advantage domestic companies over foreign ones, and other such policies. Multilateral should be the approach of the Phase 2 negotiations with China.

Chinese companies must also comply with established standards such as transparency. China's companies listed on U.S. securities exchanges must comply with the same financial transparency that non-Chinese companies do. If they don't allow financial audits, well then, Chinese companies shouldn't be allowed to list.

Then there are national security concerns. We would not ban U.S. companies from selling components to Huawei, but it makes perfect sense that we would not use Huawei technology to build a 5G or any other network. Huawei, despite protests, is essentially a state-owned enterprise. Government control is often difficult to discern in the Chinese corporate world. But a paper by Donald Clark and Christopher Balding solved this mystery.[15] The paper states, "The Huawei operating company is 100% owned by a holding company, which is in turn approximately 1% owned by Huawei founder Ren Zhengfei and 99% owned by an entity called a 'trade union committee' for the holding company." Clark and Balding assert this holding company is really the state. "Given the public nature of trade unions in China, if the ownership stake of the trade union committee is genuine, and if the trade union and its committee function as trade unions generally function in China, then Huawei may be deemed effectively state-owned." The Trump administration was right to urge countries around the world not to use Huawei for their information networks. This has been somewhat successful. The UK, which under Boris Johnson, was initially reluctant to ban Huawei technology in building their 5G network, reversed that position. A U.S. administration that did not attack ally and foe alike may have even better luck in convincing other countries to eschew Huawei technology. Despite China's propaganda, there are alternatives to Huawei that offer superior technology without the problem of China's being able to snoop throughout a country's communications network. As Christopher Balding has written, "Based upon the widely used technology industry metric of standard and essential patent, Huawei ranks generally anywhere from 4th to 6th globally. Other firms such as Nokia, Ericsson, Samsung, LG, and Qualcomm are leaders with Intel and Sharp ranking just behind Huawei and ZTE. While Huawei attempts to paint themselves as a market and technological leader, there simply is no evidence that they are a technological leader in 5G."[16] Huawei is a huge security risk to any country that uses its technology to build its communications infrastructure. Huawei is essentially government-owned, and its data would be the Chinese government's data. Yes, the U.S. government has, on occasion, tried to force American technology companies to compromise users data, but usually such companies have fought back against such efforts, including Apple fighting in court a request to open a user's iPhone. Despite Chinese propaganda, the two situations are not comparable.

Huawei represents a real and present risk to democratic countries. The U.S. must work with countries to encourage them to use non-Huawei technology to build their telecommunications infrastructure. In the many cases where China has threatened countries with economic reprisal if they do not choose Huawei (an act which more or less proves the point that Huawei is essentially a government-controlled-company), the U.S. and other countries must be willing to back up those countries. Germany is under intense pressure to use Huawei or risk its auto companies losing the lucrative Chinese market. The U.S., the EU, Japan, and others must stand as one on this issue. Again, this will be easier to accomplish with a U.S.

presidential administration that does not threaten friend and foe alike economically. A multilateral approach in pushing back against the use of Chinese technology that threatens the security of countries, whether Huawei or other Chinese technology, is a necessary prescription going forward.

Protect Taiwan

Country A has a population of 19 million people. It was run by a dictatorship until 1989 when the dictator was overthrown. Throughout the 1990s, the country continued to democratize and its economy had rapid and then steady economic growth from the time it became politically free with a GDP now totaling US$250 billion. Country B has a population of 22 million people and slowly but steadily democratized throughout the 1990s. After rapid GDP growth, it has settled into steady increases along with the usual economic down cycles. Its GDP now totals US$586 billion.

Country A is Romania, which broke free of Ceausescu and the Soviet Union, democratized, grew its economy, and eventually joined the European Union. Country B, which China demands we not call a country, is, of course, Taiwan. Economically, it has developed even more than Romania, it is a full democracy, and if space aliens landed in the East Asia Sea and reported back to headquarters, they would include in their memo that there was a remarkably successful free country called Taiwan.

But, of course, most of the world maintains a convenient fiction that Taiwan is a part of China because China is not 22 million people, it's 1.3 billion, with the second-largest economy in the world, nuclear weapons, and a thirst for reclaiming Chiang Kai-shek's gamble. Size and strength matter, at least when it comes to geopolitics.

The U.S. has been supportive of Taiwan and its rights as a free country over the years and the Trump administration, if anything, more so. Officially, under the 1979 U.S.–PRC Joint Communique, the United States only recognizes mainland China as the sole legal government of China. In other words, officially, the U.S. adheres to the PRC's position that Taiwan is a part of China. This is a bit like a court saying a woman who long ago divorced her abusive husband is still married to him even though she has her own house, job, and life. In a righteous world, the United States, and its allies, would tell China that Taiwan is a free, independent country unless and until it decides it wants to be part of the mainland again, and consequently re-open embassies with Taiwan, and tell China it will defend 22 million people's freedom with whatever it takes.

It feels good to be righteous; it is more important to be smart. The U.S. can, does and should continue to provide Taiwan with arms and moral support to defend itself. But, at the same time, we should be realistic. Is America, is the world, prepared to go to war with China over Taiwan? We presumably are not willing to use nuclear weapons. The Taiwan Relations Act of 1979 calls on the United States to provide Taiwan with the means to defend itself and asserts that the U.S. itself should "resist any resort to force or other forms of coercion that would jeopardize the security, or the social or economic system, of the people on Taiwan."[17] The Act does not explicitly command the United States to fight China should it attempt to invade Taiwan, but rather the "President and Congress, who shall determine, in accordance with constitutional processes, appropriate action by the United States in response to any such danger." Our current and future presidents and Congress will need to assess the situation and take the best course of action, which may or may not mean engaging any Chinese military action. This, frankly, is sensible. Should the U.S. fight China in a possible invasion of Taiwan? I don't know (7). It depends on the circumstances. The U.S. should make clear there would be severe consequences if they chose to invade Taiwan. These should include economic sanctions and, depending on the circumstances, military ones as well.

We should not overly provoke China with statements on Taiwan, but we and the world should note the silliness of pretending Taiwan is not a successful country with its own culture, a thriving economy (albeit one very tied to China's), and a democratic, free political system. Like any such country, it should not be overturned by the authoritarian mainland through military or cyber warfare.

China has much to learn from Taiwan about how to run a free, thriving country. Taiwan is much less unequal than China, with a much lower Gini coefficient (a measure of inequality). It has legalized gay marriage. It has a great food scene, and its president is a big fan of cats (the animal, not the play; if she was a fan of the Andrew Lloyd Weber musical we might rethink our position on Taiwan). Taiwan has also been one of the most successful countries in combatting the Covid-19 pandemic, even though the WHO continues to exclude it due to pressure from China. Back in 2003, Taiwan was hit hard by SARS—but they learned from it. They set up a National Health Command Center in 2004 "that focuses on large-outbreak response and acts as the operational command point for direct communications among central, regional, and local authorities."[18] With Covid-19 they have established a checklist of 124 actions, including "border control from the air and sea, case identification (using new data and technology), quarantine of suspicious cases, proactive case finding, resource allocation (assessing and managing capacity), reassurance and education of the public while fighting misinformation, negotiation with other countries and regions, formulation of policies toward schools and childcare, and relief to businesses." Other countries have much to learn from Taiwan.

Like any country, Taiwan has its challenges, but China has much to learn from the Taiwan development model, including what happens when your economic growth slows down after rapid increases, as happened in Taiwan and is in the process of happening in China. Taiwan stands as a conspicuous example of a country that both transitioned from authoritarianism and developing country status. It is also, as we noted earlier, a stark rebuke to those who argue that Chinese culture is not compatible with democracy. A democratic China is just 68 miles away from the mainland to observe and learn from.

We look forward to Taiwan rejoining China if and when it wants to. And we have advice for China on how to make that happen. Liberalize and democratize. Do that, and I bet Taiwan may very well want to merge with such a successful, free country.

Still cooperate where we can

The U.S., with the rest of the world, should more vigorously confront and resist China's attempts to remake the world in its authoritarian, lack-of-rule-of-law image. But that does not mean we should not also cooperate with China where it makes sense and is needed. At a time when the Trump administration called for America First and the Biden administration trumpets "Buy American," many of the world's most pressing and challenging problems are transnational. The Covid-19 pandemic is a startling and tragic example of what happens when countries don't cooperate and act transparently. Climate change is a slow burning one. Here is an area where China and the U.S. (and many other countries) could and should work together.

It is remarkable that so many U.S. politicians and climate change advocates remain U.S.-centric in developing policy recommendations for climate change. Whether it is the Green New Deal or other efforts, they live in a U.S.-centric world, which is to say in a world that does not exist. China has been the largest CO_2 emitter since 2006, much longer than a decade ago. Its CO_2 emissions are double the combined emissions of Europe and the United States. I know, I know, the U.S. still emits more per capita than China, so there is far more to do in the United States (and in other developed countries), but if you actually care about climate change, about reducing CO_2 emissions to avoid the worst scenarios of climate change, then the real game is outside the United States. Total emissions are what matters. Even if the United States somehow miraculously went to zero emissions tomorrow, the world would not have solved the climate change challenge. To solve it is to find ways that China, India, and the developing world can continue to grow economically without emitting a bunch of climate change gases.

I know Greta Thunberg and the other *New Amish* advocate for everybody changing lifestyles and accepting lower or perhaps negative economic growth. While I applaud Ms. Thunberg's raising the profile of climate change, the no-growth policy is neither realistic nor moral. It is easy for those in Sweden, the United States or other places to tell the developing world "Sorry, you can't grow economically, you'll just have to go without easy access to food, transportation, the Internet (Africans love cat videos and political squabbles, too), high paying jobs, washers and dryers, electricity, and all the other things we take for granted, but sorry, to save the world from increasing in temperature by 3 – 5 degrees Celsius you must be forever poor. Good luck selling that policy, good luck preventing these other countries from trying to grow economically. It won't work and it's morally wrong to call on people to remain deprived.

So, you argue that we merely need to transfer wealth from the developed world to the developing? Good luck with selling that policy, too. And how exactly would it work? Let's say you convince Americans, Germans, wealthy urban Chinese, and others to give some of their annual income to a fund for developing countries. Those people will take that money and do what? Well, likely want to build infrastructure that allows them to eat more and have electricity and all the other "luxuries" that we have. That means they would still emit more climate change gases in the future. And because the developed world would no longer grow, we are unlikely to further develop the clean energy and other technology needed to further reduce our emissions. Yes, the United States is still emitting too much $CO2$ and other climate change gases, but we have improved on that score, and the reason we have is mostly due to technological advances coupled with policy. The U.S. peaked at emitting 22.5 metric tons per capita in 1973 and is now down to around 16.5.[19]

The key to solving the climate change crisis is additional advances in technology coupled with smart policy decisions. And this is where the United States and China can cooperate to help the world and themselves. First, perhaps we should define what we mean by solving the climate change crisis. With current levels of emissions, an increase of 1.5 to 2 degrees Celsius is likely baked in no matter what we do at this point. Solving the climate change challenge means keeping temperature change below 3 degrees Celsius. The good news is that previous modeling based on the quantity of emissions the world was producing ten years ago showed we were on a trajectory of an increase of 4 to 5 degrees C by the end of the century. Thanks to technological advancements that have already taken place, coupled with policy changes, the world is no longer on that trajectory but rather on one that would result in warming of just over 3 degrees C. This will still bring real world challenging consequences but at least some progress has been made. And there is the possibility of even more progress, so that warming is likely to be less than 3 degrees C by the end of the century.[20]

To achieve this, we need more technological progress coupled with, or driven by, smart policy choices. One such choice is for the U.S. and China to cooperate on this issue. This is yet another area where China is showing the economy is a bakery, not a pie as it has developed and produced a variety of green energy products. China is the largest producer and consumer of electric cars, it is the largest producer of wind power[21] and solar power, too. It is a leading producer of batteries and power transmission equipment. From 2000 to 2020, China planted so many trees that the earth is greener today than it was 20 years ago.[22] For all its problems and challenges, China has been a leader in developing and implementing green technology. Of course, it is also the largest contributor to CO_2 emissions, is exporting coal-burning plants as part of its Belt and Road initiative to developing countries around the world, and continues to needlessly build additional coal-burning plants within its own borders, despite renewable energy now being cost-competitive with coal. China is nothing if not complicated.

This is all the more reason to try to work with China to confront climate change on a global scale. They are a large contributor both to the problem and to solutions. To solve climate change, we need better technology, especially in energy storage, manufacturing, and agriculture. The world has made great strides in clean energy generation, especially solar and wind, which are both, in some geographical areas, already cost-competitive with fossil fuels for generating energy. The world needs continued improvements in clean energy generation but storage, manufacturing, and agriculture are where technology is still lagging. How to address this? More research and development.

The U.S. and China should jointly fund research and development in these areas, as well as conduct joint research and development projects. They should create a Clean Energy Research and Development Fund. Further, the two countries should subsidize the results coming out of the fund for developing countries to use. A breakthrough in manufacturing cement more cleanly, or an alternative clean substance to concrete, should be given to developing countries to use, which can then grow their economies more cleanly (while compensating the institutions or companies that develop these breakthroughs). How much should the U.S. and China contribute annually to this research and development fund? I don't know (8). A number of people have suggested increases in research and development by the U.S. in these areas ranging from $30 billion to $700 billion per year. I'll let other more qualified experts determine the necessary amount, but I'll suggest the percentage the U.S. and China should contribute to the fund. For every US$1 China contributes, the U.S. should contribute US$3, which is approximately the ratio of America's per capita CO_2 emissions to China's.

Encourage and expand immigration from China

Several years ago, an agent from the FBI came to my office to meet with me. The FBI was concerned about Chinese industrial espionage and other spying in the Seattle area. Knowing that I worked closely with both American and Chinese businesses, they wanted me to keep an eye out for such spying and alert the FBI when I came across it. Putting aside the fact that my identity is most definitely not Bourne and that I have never witnessed Chinese spying in America (though I did watch that executive from a medical device company pull his device back from a potential Chinese investor he judged was eyeing his technology a little too closely), there is no doubt that China spies on America, both in its attempts to steal technology and the general spy vs. spy fun that's been occurring between countries ever since there have been nations. Unfortunately, rather than focus on these spies, many, including the Trump administration, want to throw out Chinese students, researchers, and employees with the spy bath water. This is a mistake.

As I argued in chapter 3, nothing distinguishes America more from other countries than its relative success at immigration. This holds true as much for Chinese immigrants as for any other group. In addition, one of the great exports of the United States has been higher education. Again, the United States has benefitted immensely from all the Chinese who have studied at our universities and community colleges over the years, even acknowledging that some unknown percentage of them were spying even as they memorized the periodic table for chemistry class.

The answer to Chinese spying is not to accept fewer Chinese students or immigrants into the country. Instead, if necessary, the U.S. can beef up its anti-spying efforts, including better monitoring of military bases and key assets. A number of Chinese have been caught spying at such locations, showing that America can catch spies and have students and immigrants at the same time.[23] Of course, much of spy-craft nowadays is of the cyber variety.[24] But that can be just as easily accomplished from Hangzhou as from Pittsburgh. If a Chinese student plans on hacking into American computers, they don't need to be in America to do so. The world is full of trade-offs, and the smart one here is to risk a few more Chinese spies in America in return for many more Chinese students and immigrants coming to America.

As they have been for the past decade, Chinese students are the largest source of international students in the United States, totaling just over 369,000 in 2018/2019.[25] At one point, the Trump administration considered cutting off student visas to Chinese nationals. Thankfully, that did not happen (although it may now due to the coronavirus pandemic), and indeed there was a slight increase in

Chinese students studying in the U.S. over 2017/2018. It is a large increase from the beginning of the decade when just over 127,000 Chinese studied at U.S. universities, colleges, and community colleges in 2009/2010. The smart, strategic move would not be to curtail or end the number of Chinese students in the U.S., but instead to give them a green card upon graduation. As we noted in Chapter 3, the U.S. has an aging society, though not aging as rapidly as China's, and we need more immigrants. Accepting China's best and brightest into our land would help with our demographic challenges (someone's got to pay for our social security and Medicare) and add bakers to our economy. Half of Silicon Valley's CEOs are foreign-born.[26] Undoubtedly some of these new, college-educated Chinese will either start their own companies or lead existing companies to new successes, employing Americans and producing goods and services that we will all enjoy.

Offering a green card to such graduates, and keeping track of how many accept the opportunity, would be a way to index, over time, the relative success of China and America. When many of the Chinese students decide to stay in America and start new lives, we'll know our society is relatively successful. If, at some point, we see a growing number of Chinese returning to China, we'll see that China is successfully transforming its country.

Now it should be noted there have been a number of cases, perhaps increasingly so, of Chinese students at U.S. campuses confronting other students protesting China's human rights abuses or sticking up for the protestors in Hong Kong.[27] Chinese students have every right to speak their views while here in America, even if you or I disagree with them. If they want to disagree with a student expressing concern about the internment of Uyghurs or speaking up for the rights of Hong Kongers, have at it. It will be instructive for our students to hear that point of view and learn how best to refute it. Now there are also instances where Chinese students have gone beyond freedom of speech and harassed American or other foreign students expressing concerns about China. For example, the *New York Times* reported that a Hong Kong student faced death threats from Chinese students for standing up for her fellow Hong Kongers.[28] And, at the University of California Davis, students collecting signatures in support of the Hong Kong protesters had their Hong Kong flag stolen and broken by Chinese students. U.S. educational institutions must deal with those cases forthrightly, defend freedom of speech, and protect the safety of their students. Some institutions have been reticent to do that, presumably worried about losing Chinese students and all the money they bring into their coffers. In the case of public institutions, states and even the federal government can insist that the universities and colleges live up to their responsibilities. For private institutions, let the free press, and that dreaded social media, work their magic.

The U.S. should also continue to welcome other immigrants from China. The U.S. grants more than 500,000 permanent immigrant visas each year. Much of the U.S. immigration system is family-based immigration that allows U.S. citizens to bring in their spouses, children or parents. Some have been arguing for a more skills-based immigration system where the country brings in immigrants based on their talents and skills, a sort of immigration version of *America's Got Talent*. Whichever immigration system America deploys, Chinese immigrants should be a part of it. That also includes H1B visas for skilled immigrants, as well as B1 business visas for business travelers coming into the United States. Making such visas more difficult and time-consuming to acquire harms American businesses and the U.S. economy. A classic example from our neck of the woods in Seattle is Microsoft. As U.S. immigration became tighter and visas more difficult to obtain, Microsoft opened a research facility in Vancouver, B.C., a two-and-a-half hour drive or short flight to the north from its headquarters in Redmond, Washington. Tighter visa approvals was not the sole reason for opening the research facility but as Microsoft's president Brad Smith said in a Geekwire article, "Canada's immigration policies are less stringent than the U.S., allowing Microsoft to pull top talent from all over the world for its Vancouver office."[29]

Talent is globalized nowadays (even as globalization takes hits from both the left and the right). For example, 27 percent of artificial intelligence researchers in the United States are originally from China. Through 2019, 88 percent of Chinese AI PhD students after completing their graduate work in American universities, remained to work in America (as did 85 percent of non-Chinese artificial intelligence PhD students).[30] Technology companies and other industries are on the hunt for the best talent. If we make it increasingly difficult to bring talent to the United States, including Chinese talent, then U.S. companies will increasingly set up shop outside the country. This is bad for American jobs, innovation, tax revenues and in a myriad of other ways for our economy and culture. To improve America's competitiveness, economy and standard of living, we should want more scientists, business people, artists, educators, researchers and others from China (and from other countries). We also need to ensure America continues to provide opportunities for success so that America is a better place for these immigrants, and for all Americans, to succeed, than is China. Welcoming talent and ensuring America offers more opportunities for cutting-edge research and successful business ventures by being a place of information freedom, access to capital, less corruption and other hallmarks of a liberalized society will do more to constrain China than decoupling ever will.

Again, it is true that some of these Chinese workers will be spies. Find and prosecute the spies, but welcome the Chinese workers as we should other people coming here from international destinations. Whether they are student or worker, parent or child, well-meaning aunt or crazy uncle, we should have sufficient confidence in the American way of life, our political system, and our culture to show Chinese immigrants that a society can be successful without an authoritarian government. Think for a moment of the power of talented people from China being welcomed to and thriving in America and what message they in turn will send back home.

Recently, I brought a visiting Chinese professional to the annual banquet of the Washington State China Relations Council. At the dinner, two former U.S. Ambassadors to China spoke: Stapleton Roy and Max Baucus. Neither was overly fond of the Trump administration's policies, and both were not shy to express opposition to those policies. They also discussed China, its positives and negatives. China's Economic and Commercial Counselor from San Francisco, Yang Yihang, also attended and spoke at this event designed to celebrate the Washington state-China relationship. No offense to Commercial Counselor Yihang but his speech was especially wooden—not all of us can be great orators. But, of course, it wasn't just the delivery. The difference between Americans speaking their minds at the event and the carefully, calibrated, boring words of the government official from China could not have been more stark. On the drive back from the event, my Chinese visitor, although careful with their words, noted how the American speakers spoke their minds about the American government. They noted, carefully, cautiously, that this is not possible in China. They did not criticize China for this but they noted it. They also talked about what a great night they had at the event. I do not know if this Chinese national's mind was changed by spending time in America, but certainly they will have a more nuanced view of the world, of America, not just one provided by Chinese state media or WeChat. China could be transformed by a thousand cuts of freedom, by 330,000 cuts each year.

Revolt of the Public

Allow us a speculative proposal. As you may have noticed, 2019 and 2020 were years of protests. Of course, there were the freedom protestors in Hong Kong, but in France people protested against a fuel tax increase (if even the French can't stomach a moderate increase in gas prices, what hope do we have for solving climate change?—even more reason for our joint R&D fund), in Chile a transit price increase drove masses into the streets, Iraqis took to the streets in protest against their government, Catalonians cried out for Catalonian self-determination, Indians protested Hindu nationalism—nearly every continent (penguins were strangely quiet in Antarctica) saw people rise up and give voice to one complaint or another.

Undoubtedly, your sympathy, like ours, waxes and wanes depending on the protest. But the phenomenon of increased protests is important and consequential. Many analysts have attempted to understand the root causes and whether there is something that ties together what may at first seem like disparate causes and circumstances for the protests. Over the last two years, analysts have been discovering a book published in 2014 by Martin Gurri called *The Revolt of the Public* that attempts to explain the rise of protests around the world. Gurri, a former CIA analyst, asserts that social media empowered the public to be able to organize and protest on a whole range of issues. By "public," he does not mean all the masses; he is referring to those interested in a certain issue—gas taxes, transit, extradition bills, and the like. Some of the issues may be more important than others, but the protests are all connected, Gurri says, by the new ability, brought forth by social media, of people with a common complaint to find each other, organize, and get out in the streets.

There is much to disagree with in the latter parts of Gurri's book on just how successful modern society has been and whether the public is always nihilistic or has the capability to be constructive, but Gurri does seem to hit on something with his point of social media and the ability to organize. It also perhaps provides us with another tool to help push China towards transformation.

Under Ambassador Gary Locke, the U.S. Embassy famously started displaying the air pollution level in Beijing. China, as with much of its data, often fudged this number or kept it hidden from the public. The U.S. should make information on a wider range of uncomfortable topics for China more widely accessible. Analysis and data on China's actual GDP growth, rather than the fake 6.0 numbers China publishes could be one example. The high inequality in China another. The vast, hidden wealth of Chinese leaders, including Xi Jinping's relatives, yet another.[31] China's crackdown on feminists in the Xi era should be emphasized. The World Economic Forum's 2020 Global Gender Gap Index ranks China 106th out of 153 countries.[32] During the Xi era, as Leta Hong Fincher states in her book *Betraying Big Brother: The Feminist Awakening in China*, "The term 'feminist' suddenly became a politically sensitive keyword, subject to waves of censorship."[33] Let's shed light on this dissent and worthy cause (even as we continue to work on our own gender equality problems here). We should work to get out into the Chinese public a wide range of the equivalent of air pollution data. Then we shall see whether various Chinese publics start to organize and put pressure on China's government. Granted China makes this difficult with its heavy-handed censorship of WeChat and other social media platforms, but information does find its way through society. And there are already many environmental and other types of protests in China. As Carl Minzner has noted, large protests in China have increased tremendously over the years, "from 10,000 in 1994 to 74,000 in 2004 to more than 120,000 in 2008."[34] At that point, the Chinese government, protesting all the protests, stopped publishing the data. But it is likely, according to a number of analysts, that the number of large protests has continued to increase. It is possible that China is just as vulnerable to the organization of the streets as Paris, Santiago, and Hong Kong are.

Of course, there is a risk to implementing this policy. Xi and the CCP are a big problem. A revolt of the public could lead to liberalization and democratization. But mobilizing the masses could also lead to something worse, perhaps even a government more authoritarian, or more nationalist, or more expansionistic. The Arab Spring did not lead to a necessarily better government in Egypt, for example. For many reasons, a revolt-of-the-public strategy is a speculative proposal.

Utopianism is the enemy of optimism. It helps fuel the Revolt of the Public. If we think we can create Eden here on earth, we will forever be disappointed, leading to rage and destruction. If we believe we can over time make things better, in fits and starts, with missteps and occasional setbacks, then we have every right to be optimistic. Perhaps wary optimism is the order of the day. That China has not liberalized yet, did not follow the trajectory of other Asian tigers, who were mere cubs, of course, in size, does not mean China will never liberalize. It does not ordain it either. But if we examine and deal with China clear-eyed. If we call out its excesses, misdeeds, and mistakes. If we call its government what it is—an authoritarian beast interested in its own survival. If we secure our institutions from their spying and meddling but remain open and welcoming to their students and workers. If we implement the recommendations I make in this book but also evolve them as we learn from experience and circumstances change. If we continue to improve America and work with our allies. Then we have every reason to think someday, China will be transformed too.

The truth is, over the last few centuries, the world has improved tremendously. And there is evidence that, despite all the missteps and back-tracking of recent years and the great challenges confronting us, the world will be better yet tomorrow.

CHAPTER 8

The World Is Getting Better and Can Get Better Yet

When I was a younger man, out at parties or social occasions with friends, I would occasionally, often jokingly, but not always so, say, "I sense trouble." It could be at a ballgame where it appeared my beloved Seattle Mariners might be about to blow a lead (In this case, my trouble sense was almost always infallible, so fallible are the Mariners.) It could be about some dark turn to a party I was at, or a rumble about to take place at a bar, or just a general sense of darkness in the world. I was not, am not, a particularly optimistic person, as any of my close friends will tell you. And yet, as we enter the third decade of the twenty-first century, as the whole world turns towards pessimism, as nearly everyone foresees nothing but danger and dark times ahead, we find ourselves, if not sunnily optimistic, at least often seeing more of the positive than others. This may merely indicate we are more of a contrarian than a pessimist. Or perhaps as we read, analyze data, and travel through this mixed-up, muddled world of ours, we can see all the good things that have happened in our lifetime…and the possibilities for a better future.

As this book noted earlier, we live in the most prosperous, healthy time in human history.[1] Some argue it is the most peaceful time,[2] while others claim evidence does not show that.[3] Either way, peaceful or violent, humans have made remarkable progress since the dawn of the industrial revolution and certainly in the post-world War II period. Thanks to China and other developing countries, more people have risen out of poverty over the last forty years than at any other time in history. Poverty even fell in the United States, though you are unlikely to hear about it on your local or national news, in your Instagram or Facebook feeds. In fact, since the late 1960s, poverty has fallen nearly in half in the United States (though racial disparities unfortunately still persist). The number of deaths of children under the age of five has dropped from over 12 million per year in 1990 to just under six million. Certainly still too high but remarkable progress nonetheless. Literacy and education are way up all over the world. In 1950, just over 60 percent of the world was illiterate. Today it is less than 20 percent. The share of the world with electricity has risen from less than 80 percent in 1990 to today nearly 90 percent and rising. India alone went from under 50 percent of the population having access to electricity to now 80 percent.

The world, by nearly any measure, is better today than at the end of World War II, or the Cold War and even ten years ago. Of course, huge challenges confront the world, from climate change, to navigating the cacophony of voices created by communications technology, to the subject of this book: the rise of a still authoritarian, more expansionistic China. We should be clear-eyed, but there is no reason to be pessimistic about these and other challenges (Even the Seattle Mariners, with a restocked minor league system, give room for hope—if not optimism, given their long, cursed history.)

There is a myth that Chinese leaders are smarter than other countries' and that they think longer term. Often this myth is promoted by the Chinese leaders themselves. It's essentially racist, a sort of blacks-are-all-good-at-basketball version of a distorted view of the Chinese. China's leaders are prone to the same pratfalls, mistakes, over confidence, and short-term thinking as any other country's leaders. China deserves praise for the last forty years of remarkable economic success, but their leaders are no more infallible than anyone else. The one-child policy was misguided and is coming back to bite them, with difficult demographics. By coming down so hard on the NBA, all China did was inform millions of American (and other) basketball fans who never thought about China at all to now have a negative image of the country's government. It was probably the most effective tactic for providing American support for get-tough-on-China policies that could have been implemented, other than if Xi Jinping had come down hard on the NFL. Their efforts to continue high GDP growth have created hard-to-sustain debt and financial challenges.

It is rare to have a Lex Luthor villain, someone who is doing something for the pure reason of doing evil. Xi and his cadres are not Lex Luther. Their motivations are to maintain power for the CCP. But they undoubtedly believe this is a good thing for China. They have convinced themselves this is so. We all rationalize actions and decisions in our own lives this way, whether rationalizing why we chose to break up with a girlfriend or boyfriend by text or making a business decision or personal decision that is less than savory. We do not take such actions while cackling evilly, twirling our mustaches, and lacing our fingers together as we actively try to do evil. Rather, we convince ourselves this is what needs to be done, has to be done, that this action is for the best. China's leaders are no different, other than the scale of the impact of their decisions and actions. They undoubtedly believe, or have convinced themselves to believe, that keeping the CCP in power is what is best for China, not just what is best for themselves individually. And, of course, given China's remarkable success the last forty years, this is not a difficult task.

With all that in mind, the key to changing China is to reframe their thinking so they believe liberalization will help the CCP and China. As China's economy slows, if the world coalesces in pushing back against China's current extremist tendencies, perhaps they will see that for China to continue to be successful, they will have to operate differently than they have in the past, that perhaps liberalization is what will keep the country moving forward and the CCP in power. Xi has specifically studied the Soviet Union to ensure that they don't liberalize and lose power. But as China leaves the era of rapid economic growth, as the Revolt of the Public phenomenon continues its onward pressure, as the worst excesses of the regime continue to be exposed to the world, perhaps China, despite Xi's best intentions, will change. Remember that the increasing repression by China is a sign of weakness, not strength. If its leaders were fully confident in their system and ability to maintain power, there would be no need to censor the Internet, imprison human rights advocates, install an internment system on 2 million Uyghurs, destroy the cultural heritage of Tibet, eradicate a small-time, somewhat odd religion of the Falun Gong, create imaginary GDP growth numbers, and all the myriad of other measures that are signs of cowardice and weakness, not strength.

Perversely, perhaps why we're optimistic is we are pessimistic about China. Or, to be more precise, we are pessimistic that in the long run China's authoritarian system can continue to sustain success and keep up with the dreams and aspirations of the Chinese people. Carl Minzner points out that, beginning in 2011, spending on public security surpassed spending on the military—China's government was more afraid of its own people than outsiders. Or as Minzner puts it, "…authorities find themselves trapped in a vicious cycle wherein the harder they try to preserve stability, the greater instability they face."[4]

This book was meant to highlight how China has changed, why that is a risk to the world, why we need to address that risk, and how we should do it. Will my recommendations work? I don't know (9). China is large and complicated. Like the businessperson I had coffee with many years ago, I will never understand China. But there is an intrinsic yearning for freedom in the human psyche that I do understand, and that Chinese, like any people, yearn for too. Ultimately, I am hopeful and relatively confident that this yearning will win out.

On occasion, I ponder the Xi Jinpings of the world, the Vladimir Putins and others of their ilk, so intent on gaining and holding onto power and wielding the muscles of the state ruthlessly and expensively to such endeavors. Such leaders are ultimately to be pitied and ridiculed. Their inability to look at the bigger picture—the vast universe still awaiting understanding and exploration; the mysteries of the human mind, how it functions and the intricacies that are perhaps still as unfathomable as the universe; the complicated biology of the human body that still awaits ways to heal it more efficiently and fully from disease and injury; how music came to be and is so universal to nearly every culture, with all genres connected and building upon each other; the dynamics of the family and the many loves that permeate all humans—displays a remarkable shortsightedness of such leaders that they use their powers to concentrate on other, much more mundane and prosaic matters.

For all these reasons we are hopeful, cautiously optimistic, that China will again start reforming, eventually liberalize, and be a leader in drawing a beautiful bigger picture.

A Tree Grows in Beijing
(And Scranton)

A t the house we owned before marrying, we decided to transplant a dwarf Japanese maple tree from a rather random spot in the front yard to a new area we had landscaped near the front drive. We began digging. And digging. And digging. Until nearly half of our front yard was a big hole. The roots of this little tree were far broader and deeper than the height of the tree itself. But determined and resolute, we launched the shovel once more into the ground—CLANG! We stopped digging and investigated what we had struck with our shovel. It was a metal pipe. We looked up from the hole to our house and saw the gas meter directly parallel to where we stood. We had hit the gas line. Fortunately, we had not severed it. We stopped digging, clipped the remaining roots, and successfully transplanted the small, beautiful, resilient maple to its new spot.

We were proud of our work, even though we were lucky we did not blow up the entire neighborhood, and when we moved into a new house a few years later with our bride, we felt we had left the old home a better, more aesthetically pleasing, more useful place through sweat of brow and diligent work. We had left our mark for posterity.

A few years later we found ourselves not far from our old home, and took a minor detour to drive by the house to see our old haunts. As we slowed in front of the house, we were astonished to find the front yard transformed yet again. The Japanese dwarf maple had been re-transplanted, this time in front of a window of the street-facing part of the house. The front landscaped area was gone. It was then we first confronted the reality that nothing is permanent.

When Joseph Robinette Biden walked into the Oval Office on January 20, 2021 beginning his duties as the 46th president of the United States, he looked out at a world that was very different from when he was vice president only four years earlier. The U.S. is not the same, with its standing and influence both lesser and different than it was in the 2010s. The world—democracies, authoritarian countries and those between—adapted and moved on from one where the U.S. was the undisputed leader. Multilateral organizations—from the UN to the World Bank to WTO and WHO—also changed. New alliances are being built. Japan, India and Australia, for example, began developing a supply chain coalition to counter China's dominance in the supply chain.[1] Various countries work together to battle Covid-19, to develop new defense networks and to cooperate in a world no longer dominated or led by the United States. Even with a new U.S. president, this trend is unlikely to abate.

China has changed as well. At least as of this writing, after initial missteps, it has contained Covid-19 better than most. But its economy, like all economies, slowed during the pandemic no matter what official data may claim.[2] And China finds itself less popular than ever.[3]

Biden is intent on restoring America at home and its moral leadership abroad. I wish him well but even if successful, an invigorated America will still find its rejuvenated self in a different world. Biden can rebuild America but cannot bring us back to the old age. He must work within this new era, repair what should be fixed but build anew in concert with others where circumstances dictate. Given the narrowness of the election outcome and a divided government, indeed a divided America, none of this will be easy.

Biden will find competing pressures from within his party and from Republicans but also from the rest of the world. China's large market still beckons—potential allies will not always align with what America wants in regards to China. And even as Biden acts more strategically and provides a much different tone than Trump, all the world knows that 2024 or 2028 could bring yet another different

America. The vapid, irresponsible American genie is out of the lamp, at least for the foreseeable future, and the world's planning has adjusted accordingly.

Many Republicans will push for radical decoupling from China. Senator Josh Hawley from Missouri calls for a complete withdrawal from the WTO.[4] He has said, "I'd like to see as much production brought back to our shores as we can."[5] In the coming months and years there will be continued calls for complete disengagement from China.

But even within the Democratic party, Biden will be pulled in different directions. Some Obama stalwarts populating the Biden administration are not convinced that China has become more authoritarian and do not believe China is trying to transform the world order into one more accommodating of authoritarianism. As Thomas Wright, at the Brookings Institution puts it, "…they tend to be less willing to accept that Xi has transformed China into a different type of regime that is dictatorial, ideologically motivated, and determined to overturn key parts of the liberal international order."[6] They would counsel Biden to continue whispering and carrying a very small stick as did the Obama administration.

But there are other Democrats who do recognize China has evolved for the worse over the last decade and the challenge that presents to the world. They advocate for speaking up on human rights more forthrightly, pushing back on China's closed market in cooperation with allies, and implementing targeted decoupling where it makes national security sense.

In our binary, black and white, choose-a-side world, the debate will unfortunately probably be framed as either completely decoupling from China or full-on engagement. The loudest voices, the ones amplified by media for ratings and clicks, will accuse the other side of either not taking the China threat seriously or of acting dangerously and risking war. President Biden will be pressured to choose a side. But that would be a vice and since he's already eliminated that part of his title, he should resist it. We do not live in a binary world despite so many painting it that way. President Biden should strategically choose where to more forcefully confront China, where to tread more quietly and where to cooperate and collaborate. And, of course, Biden will need to do this in alliance with other like-minded countries and within the context of a more multi-polar world.

Of course, as we argued in chapter 3, the most important step America can take to encourage China's liberalization is to improve our own country. America's problems didn't go away merely by replacing Trump with Biden. Indeed many of our country's problems are long-standing and were ignored or ineffectually addressed pre-Trump. The Biden administration is likely to address health care but will the reform provide universal health care efficiently utilizing competition and encouraging medical innovation? The Biden administration will likely work to remedy racial injustice but the policing issue is mostly a state and local problem that has existed in localities run by progressives, standard issue Democrats and Republicans. The black-white wealth gap remains. It is not obvious that a Biden administration can solve this long-standing American stain any more than others have. Immigration has been difficult to solve under both Democratic and Republican presidents. And, the undue expense and time of building infrastructure, not to mention other regulatory problems, is not even on the Democrat policy radar. The Biden team has proposed ambitious domestic policies to combat climate change but will they help emerging markets, where the real climate game is played, transform to reduce climate change emissions? So just because Biden is president and Trump is not does not mean America will tackle and solve its most vexing issues.

But defeating Trump in a democratic process was a prerequisite for solving our problems. Under the Trump administration most important challenges were ignored, subverted or made worse. America declined under the Trump administration, and to have any hope of rebuilding, his defeat in the election was necessary.

China also believes that America is a country on the decline. According to some reports, they believe that Trump accelerated the deterioration but also judge America's long-term ebb is inevitable. Wu Xinbo, the Dean of Fudan University's Institute of International Studies, said in an interview, "For the United States, its world status and influence are gradually declining, and its international reputation has been severely weakened."[7] Rush Doshi, in a *Foreign Policy* article, documents a variety of Chinese scholars and officials who view America in descent, including President Xi himself, who asserted in a 2018 speech, "the world is in a state of great changes unseen in a century."[8] Indeed, as we noted near the beginning of this book, Xi said China "must diligently prepare for a long period of cooperation and of conflict between these two social systems in each of these domains." But that China must lay "the foundation for a future where we will win the initiative and have the dominant position." China appears to believe that future was moved up by the actions and words of Trump.

But America, in its democratic system, was able to vote Trump out, and begin charting a new course. Chinese, and the world, are stuck with Xi, who through his strategies has made China less popular, spurred alliances against its new assertiveness, and must combat a variety of economic and social challenges ranging from an aging population to a slower growing economy to inequality to a weak social safety net. Americans voted out Trump. If China's challenges mount, Chinese may increasingly wish they had the same power. They, too, may want to transplant a tree.

Acknowledgments

I t was a long journey from idea to publication, one full of help, advice, criticism and Montepulciano wine. From the train ride and rooftop hotel bar in Italy where the spark first lit (and the wine drunk), to what I imagine are the sturdy oak desks of the good offices of Tuttle Publishing, though I haven't seen them so for all I know they're nouveau art deco or rickety aluminum, I was greatly aided by a variety of people in writing this book.

Spencer Cohen was generous with his time, knowledge, wisdom and experience as he read early drafts, pointed in the direction of additional approaches and suggested books and articles to read. Over beers and food, an occasional socially distanced whiskey, we robustly discussed the ideas in this book. There are undoubtedly many ideas and proposals in this book Spencer still disagrees with but he enabled me to articulate and defend them better due to his helpful, intellectual prodding. Similarly, thanks to Fraser Mendel who over drinks and food also prodded my thoughts and ideas, also occasionally challenging them. Scott Hilton and Rachel Tritt's skepticism over an excellent lunch in midtown Manhattan, forced me to think through my assertions and either change them or buttress them with more research.

Marc Freeman, my fellow writer, inspired me with his own book on a very different subject and took an early look at the beginnings of this one.

Thanks to Scott Johnson for his advice, help and long friendship.

Many thanks to the legendary Chris Johns without whom this book would not be published. More pleasurable and gratifying than having my book published is reconnecting and rekindling an old friendship.

Thanks to Robert Goforth for his edits.

And, of course, Danielle, my wife, who I subject to editorial responsibilities whether she wants them or not. The first and most important editor and collaborator.

Dedication

To, of course, Danielle. Someday, though now not likely for a while, we will travel together to China. But, first, back to New Orleans.

And to Putter and Willow, who warmed our lap and our household throughout.

Selected Bibliography

I kneel at the knowledge and information provided by these books, newsletters, and journals. They may not have made me a China expert, but over the years they have made me far more knowledgeable, even when I disagree with what they write, perhaps especially when I disagree. Not all, of course, are strictly about China. In those cases, they had a direct relevance to the subjects in this book, even if not strictly focused on China. This is by no means an exhaustive list, but they will set you down the road to understanding and keeping up to date on China.

Books

Ang, Yuen Yuen. *China's Gilded Age: The Paradox of Economic Boom and Vast Corruption*. Cambridge University Press, 2020.

Clements, Jonathan. *A Brief History of China: Dynasty, Revolution and Transformation: From the Middle Kingdom to the People's Republic*. Tuttle Publishing, 2019.

Cowen, Tyler. *Stubborn Attachments*. Stripe Press, 2018.

Fincher, Leta Hong. *Betraying Big Brother: The Feminist Awakening in China*. Verso, 2018.

French, Paul. *Midnight in Peking: How the Murder of a Young Englishwoman Haunted the Last Days of Old China*. Pengiun Books, 2014.

Gurri, Martin. *The Revolt of the Public and the Crisis of Authority in the New Millennium*. Stripe Press, 2018.

Huang, Yasheng. *Capitalism with Chinese Characteristics: Entrepreneurship and the State*. Cambridge University Press, 2008.

Keay, John. *China: A History*. HarperCollins, 2009.

Kroeber, Arthur. *China's Economy: What Everyone Needs to Know*. Oxford University Press, 2020.

Lardy, Nicholas. *The State Strikes Back: The End of Economic Reform in China?* Peterson Institute for International Economics, 2019.

Lindsey, Brink, and Steven M. Teles. *The Captured Economy: How the Powerful Enrich Themselves, Slow Down Growth and Increase Inequality*. Oxford University Press, 2017.

Liu, Cixin. *The Three Body Problem*. Tor Books, 2014.

Maçães, Bruno. *Belt and Road: A Chinese World* Order. Hurst, 2019.

_____. *The Dawn of Eurasia: On the Trail of the New World Order*. Yale University Press, 2018.

Mauldin, John, and Worth Wray, eds. *A Great Leap Forward?: Making Sense of China's Cooling Credit Boom, Technological Transformation, High Stakes Rebalancing, Geopolitical Rise, & Reserve Currency Dream*. Mauldin Economics, 2015.

McGregor, Richard. *Xi Jinping: The Backlash*. Pengiun Books, 2019.

Minzner, Carl. *End of an Era: How China's Authoritarian Revival is Undermining its Rise*. Oxford University Press, 2018. Henry Holt & Co., 2015.

Pillsbury, Michael. *The Hundred-Year Marathon: China's Secret Strategy to Replace America as the Global Superpower*. Henry Holt & Co., 2015.

Shobert, Benjamin. *Blaming China: It Might Feel Good But It Won't Fix America's Economy*. Potomac Books, 2018.

Sun, Irene Yuan. *The Next Factory of the World: How Chinese Investment is Reshaping Africa*. Harvard Business Review Press, 2017.

Walter, Carl, and Fraser Howie. *Red Capitalism: The Fragile Financial Foundation of China's Extraordinary Rise*. Wiley, 2012.

Newsletters and Websites

Asia on Tap by The National Bureau on Asian Research (https://www.nbr.org/publication/asia-on-tap)

Axios China Newsletter by Bethany Allen-Ebrahimian (https://www.axios.com/newsletters/axios-chin)

Baldings World (https://www.baldingsworld.com)

China Econ Talk by Jordan Schneider (https://jorschneider.com)

ChinaFile (http://chinafile.com)

China Law Blog (https://www.chinalawblog.com)

China Neican edited by Yun Jiang and Adam Ni (https://neican.sub-stack.com)

ChinaTalk (https://chinatalk.substack.com)

Sinocism by Bill Bishop (https://sinocism.com)

Sixth Tone (http://www.sixthtone.com)

The Wire China (https://www.thewirechina.com)

Twitter Feeds
@akugariaherrer0
@Baldingsworld
@BethanyAllenEbr
@Brad_Setser
@ChinaBeigeBook
@michaelxpettis
@niubi
@sbanjo

Podcasts
The China History Podcast by Laszlo Montgomery
The Little Red Podcast by Graeme Smith and Louisa Lim

Notes

Chapter 1—Regression and Expansion: Why a New Strategy in China

1. "Xi Jinping's Visit to Seattle will Shut Down Entire City Blocks," Huffington Post: https://www.huffpost.com/entry/xi-jinping-visit-seattle-shutdown_n_55ff15cae4b0fde8b0ceb25f.

2. "Bo Xilai Scandal: Timeline," BBC: http://bbc.com/news/world-asia-china-17673505.

3. "Visualizing China's Anti-Corruption Campaign," August, 2015, *ChinaFile*: http://www.chinafile.com/infographics/visualizing-chinas-anti-corruption-campaign.

4. *Xi Jinping: The Backlash*, by Richard McGregor, Location 337 (Kindle version).

5. *China's Gilded Age: The Paradox of Economic Boom and Vast Corruption* by Yuen Yuen Ang, Chapter 6, "All the King's Men."

6. "Revealed: the far-reaching powers of China's new super anticorruption agency," March 13, 2018, *South China Morning Post*: https://www.scmp.com/news/china/policies-politics/article/2136949/far-reaching-powers-chinas-new-super-anti-corruption.

7. Ibid.

8. *China's Gilded Age: The Paradox of Economic Boom and Vast Corruption* by Yuen Yuen Ang, Chapter 6, "All the King's Men," p. 175.

9. "Coup plotters foiled: Xi Jinping fended off threat to 'save Communist Party,'" *South China Morning Post*: https://www.scmp.com/news/china/policies-politics/article/2116176/coup-plotters-foiled-xi-jinping-fended-threat-save.

10. Xi Jinping speech, November 16, 2012, *China Daily*, https://www.chinadaily.com.cn/china/2012cpc/2012-11/16/content_15934514.htm.

11. "The symbolism of Xi Jinping's trip south," BBC News, December 10, 2012, https://www.bbc.com/news/world-asia-china-20662947.

12. "Leaked Speech Shows Xi Jinping's Opposition to Reform," *China Digital Times*, https://chinadigitaltimes.net/2013/01/leaked-speech-shows-xi-jinpings-opposition-to-reform/.

13. More on Chinese feminists' attempts to reform China later, but for a longer examination of the subject, read "Betraying Big Brother: The Feminist Awakening in China" by Leta Hong Fincher.

14. "Xi inaugurates Asian Infrastructure Investment Bank, says China will take more international responsibility," *Japan Times*, https://www.japantimes.co.jp/news/2016/01/17/business/xi-inaugurates-asian-infrastructure-investment-bank-says-china-will-take-international-responsibility/#.XbYywm5FydI.

15. China's unilateral, geographic claims on the South China Sea, defying international law.

16. "Viral Alarm: When Fury Overcomes Fear," an essay by Xu Zhangrun, translated and annotated by Geremie R. Barmé: February 10, 2020: *ChinaFile*, https://www.chinafile.com/reporting-opinion/viewpoint/viral-alarm-when-fury-overcomes-fear.

17. "Xi Jinping in Translation: China's Guiding Ideology," *Palladium*: https://palladiummag. com/2019/05/31/xi-jinping-in-translation-chinas-guiding-ideology/

18. Human Rights Watch 2018 China Report: https://www.hrw.org/world-report/2019/ country-chapters/china-and-tibet.

19. "2017/2018 Amnesty International Human Rights Report": https://www.amnesty.org/ en/latest/news/2019/01/china-disgraceful-prison-term-fo-human-rights-lawyer-wang-quanzhang/.

20. "The great firewall of China: Xi Jinping's internet shutdown," *The Guardian*, June 29, 2018: https://www.theguardian.com/news/2018/jun/29/the-great-firewall-of-china-xi-jinpings-internet-shutdown.

21. "China's Xi Jinping says internet users must be free to speak their minds," *The Guardian*, December 16, 2015: https://www.theguardian.com/world/2015/dec/16/china-xi-jinping-internet-users-freedom-speech-online.

22. "FCCC Statement on the Blocking of Foreign News Websites in China," https://twitter. com/fccchina/status/1186541607362990081/photo/1.

23. "China enacted a sweeping new law that bars people from posting negative content online" by Bill Bostok, March 2, 2020, *The Guardian*: https://www.businessinsider.com/ china-internet-ban-criticism-could-suppress-coronavirus-news-2020-3.

24. "The complicated truth about China's social credit system," *Wired*, June 7, 2019: https:// www.wired.co.uk/article/china-social-credit-system-explained.

25. "About the China Cables Investigation," *ICIJ*, November 23, 2019: https://www.icij.org/ investigations/china-cables/about-the-china-cables-investigation/.

26. "China cuts Uighur births with IUDs, abortion, sterilization," *The Associated Press*, June 28, 2020: https://apnews.com/269b3de1af34e17c1941a514f78d764c.

27. "A Million People Are Jailed at China's Gulags," *Haaretz*, October 17, 2019: https:// www.haaretz.com/world-news/.premium.MAGAZINE-a-million-people-are-jailed-at-china-s-gulags-i-escaped-here-s-what-goes-on-inside-1.7994216?utm_source=dlvr. it&utm_medium=twitter.

28. "Analysis of official deceased organ donation data casts doubt on the credibility of China's organ transplant reform" by Matthew P. Robertson, Raymond L. Hinde and Jacob Lavee, *BMC Medical Ethics*, November 14, 2019: https://bmcmedethics. biomedcentral.com/articles/10.1186/s12910-019-0406-6.

29. China Tribunal: Final Judgment Report, June 17, 2019: https://chinatribunal.com/final-judgement-report/.

30. "Case of Hong Kong's Missing Booksellers " *New York Times*, April 3, 2018: https://www. nytimes.com/2018/04/03/magazine/the-case-of-hong-kongs-missing-booksellers.html.

31. "Specter of Meddling by Beijing Looms Over Taiwan's Elections," *New York Times*, November 22, 2018: https://www.nytimes.com/2018/11/22/world/asia/taiwan-elections-meddling.html.

32. "Chinese Cyber-Operatives Boosted Taiwan's Insurgent Candidate," *Foreign Policy Magazine*, June 26, 2019: https://foreignpolicy.com/2019/06/26/chinese-cyber-operatives-boosted-taiwans-insurgent-candidate/.

Chapter 2—The Economy is a Bakery, Not a Pie

1. Using World Bank Numbers.

2. World Bank and OECD data: https://data.worldbank.org/indicator/NE.TRD.GNFS. ZS?locations=CN.

3. "Who Deserves the Nobel for China's Economic Development?" October 25, 2019: https://andrewbatson.com/2019/10/25/who-deserves-the-nobel-for-chinas-economic-development/.

4. *China's Economy: What Everyone Needs to Know* by Arthur R. Kroeber, Locations 873 and 887 in Kindle edition.

5. *China's Gilded Age: The Paradox of Economic Boom and Vast Corruption* by Yuen Yuen Ang.

6. "What's Happening with China's Fintech Industry?" Brookings Institution, February 8, 2018: https://www.brookings.edu/blog/order-from-chaos/2018/02/08/whats-happening-with-chinas-fintech-industry/.

7. "China Now Boasts More Than 800 Million Internet Users," *Forbes*, August 23, 2018: https://www.forbes.com/sites/niallmccarthy/2018/08/23/china-now-boasts-more-than-800-million-internet-users-and-98-of-them-are-mobile-infographic/?sh=772b88747092.

8. "Breakdown of internet users in China from December 2016 to March 2020, by age," *Statista*: https://www.statista.com/statistics/265150/internet-users-in-china-by-age/.

9. Stanford-New America Digichina Project, AI Policy and China, October 29, 2019.

10. "The Rise of Chinese Innovation in the Life Sciences," National Bureau of Asian Research, April 5, 2016: https://www.nbr.org/wp-content/uploads/pdfs/publications/special_report_56_china_life_science_april2016.pdf.

11. "China's population numbers are almost certainly inflated to hide the harmful legacy of its family planning policy" by Yi Fuxian, *South Morning China Post*, July 20, 2019: https://www.scmp.com/comment/opinion/article/3018829/chinas-population-numbers-are-almost-certainly-inflated-hide.

12. "Economic Development and Democracy: Predispositions and Triggers, August 8, 2019" by Daniel Triesman: https://static1.squarespace.com/static/5a4d2512a803bb1a5d9aca35/t/5d7fb1ad3d119516bfba6792/1568649647235/treisman+complete+ms+Jul+28+-revised+for+website.pdf.

13. "Is Tony Soprano Dead or Not" by Christopher Orr, *The Atlantic*, January 8, 2019: https://www.theatlantic.com/entertainment/archive/2019/01/tony-soprano-dead-or-not/579736/.

14. International Labor Organization data: https://www.ilo.org/shinyapps/bulkexplorer21/?lang=en&segment=indicator&id=SDG_B821_NOC_RT_A; "China's Productivity Slowdown and Future Growth Potential," World Bank Group Policy Research Working Paper, Multiple Authors, June 2020: http://documents1.worldbank.org/curated/en/839401593007627879/pdf/Chinas-Productivity-Slowdown-and-Future-Growth-Potential.pdf.

15. "Fertility, mortality, migration, and population scenarios for 195 countries and territories from 2017 to 2100: a forecasting analysis for the Global Burden of Disease Study," Numerous Authors, July 14, 2020, *The Lancet*: https://www.thelancet.com/journals/lancet/article/PIIS0140-6736(20)30677-2/fulltext.

16. "Revised demographic forecasts for China: key takeaways," *Economist Intelligence Unit*, July 2, 2019: http://country.eiu.com/article.aspx?articleid=1098186693&Country=China&topic=Economy.

17. "Book Review Roundtable: Nicholas Lardy's The State Strikes Back," *Asia Policy*,

Volume 14, Number 4, Lardy response: https://www.nbr.org/wp-content/uploads/pdfs/publications/ap14-4_statestrikesback_brrt_oct2019.pdf.

18. "China's social security system," *China Labour Bulletin*: https://clb.org.hk/content/china%E2%80%99s-social-security-system.

19. World Bank based on International Labour Organization Data: https://data.worldbank.org/indicator/SL.TLF.CACT.ZS?locations=N.

20. "The Impact of Workforce Aging on European Productivity" by Shekhar Aiyar, Christian Ebeke and Xiaobo Shao, IMF Working Paper, December 2016: https://www.imf.org/external/pubs/ft/wp/2016/wp16238.pdf.

21. "Human Capital and China's Future Growth" by Hongbin Li, Prashant Loyalka, Scott Rozelle and Binzhen Wu, *The Journal of Economic Perspectives*, Winter 2017: https://www.jstor.org/stable/pdf/44133949.pdf?refreqid=excelsior%3A350492110f91bd28d18561a698b6c7bd.

22. IMF figures. Nice explanation here: *Mercator Institute for China Studies*, August 22, 2019: https://www.merics.org/en/china-monitor/chinas-corporate-debt.

23. "Less Savings, More Debt: How Chinese Manage Money American-Style, in 17 Charts," *Wall Street Journal*: https://www.wsj.com/articles/less-savings-more-debt-how-chinese-manage-money-american-style-in-17-charts-11572427805.

24. "China's High and Rising Corporate Debt," *Mercator Institute for China Studies*, August 22, 2019: https://www.merics.org/en/china-monitor/chinas-corporate-debt.

25. "Chart of the Week: Inequality in China," *Chart of the Week*, IMF Blog, September 20, 2018: https://blogs.imf.org/2018/09/20/chart-of-the-week-inequality-in-china/.

26. "China refuses to release Gini coefficient," *Market Watch*, January 19, 2012: https://www.marketwatch.com/story/china-refuses-to-release-gini-coefficient-2012-01-18.

27. "Forced or Not? Why U.S. Says China Steals Technology", *Bloomberg*, October 30, 2019: https://www.washingtonpost.com/business/forced-or-not-why-us-says-china-steals-technology/2019/10/29/2ae368fa-fab2-11e9-9e02-1d45cb3dfa8f_story.html.

28. "Microsoft offices in China raided again in antitrust probe," *CNET*: https://www.cnet.com/news/microsoft-offices-in-china-raided-again-in-antitrust-probe/.

29. A chain of coffee shops founded in Beijing in 2017. Note that after I wrote this, Luckin's CEO was fired as the result of an accounting scandal, including fabricating over 2 billion yuan in sales. Turns out they really did need Xi to label them a strategic company.

30. "Statement of the Government of the People's Republic of China and the Government of the Kingdom of Norway on Normalization of Bilateral Relations," https://www.regjeringen.no/globalassets/departementene/ud/vedlegg/statement_kina.pdf.

Chapter 3: We Succeed in Changing China by Being Successful Ourselves

1. *The State Strikes Back: The End of Economic Reform in China* by Nicholas Lardy.

2. "China's Success Explains Authoritarianism's Allure" by Tyler Cowen, *Bloomberg*, April 3, 2017: https://www.bloomberg.com/opinion/articles/2017-04-03/china-s-success-explains-authoritarianism-s-allure?cmpid%3D=socialflow-twitter-view&utm_campaign=socialflow-organic&utm_content=view&utm_medium=social&utm_source=twitter.

3. Japan is actually doing much better than people realize—its GDP per capita growth rate compares favorably to many advanced economies, it is starting to accept immigrants, and it has a fine quality of life. But unfortunately perceptions of Japan, rather than reality, drive the China story here.

4. Along with a good dose of racism, misogyny and James Comey releasing a letter the week before the election stating he was reopening the Clinton email investigation (see FiveThirtyEight.com—"The Comey Letter Probably Cost Clinton the Election, by Nate Silver, May 3, 2017).

5. "Presidential Executive Order Addressing Trade Agreement Violations and Abuses," April 29, 2017: https://www.whitehouse.gov/presidential-actions/presidential-executive-order-addressing-trade-agreement-violations-abuses/.

6. "How's the Steel Industry Doing?" Kevin Drum Blog on *Mother Jones*, April 16, 2019: https://www.motherjones.com/kevin-drum/2019/04/hows-the-steel-industry-doing/.

7. "Trump Discussed Pulling U.S. From NATO, Aides Say Amid New Concerns Over Russia," *New York Times*, January 14, 2019: https://www.nytimes.com/2019/01/14/us/politics/nato-president-trump.html.

8. "Donald Trump Expounds on his Foreign Policy Views," *New York Times*, March 26, 2016.

9. "America First: A Phrase with a Loaded Anti-Semitic and Isolationist History" by Brian Bennett, *Los Angeles Times*, January 20, 2017.

10. "20 Times Donald Trump Praised Dictators And Controversial Leaders," *The Hill*, April 18, 2019: https://hillreporter.com/times-donald-trump-praised-dictators-and-controversial-leaders-31009.

11. "Donald Trump fakes accent to mock leaders of South Korea and Japan, angering Asian-American voters," *South Morning China Post*, August 22, 2019: https://www.scmp.com/news/world/united-states-canada/article/3023828/donald-trump-fakes-accent-mock-leaders-south-korea.

12. NBC News/Wall Street Journal August 2019 Poll: https://www.nbcnews.com/politics/meet-the-press/deep-boiling-anger-nbc-wsj-poll-finds-pessimistic-america-despite-n1045916.

13. Pew Research Center, March 2019 Poll: https://www.courthousenews.com/wp-content/uploads/2019/03/pew-future.pdf.

14. "Decades-Old Housing Discrimination Case Plagues Donald Trump," *National Public Radio's All Things Considered*, September 29, 2016: https://www.npr.org/2016/09/29/495955920/donald-trump-plagued-by-decades-old-housing-discrimination-case.

15. "Ta Nehisi Coates is not here to comfort you" by Ezra Klein, Vox, October 29, 2017: https://www.vox.com/2017/10/9/16430390/ta-nehisi-coates-podcast-hope-book.

16. U.S. Census Bureau figures.

17. "Incarceration rate down again in 2017" by Kevin Drum, *Mother Jones*, May 2, 2019: https://www.motherjones.com/kevin-drum/2019/05/incarceration-rate-down-again-in-2017/.

18. "3 more years of I-5 construction in Tacoma before decade-old HOV project is finished," *Tacoma News Tribune*, January 28, 2019: https://www.thenewstribune.com/news/local/traffic/article225135305.html.

19. "High Costs May Explain Crumbling Support for U.S. Infrastructure" by Tracy Gordon and David Schleicher, March 30, 2015, *Real Clear Policy*: https://www.realclearpolicy.com/blog/2015/03/31/high_costs_may_explain_crumbling_support_for_us_infrastructure_1249.html.

20. "America's political economy: The inefficiency of construction and the politics of

infrastructure" by Adam Tooze, June 6, 2017: https://adamtooze.com/2017/06/06/americas-political-economy-inefficiency-construction-politics-infrastructure/.

21. "This bill would let new homeless shelters and affordable housing bypass environmental law," *Los Angeles Times*, January 8, 2020: https://www.latimes.com/california/story/2020-01-08/affordable-housing-homeless-shelter-bill-bypass-environmental-law-ceqa.

22. "What is the Cost of Building a Subway?" by Alon Levy, November 19, 2019: https://pedestrianobservations.files.wordpress.com/2019/11/costspresentation2.pdf.

23. "The 4 Key Reasons the U.S. Is So Behind on Coronavirus Testing" by Olga Khazan March 13, 2020, *The Atlantic*: https://www.theatlantic.com/health/archive/2020/03/why-coronavirus-testing-us-so-delayed/607954/.

24. Peterson-Kaiser Health System Tracker: https://www.healthsystemtracker.org/chart-collection/health-spending-u-s-compare-countries/#item-average-wealthy-countries-spend-half-much-per-person-health-u-s-spends.

25. Department of Justice Report on shooting of Michael Brown, March 4, 2015: https://www.justice.gov/sites/default/files/opa/press-releases/attachments/2015/03/04/doj_report_on_shooting_of_michael_brown_1.pdf.

26. Investigation of the Ferguson Police Department, March 4, 2015: https://www.justice.gov/sites/default/files/opa/press-releases/attachments/2015/03/04/ferguson_police_department_report.pdf.

27. "Study claims white police no more likely to shoot minorities draws fire" *Science Magazine*, August 15, 2019: https://www.sciencemag.org/news/2019/08/study-claims-white-police-no-more-likely-shoot-minorities-draws-fire; "It took us months to contest a flawed study on police bias. Here's why that's dangerous" by Dean Knox and Jonathan Mummolo, January 28, 2020, *Washington Post*: https://www.washingtonpost.com/opinions/2020/01/28/it-took-us-months-contest-flawed-study-police-bias-heres-why-thats-dangerous/; "Stories and Data, Reflections on race, riots, and police" by Coleman Hughes, June 14, 2020, *City Journal*: https://www.city-journal.org/reflections-on-race-riots-and-police?utm_source=Twitter&utm_medium=Organic_Social; "What the data say about police brutality and racial bias — and which reforms might work" by Lynne Peeples, June 19, 2020, *Nature*: https://www.nature.com/articles/d41586-020-01846-z.

28. Clinton proposes $5,000 "baby bonds" September 28, 2007, *Reuters*: https://www.reuters.com/article/us-usa-politics-democrats-idUSN2834292620070928.

29. "Better Baby Bonds," byAlex Tabarrok, October 17, 2007, *Marginal Revolution*: https://marginalrevolution.com/?s=baby+bonds.

30. "Universal Baby Bonds Reduce Black- White Wealth Inequality, Progressively Raise Net Worth of all Young Adults" by Naomi Zewdi, 2018: https://static1.squarespace.com/static/5743308460b5e922a25a6dc7/t/5c4339f67ba7fc4a9add58f9/1547909624486/Zewde-Baby-Bonds-WP-10-30-18.pdf.

31. Trump announcement speech, June 16, 2015: https://time.com/3923128/donald-trump-announcement-speech/.

32. June 21, 2018 Gallup Poll: https://news.gallup.com/poll/235793/record-high-americans-say-immigration-good-thing.aspx.

33. "Why are immigrants more entrepreneurial?" *Harvard Business Review*, October 27, 2016, https://hbr.org/2016/10/why-are-immigrants-more-entrepreneurial.

34. "Immigrants do a great job at becoming Americans" by Noah Smith, *Daily Journal*, November 27, 2017: https://www.daily-journal.com/opinion/columnists/national/immigrants-do-a-great-job-at-becoming-americans/article_6329389f-46e3-57bc-94b0-91081b433eb3.html.

35. "What ails the right isn't (just) racism" by Conor Friedersdorf, *The Atlantic*, August 9, 2019: https://www.theatlantic.com/ideas/archive/2019/08/what-if-left-was-right-race/595777/.

36. *Dolly Parton's America*, Episode 4 Neon Moss, hosted by Jad Abumrad: https://www.wnycstudios.org/podcasts/dolly-partons-america.

Chapter 4: Promoting Human Rights is Underrated

1. *Human Rights in American Foreign Policy* by Joe Renouard, 2016.

2. Presidential Inaugural Address of Jimmy Carter, January 20, 1977: https://jimmycarter.info/presidential-inaugural-address-of-jimmy-carter/.

3. Address at Commencement Exercises at the University of Notre Dame, President Jimmy Carter, May 22, 1977: https://teachingamericanhistory.org/library/document/address-at-commencement-exercises-at-the-university-of-notre-dame/.

4. "The Defeat of Ernest Lefever's Nomination," Chapter 10 of *Challenging U.S. Foreign Policy* by Sarah Snyder, 2011.

5. President Ronald Reagan 1982 Speech to British Parliament: http://www.historyplace.com/speeches/reagan-parliament.htm.

6. "The Reagan Turnaround on Human Rights" by Tamar Jacoby, *Foreign Affairs*, June 1, 1986: https://www.foreignaffairs.com/articles/1986-06-01/reagan-turnaround-human-rights.

7. Speech at Westminster, President Ronald Reagan, June 8, 1982: https://teachingamericanhistory.org/library/document/speech-at-westminster/.

8. Gorbachev to 19th Party Congress, June 28, 1988: https://www.upi.com/Archives/1988/06/28/Gorbachev-wants-to-limit-power-of-Communist-Party/1981821841247/.

9. 1989 Rand Corporation Report.

10. "'Torture Report': A Closer Look At When And What President Bush Knew," NPR, December 16, 2014: https://www.npr.org/sections/thetwo-way/2014/12/16/369876047/torture-report-a-closer-look-at-when-and-what-president-bush-knew.

11. "Critics Say China Has Suppressed and Censored Information In Coronavirus Outbreak," by Emily Feng and Amy Cheng, *NPR*, February 8, 2020: https://www.npr.org/sections/goatsandsoda/2020/02/08/803766743/critics-say-china-has-suppressed-and-censored-information-in-coronavirus-outbrea.

12. See www.testandtrace.com and https://covid19.osinthk.org/ among others for data-driven evidence for the effectiveness of these strategies. This approach has been successful in South Korea, Taiwan, Vietnam, and, yes, in Wuhan, after China's initial stumbles.

13. Twitter Thread on human rights theory by Paul Poast, International Relations Professor at the University of Chicago: https://twitter.com/ProfPaulPoast/status/1206362233766322177.

14. "Backlash against human rights shaming: emotions in groups" by Jack Snyder, September 13, 2018: https://www.cambridge.org/core/services/aop-cambridge-core/content/view/D810A755EF58CA80559E98F9ED73D43F/S1752971919000216a.pdf/backlash_against_human_rights_shaming_emotions_in_groups.pdf.

15. The paper is frankly a mess, applying psychological concepts of "shaming" to human rights advocacy against a country's policies. We found the whole work remarkably dubious. But in the interest of transparency and openness, we present this academic research for your consideration.

Chapter 5: Better To Hang Together: Multilateralism

1. "Swedish PM hits back at China over literature prize threat," November 15, 2019, *The Local*, November 15, 2019: https://www.thelocal.se/20191115/china-threatens-sweden-over-prize-to-dissident-author/amp.

2. Ibid.

3. "Denmark's China Challenge" by Luke Patey, October 29, 2019, *Dansk Institut for Internationale Studier*: https://www.diis.dk/publikationer/denmarks-china-challenge.

4. "The Announcement on Shanghai Municipality's Decision to Terminate Sister-City Relationship with the City of Prague of the Czech Republic," January 14, 2020: http://www.shanghai.gov.cn/shanghai/n46669/n48081/u22ai127345.html.

5. P"laything to Player: How Europe Can Stand Up for itself in the next 5 years," European Council Policy Brief by Carl Bildt and Mark Leonard, July 17th, 2019.

6. European Commission report on China: https://ec.europa.eu/trade/policy/countries-and-regions/countries/china/.

7. "EU Commissioner on the U.S.-China Trade War," *Der Spiegel*, June 26, 2019: https://www.spiegel.de/international/europe/eu-commissioner-cecilia-malmstraem-on-the-u-s-china-trade-war-a-1274479.html.

8. European Chamber European Business in China Position Paper 2019/2020: file:///C:/Users/munsr/OneDrive/Documents/China%20US%20Book/European_Business_in_China_Position_Paper_2019_2020[756].pdf.

9. European Council Policy Brief by Carl Bildt and Mark Leonard, July 17th, 2019: https://www.ecfr.eu/publications/summary/how_europe_can_stand_up_for_itself_in_the_next_five_years_eu_foreign_policy.

10. "Europe and China must keep conversation going: Merkel," August 28, 2020, *Reuters*: https://www.reuters.com/article/us-germany-merkel-china/europe-and-china-must-keep-conversation-going-merkel-idUSKBN25O1JZ?ocid=uxbndlbing.

11. "China offers hope for German cars after stimulus snub," *Deutsche Welle* (DW), April 6, 2020: https://www.dw.com/en/china-offers-hope-for-german-cars-after-stimulus-snub/a-53683919.

12. "Japan's TPP Architect Warns China could set global trade rules," *Boomberg*, February 27, 2018: https://www.bloomberg.com/news/articles/2018-02-28/japan-s-tpp-architect-warns-china-could-set-global-trade-rules.

13. "Japan and Vietnam defense ministers agree to peacefully tackle Beijing's South China Sea expansion," *Japan Times*, May 3, 2019: https://www.japantimes.co.jp/news/2019/05/03/national/japan-vietnam-defense-ministers-agree-peacefully-tackle-beijings-south-china-sea-expansion/.

14. "Indonesia 'a friend to all' and won't play favourites with US and China, says former foreign minister Marty Natalegawa" by Amy Chew, *South China Morning Post*, June 27, 2019: https://www.scmp.com/week-asia/geopolitics/article/3016241/indonesia-friend-all-and-wont-play-favourites-us-and-china.

15. Indonesians optimistic about their country's democracy and economy as elections near, Pew Research Center, April 4, 2019: https://www.pewresearch.org/fact-tank/2019/04/04/indonesians-optimistic-about-their-countrys-democracy-and-economy-as-elections-near/.

16. "Understanding Indonesians' Souring Sentiment Toward China," *The Diplomat*, November 15, 2019: https://thediplomat.com/2019/06/understanding-indonesians-souring-sentiment-toward-china/.

17. "Indonesia rejects China's claims over South China Sea," *Reuters*, January 1, 2020: https://twitter.com/michaelxpettis/status/1214054602053603328?s=20.

18. "India will soon overtake China to become the most populous country in the world," *Our World in Data*, April 26, 2019: https://ourworldindata.org/india-will-soon-overtake-china-to-become-the-most-populous-country-in-the-world.

19. "A Forensic Examination of China's National Accounts," Brookings Institution, March 7-8, 2019: https://www.brookings.edu/wp-content/uploads/2019/03/BPEA-2019-Forensic-Analysis-China.pdf.

20. "World's Fastest-Growing Economy May Not Be So Fast After All," *Bloomberg News*, June 11, 2019, : https://www.bloomberg.com/news/articles/2019-06-11/world-s-fastest-growing-economy-may-not-be-so-fast-after-all.

21. "Corruption Perceptions Index 2019," *Transparency International*: https://www.transparency.org/en/cpi/2019/results/chn.

22. "Corruption, securing funding key challenges for startups in 2019," *Times of India*, January 3, 2019, : https://timesofindia.indiatimes.com/business/india-business/corruption-securing-funding-key-challenges-for-startups-in-2019-report/articleshow/67365849.cms.

23. "Global Corruption Barometer," *Transparency International*: https://www.transparency.org/en/gcb.

24. *China's Gilded Age: The Paradox of Economic Boom and Vast Corruption* by Yuen Yuen Ang, p. 42.

25. "The impact of exposure to air pollution on cognitive performance" by Xin Zhang, Xi Chen, and Xiaobo Zhang, *Proceedings of the National Academy of the Sciences of the United States of America*, September 11, 2018: https://www.pnas.org/content/115/37/9193.

26. "Economic Center of Gravity" created by McKinsey Global Institute, "Urban world: Cities and the rise of the consuming class," June 1, 2012: https://www.mckinsey.com/featured-insights/urbanization/urban-world-cities-and-the-rise-of-the-consuming-class; Quote is from "Model of Decision Support for Alternative Choice in the Large Scale Transportation System" by Igor Kabashkin, October 2014.

27. "Where The Global Economic Center Of Gravity Is Moving And Why?" *Financial Nerd*, January 14, 2014: https://financialnerd.com/global-economic-center-gravity-moving/#:~:text=Researchers%20at%20the%20London%20School%20of%20Economics%20calculated,gravity%20in%201950%20was%20in%20the%20Atlantic%20Ocean.

28. "India looks to lure more than 1,000 U.S. companies out of China" by Archana Chaudhary, May 7, 2020, Bloomberg: https://www.msn.com/en-us/money/markets/india-looks-to-lure-more-than-1000-us-companies-out-of-china/ar-BB13I7Ha.

29. "Govt plans ¥200 bil. in subsidies to reduce firms' dependence on China" March 28, 2020, *The Japan News*: https://the-japan-news.com/news/article/0006454030 and "China's Coronavirus Policy Has Finally Pushed Europe Too Far", April 21, 2020,

Bloomberg: https://www.bloomberg.com/news/articles/2020-04-21/china-s-coronavirus-diplomacy-has-finally-pushed-europe-too-far.

30. "Generally low confidence in Xi Jinping," October 18, 2018, *Pew Research Center*: https://www.pewresearch.org/fact-tank/2018/10/19/5-charts-on-global-views-of-china/ft_18-10-19_chinaviews_generallylowconfidence/.

31. "5 charts on global views of China," October 19, 2018, *Pew Research Center*: https://www.pewresearch.org/fact-tank/2018/10/19/5-charts-on-global-views-of-china/ft_18-10-19_chinaviews_generallylowconfidence/.

32. "The State of Southeast Asia 2020 Survey Report," *ASEAN Studies Centre, Yusof Ishak Institute*, https://www.iseas.edu.sg/images/pdf/TheStateofSEASurveyReport_2020.pdf

33. "Japan and EU sign deal in riposte to China's Belt and Road," *Financial Times*, September 27, 2019: https://www.ft.com/content/dd14ce1e-e11d-11e9-9743-db5a370481bc.

34. "Quality Infrastructure: Japan's robust challenge to China's Belt and Road," April 9, 2019, *War on the Rocks*: https://warontherocks.com/2019/04/quality-infrastructure-japans-robust-challenge-to-chinas-belt-and-road/.

Chapter 6: A New World Order with Chinese Characteristics

1. Full text: Obama's 2015 State of the Union Address: https://www.usatoday.com/story/news/politics/2015/01/20/full-text-obama-2015-state-of-the-union/22064089/.

2. "The 'China Inc' Challenge to Global Trade Governance" by Mark Wu, *Harvard International Law Journal*: https://rameznaam.com/2019/04/02/the-third-phase-of-clean-energy-will-be-the-most-disruptive-yet/.

3. *The Captured Economy* by Brink Lindsey and Steven Teles, p. 21.

4. *China's Gilded Age: The Paradox of Economic Boom and Vast Corruption* by Yuen Yuen Ang, p. 44.

5. "Who's Afraid of the Trans-Pacific Partnership?" by Kevin Drum, *Mother Jones*, January 25, 2017: https://www.motherjones.com/kevin-drum/2017/01/whos-afraid-trans-pacific-partnership/.

6. "The Impact of Chinese Trade on U.S. Employment: The Good, The Bad, and The Apocryphal" by Nicholas Bloom, Kyle Handley, Andrew Kurmann and Philip Luck, March 19, 2019: https://d101vc9winf8ln.cloudfront.net/documents/30626/original/BHKL_3-20-19_v2.pdf?1554902707.

7. *China's Economy: What Everyone Needs to Know* by Arthur R. Kroeber, p. 49.

8. "The 'China, Inc.' Challenge to Global Trade Governance" by Mark Wu, Harvard Law School, *Harvard International Law Journal*, Vol. 57, 1001-1063 (2016), May 15, 2016: https://papers.ssrn.com/sol3/papers.cfm?abstract_id=2779781.

9. *Disciplining China's Trade Practices at the WTO: How WTO Complaints Can Help Make China More Market-Oriented* by James Bacchus, Simon Lester and Huan Zhu, November 15, 2018, Cato Institute: https://www.cato.org/publications/policy-analysis/disciplining-chinas-trade-practices-wto-how-wto-complaints-can-help.

10. "World Trade Statistical Review 2019," *World Trade Organization*: https://www.cnn.com/2020/05/12/investing/luckin-coffee-ceo-fired/index.html.

11. The Covid-19 pandemic has cratered global trade and is likely to reset trade patterns and global supply chains profoundly, but as of this writing it is not possible to predict or understand how this will play out.

12. "U.S. China Trade Deal: Trump is the Winner of Round One" by Tyler Cowen, *Bloomberg*, January 15, 2020: https://www.bloomberg.com/opinion/articles/2020-01-15/u-s-china-trade-deal-trump-is-the-winner-of-round-one.

13. "Biden Says He Will End Trump's Tariffs On Chinese-Made Goods, Aide Walks Back Statement" by Stuart Anderson, August 6, 2020, Forbes: https://www.forbes.com/sites/stuartanderson/2020/08/06/biden-says-he-will-end-trumps-tariffs-on-chinese-made-goods/#17734c02523a.

14. "A New Approach To Trade," Elizbeth Warren campaign website: https://elizabethwarren.com/plans/new-approach-trade.

15. "China and the United Nations: A New Battleground," *The Economist*, December 7, 2019.

16. "Chinese tech groups shaping UN facial recognition standards," *Financial Times*, December 1, 2019: https://www.ft.com/content/c3555a3c-0d3e-11ea-b2d6-9bf4d1957a67.

17. "1 big thing: The debate over U.S. restrictions on Chinese journalists," *Axios*, March 4, 2020, Bethany Allen-Ebrahimian: https://www.axios.com/newsletters/axios-china-c22a1a6a-cb47-4631-a655-af74883e378f.html?utm_source=newsletter&utm_medium=email&utm_campaign=newsletter_axioschina&stream=china.

18. "Congress seeks answers from World Bank over hiring rules for Taiwan nationals," *Axios*, January 10, 2020: https://www.axios.com/world-bank-congress-hiring-rules-china-taiwan-c6ce49b2-8d66-466b-b31c-2bcc5647d136.html.

19. https://www.documentcloud.org/documents/6297116-NBCWSJ-August-2019-Poll.html.

20. "The Rules When Manufacturing Overseas" by Dan Harris, *China Law Blog*, December 20, 2019: https://www.chinalawblog.com/2019/12/the-rules-when-manufacturing-overseas.html.

21. "Democracy Does Cause Growth" by Daron Acemoglu, Massachusetts Institute of Technology; Suresh Naidu, Columbia University; Pascual Restrepo, Boston University; James A. Robinson, University of Chicago: *Journal of Political Economy*, February 2019: https://www.journals.uchicago.edu/doi/abs/10.1086/700936?mobileUi=0&.

22. "The whistleblower doctor who fell victim to China's coronavirus" by Emma Graham Harrison, February 6, 2020, The *Guardian*: https://www.theguardian.com/world/2020/feb/06/li-wenliang-coronavirus-whistleblower-doctor-profile.

23. "Timeline: The early days of China's coronavirus outbreak and cover-up" by Bethany Allen-Ebrahimian, March 18, 2020, *Axios*: https://www.axios.com/timeline-the-early-days-of-chinas-coronavirus-outbreak-and-cover-up-ee65211a-afb6-4641-97b8-353718a5faab.html?utm_source=twitter&utm_medium=social&utm_campaign=organic&utm_content=1100.

24. Genetic analysis has found most of the infections found in the U.S. came from Europe and appear to be a different, more infectious strain of Covid-19. Nonetheless, it is irresponsible to allow people potentially carrying a novel virus to freely travel hither and yon.

25. "Coronavirus: Chinese official suggests U.S. Army to blame for outbreak" by Henry Austin and Alexander Smith, March 13, 2020, *NBC News*: https://www.nbcnews.com/news/world/coronavirus-chinese-official-suggests-u-s-army-blame-outbreak-n1157826.

26. "Timeline: The early days of China's coronavirus outbreak and cover-up" by Bethany Allen-Ebrahimian, *Axios*, March 18, 2020: https://www.axios.com/timeline-the-early-days-of-chinas-coronavirus-outbreak-and-cover-up-ee65211a-afb6-4641-97b8-353718a5faab.

html?utm_source=twitter&utm_medium=social&utm_campaign=organic&utm_
content=1100.

27. "Coronavirus, la riabilitazione della Cina passa attraverso le fake news" by Mario
D'Angelo, March 15, 2020, *Money.it:* https://www.money.it/coronavirus-il-virus-
portato-in-cina-da-usa-e-altre-fake-news.

28. "As world combats coronavirus, Commerce secretary says it could be good for US jobs"
by Ben Gittleson, January 30, 2020, ABC News: https://abcnews.go.com/Politics/
commerce-secretary-wilbur-ross-chinas-coronavirus-bring-jobs/story?id=68640164.

29. "AP Fact Check: Trump's False Assurances on Coronavirus," *Associated Press,* March 2,
2020: https://www.usnews.com/news/politics/articles/2020-03-02/ap-fact-check-
trumps-false-assurances-on-coronavirus.

30. "China Media Group doubling down on suggesting US is the source of the virus, &
maybe it came from a US army lab," Bill Bishop Tweet, March 24, 2020: https://twitter.
com/niubi/status/1242456215868841988.

31. "An Italian doctor is now key to China's efforts to sow confusion over the coronavirus's
origins," *Quartz:* https://qz.com/1823417/italy-now-key-to-china-coronavirus-origin-
propaganda-efforts/.

Chapter 7: Dealing with China

1. "World Bank data and The Soviet Union: GDP growth," *Nintil,* March 26, 2016: https://
nintil.com/the-soviet-union-gdp-growth/.

2. "Explained: US, China's undersea battle for control of global internet grid,"By Jeremy
Page, Kate O'Keeffe, Rob Taylor, July 09, 2019, *Business Standard*: https://wap.business-
standard.com/article-amp/international/explained-us-china-s-undersea-battle-for-
control-of-global-internet-grid-119031300168_1.html.

3. "Ecuador monitoring fleet of fishing vessels near Galapagos," *Reuters,* July 23, 2020:
https://www.reuters.com/article/us-ecuador-fishing/ecuador-monitoring-fleet-of-
fishing-vessels-near-galapagos-idUSKCN24O369.

4. "Secret Chinese documents reveal inner workings of Muslim detention camps" by
Chelsea Stahl, November 24, 2019, *NBC News*: https://www.nbcnews.com/news/all/
secret-chinese-documents-reveal-inner-workings-muslim-detention-camps-n1089941.

5. "Guy Who Reverse-Engineered TikTok Reveals the Scary Things He Learned, Advises
People To Stay Away From It" by Rokas Laurinavičius and Ilona Baliūnaitė, July 22,
2020, Boredpanda.com: https://www.boredpanda.com/tik-tok-reverse-engineered-
data-information-collecting/?utm_source=twitter&utm_medium=social&utm_
campaign=organic.

6. "Does time spent using social media impact mental health? An eight year longitudinal
study," *Computers in Human Behavior,* Volume 104: https://www.sciencedirect.com/
science/article/pii/S0747563219303723.

7. "Social media's enduring effect on adolescent life satisfaction, Proceedings of the
National Academy of Sciences of the United States of America," May 21, 2019: https://
www.pnas.org/content/116/21/10226.

8. "Ring-wing populism, social media, and echo chambers in Western Democracies,"
March 2019: https://academic.macewan.ca/bouliannes/files/2019/09/NMS_FINAL_
March2019all.pdf.

9. Again, Facebook didn't elect Donald Trump, James Comey did. (see "Say It With Me Again: James Comey Elected Donald Trump President" by Kevin Drum, *Mother Jones*: https://www.motherjones.com/kevin-drum/2017/03/say-it-me-again-james-comey-elected-donald-trump-president/).

10. Congressional-Executive Commission on China 2019 Annual Report: https://www.cecc.gov/sites/chinacommission.house.gov/files/documents/EMBARGOED_CECC%20 2019%20Annual%20Report.pdf.

11. "Uyghurs for Sale," *Australian Strategic Policy Institute*: https://www.aspi.org.au/report/uyghurs-sale.

12. "'South Park' creators shade China in faux apology for banned episode" by Nardine Saad, *Los Angeles Times*, October 7, 2019: https://www.latimes.com/entertainment-arts/tv/story/2019-10-07/south-park-china-apology.

13. "'Something has to change': Michael Kovrig's letters detail life in a Beijing jail cell. His wife wants Canada to do more to free him" by Robert Fife and Nathan Vanderklippe, June 22, 2020, *The Globe and Mail*: https://www.theglobeandmail.com/canada/article-something-has-to-change-michael-kovrigs-letters-detail-life-in-a/?cmpid=rss&utm_source=dlvr.it&utm_medium=twitter.

14. "Disentangling the Effects of the 2018-2019 Tariffs on a Globally Connected U.S. Manufacturing Sector" by Aaron Flaaen and Justin Pierce, December 3, 2019, Federal Reserve Board: https://www.federalreserve.gov/econres/feds/files/2019086pap.pdf.

15. "Who owns Huawei" by Christopher Balding and Donald C. Clarke, April 17, 2019: https://papers.ssrn.com/sol3/papers.cfm?abstract_id=3372669.

16. The Case Against Huawei, Christopher Balding, Baldingsworld.com, January 15, 2020: https://www.baldingsworld.com/.

17. Taiwan Relations Act: https://www.ait.org.tw/our-relationship/policy-history/key-u-s-foreign-policy-documents-region/taiwan-relations-act/.

18. "Response to COVID-19 in Taiwan Big Data Analytics, New Technology, and Proactive Testing" by C. Jason Wang, MD, PhD1,2; Chun Y. Ng, MBA, MPH2; Robert H. Brook, MD, ScD, March 3, 2020, JAMA Network: https://jamanetwork.com/journals/jama/fullarticle/2762689?guestAccessKey=2a3c6994-9e10-4a0b-9f32-cc2fb55b61a5&utm_source=For_The_Media&utm_medium=referral&utm_campaign=ftm_links&utm_content=tfl&utm_term=030320.

19. "CO2 Emissions," *Our World In Data*: https://ourworldindata.org/co2-emissions.

20. "The sad truth about our boldest climate target" by David Roberts, January 3, 2020, *Vox*: https://www.vox.com/energy-and-environment/2020/1/3/21045263/climate-change-1-5-degrees-celsius-target-ipcc and Tweet by Michael Liebreich: https://twitter.com/MLiebreich/status/1200508263403597824.

21. World Economic Forum: https://www.weforum.org/agenda/2016/06/china-green-energy-superpower-charts/.

22. "Human Activity in China and India Dominates the Greening of Earth, NASA Study Shows," NASA, February 11, 2019: https://www.nasa.gov/feature/ames/human-activity-in-china-and-india-dominates-the-greening-of-earth-nasa-study-shows.

23. "Fears grow over Chinese spy ring after arrest at U.S. Navy base," *The Times*, December 30, 2019: https://www.thetimes.co.uk/article/fears-grow-over-chinese-spy-ring-after-arrest-at-us-navy-base-pb2bdb883.

24. See, for example, "Shattered: Inside the secret battle to save America's undercover spies in the digital age," *Yahoo News*, December 30, 2019: https://news.yahoo.com/shattered-inside-the-secret-battle-to-save-americas-undercover-spies-in-the-digital-age-100029026.html?guccounter=1.

25. IIE's Fast Facts: https://www.iie.org/Research-and-Insights/Open-Doors/Fact-Sheets-and-Infographics/Fast-Facts.

26. "The Heroes of America's Startup Economy Weren't Born in America," *INC Entrepreneurship Index*: https://www.inc.com/arnobio-morelix/inc-entrepreneurship-index-2018-q1.html.

27. "My Chinese students don't want you to talk about Hong Kong. Clearly, we're failing them" by Jonathan Zimmerman, *USA Today*, November 13, 2019: https://www.usatoday.com/story/opinion/voices/2019/11/13/chinese-international-students-college-education-hong-kong-column/2575189001/.

28. "Hong Kong protests spread to U.S. colleges, and a rift grows," *New York Times*, October 26, 2019: https://www.nytimes.com/2019/10/26/us/hong-kong-protests-colleges.html.

29. "Microsoft opening new Vancouver, B.C., development center with visit from PM Trudeau," *GeekWire*, June 17. 2016: https://www.geekwire.com/2016/trudeau-speak-opening-microsoft-vancouver-facility/.

30. The Global AI Talent Tracker, Marc Polo: https://macropolo.org/digital-projects/the-global-ai-talent-tracker/.

31. "Chinese leader's family worth a billion," *The Sydney Morning Herald*, June 30, 2012: https://www.smh.com.au/world/chinese-leaders-family-worth-a-billion-20120629-218qi.html.

32. Global Gender Gap Report 2020, World Economic Forum: http://www3.weforum.org/docs/WEF_GGGR_2020.pdf.

33. *Betraying Big Brother: The Feminist Awakening in China* by Leta Hong Fincher, Location 75, Kindle Edition.

34. *End of an Era: How China's Authoritarian Regime is Undermining its Rise* by Carl Minzner, p. 87.

Chapter 8: The World Is Getting Better and Can Get Better Yet

1. Pandemics aside. But even Covid-19, as bad as it is, will likely be far less deadly than the Spanish Flu thanks to advances in medicine. And it may even accelerate advances in medicine.

2. *The Better Angels of Our Nature: Why Violence Has Declined* by Stephen Pinker, 2011.

3. "Steven Pinker: This Is History's Most Peaceful Time—New Study: 'Not So Fast'" by Bret Stetka, *Scientific American*, November 9, 2017: https://www.scientificamerican.com/article/steven-pinker-this-is-historys-most-peaceful-time-new-study-not-so-fast/.

4. *End of an Era, How China's Authoritarian Revival is Undermining its Rise* by Carl Minzner, p. 101.

Epilogue: A Tree Grows in Beijing (And Scranton)

1. "India-Japan-Australia supply chain in the works to counter China," August 19, 2020, *The Economic Times*: https://economictimes.indiatimes.com/news/economy/foreign-trade/india-japan-australia-supply-chain-in-the-works-to-counter-china/articleshow/

77624852.cms?utm_source=contentofinterest&utm_medium=text&utm_campaign=cppst.

2. "Why China's dramatic economic recovery might not add up" by Emma Graham-Harrison, *The Guardian*, October 25, 2020: https://www.theguardian.com/business/2020/oct/25/why-chinas-dramatic-economic-recovery-might-not-add-up?ref=hvper.com; "Why China's official data don't add up" by Shehzad Qazi, *Asia Financial Times*, October 29, 2020: https://www.asiatimesfinancial.com/why-china-s-official-data-don-t-add-up.

3. "Unfavorable Views of China Reach Historic Highs in Many Countries," October 6, 2020, *Pew Research Center*: https://www.pewresearch.org/global/2020/10/06/unfavorable-views-of-china-reach-historic-highs-in-many-countries/.

4. "Senator Hawley Gives Floor Speech on Reforming the Global Economy, Preventing China's Domination," Wednesday, May 20, 2020: https://www.hawley.senate.gov/senator-hawley-gives-floor-speech-reforming-global-economy-preventing-chinas-domination.

5. *The Great Decoupling* by Keith Johnson and Robbie Gramer, May 14, 2020: *Foreign Policy*: https://foreignpolicy.com/2020/05/14/china-us-pandemic-economy-tensions-trump-coronavirus-covid-new-cold-war-economics-the-great-decoupling/.

6. "Between Restoration and Change" by Thomas Wright, October 1, 2020, *Brookings*: https://www.brookings.edu/blog/order-from-chaos/2020/10/01/between-restoration-and-change/.

7. "For the United States, its world status and influence are gradually declining, and its international reputation has been severely weakened," *U.S.-China Perception Monitor*, January 7, 2020: https://uscnpm.org/2020/01/07/wu-xinbo-america-cannot-afford-to-forgo-u-s-china-cooperation/.

8. "Beijing Believes Trump is Accelerating American Decline," by Rush Doshi, October 12, 2020, *Foreign Affairs*: https://foreignpolicy.com/2020/10/12/china-trump-accelerating-american-decline/.